Dorothy's
INCREDIBLE HEALING HANDS

Dorothy's
INCREDIBLE HEALING HANDS

Dorothy Nancy Lily Rodgers

Riverside Publishing Solutions

Dorothy Rodgers asserts her moral right to be identified as the author of this book.

The views expressed in this book are solely those of the author and Riverside Publishing Solutions accept no liability.

Typeset by Riverside Publishing Solutions
www.riversidepublishingsolutions.com

Copyright © 2019 Dorothy Nancy Lily Rodgers

ISBN: 978-1-913012-15-1 (Paperback)

All rights reserved. No part of this publication may be reproduced, distributed, or transmitted in any form or by any means, including photocopying, recording, or other electronic or mechanical methods, without the prior written permission of the publisher, except in the case of brief quotations embodied in critical reviews and certain other non-commercial uses permitted by copyright law.

Printed and bound in the UK.

Contents

Chapter One – Childhood	1
Chapter Two – Marriage	10
Chapter Three – Healing	31
Chapter Four	65
Chapter Five – Shirley Bassey's Sister	68
Chapter Six	70
Chapter Seven	72
Chapter Eight	75
Chapter Nine – Malta	87
Chapter Ten	89
Chapter Eleven	109

Chapter One

Childhood

I was born in Manchester, England, at Rusholme Hospital to an English-Jewish woman. My birth father was from Liberia and boarded at the woman's house who gave birth to me. I was always known as a little brown-skinned child.

Why the woman never got me adopted from the hospital I will never know. She knew I would never be accepted as I was of a tanned complexion. Her husband told her either to "Get that brat out or she'd have to get out". She then took me to the attic and tied my little legs to a chair. Can you imagine how twisted that made my body feel after I had been there for two years?

The neighbours used to visit the home and ask how the baby was; they could not understand why she never took me out. She always told them I was sleeping, but every time they left, they would always hear me screaming and crying. Of course, in those days people did not like to intervene. I suppose that was why it went on so long. By this time the neighbours, especially the ladies on both sides of the house, started to get very suspicious. They called in the welfare and saved my life.

When the ambulance came to pick me up, the lady next door told me that neighbours from all over the district came to observe what was going on. She told me that I was full of sores all over my body. The vest I was wearing was so stuck that it had to be cut off. I was then taken straight to the hospital and I stayed there for around two years. I know the woman who had me wished I had died. I never knew her and never saw her again.

I was adopted, unofficially, by a lovely Christian lady (Mother Connie) who ran a small orphanage for teenage girls in Manchester. I was the youngest child there; I was only four years old.

My new mother, Connie, was an angel, very caring and she taught me a lot, even what to wear when I was older. Mother Connie was a Christian and her father, a priest – I was brought up a Christian. My mother did all she could do for my legs to see if she could get them right, and she always bought me expensive ankle boots. I was very happy with her; I loved her very much. I did not go to school until I was seven years old. I could not walk very well.

Living with Mother Connie, I felt very secure. Every year we all (myself and the teenage girls from the orphanage) went on holiday for two weeks to St Anne's on the Sea. We would have a wonderful time. Christmas was also fantastic. We had lots of presents and at New Year we would have lots of new clothes. We always went to church on Saturday mornings, and on Sunday three times a day. I loved going there and I still do, but definitely not three times a day; one time is enough! Once when we were at church the priest asked me, "What is your name?" I told him "Dorothy" and he said, "Dorothy, that means Gift of God". Well I felt extremely fortunate and proud and it makes a bit more sense to me now knowing what God had blessed me with – more about that later.

We were all ladies of leisure. Once every year we would visit a lord's home, we would spend all day there being waited on by butlers and could choose anything we wanted to eat. We were allowed to walk anywhere in the house, even in the ten gardens. It was so beautiful. The house was full of paintings – most times I felt the eyes of the portraits seemed to follow me when I walked up the stairs. I had never seen so many beautiful things in one place.

We would always dress up in white, even down to my gloves. I used to ask Mother Connie, "Why has God given me such big hands?" She always had to buy the biggest gloves she could get. She told me I was going to do wonderful things with my hands, but she never told me what they were going to do.

On our annual holiday to St Anne's on the Sea the homeowners would share their animals with us. This was such a wonderful time. Their daughter, Barbie, took me to the horses and showed me how to ride. She was a super rider. I was not such a good one as her, but I always enjoyed it. Barbie was a lovely girl and her father was a nice man, but I do not think her mother liked me!

One day a week while we were there we would walk to Blackpool where all the amusements were. On one of our trips, when I was about seven years old, one of the gypsies managed to steal me away. Mother Connie went to the police. Everyone was looking for me. I was found holding a big teddy bear that the gypsy had given me. The police officer who found me asked me my name and I told him, "Dorothy". He then told off the gypsy and told her to stop taking children or she would get locked up.

Back home at the orphanage there was a housekeeper who did not like me. Her name was Miss Aysie. She was always hitting me and making me stand on the landing. I do not know why she did it. I think she was jealous of the relationship I had with Mother Connie and she did not like the colour of my skin.

One day it all stopped when Mother Connie came to bed and saw me on the landing. She told me to go to bed and she would sort it out.

In the morning I overheard Mother Connie telling her off; she did not want her to hit me or make me stand on the landing and if she continued to do this she would have to leave. After that I was left in peace but always got dirty looks.

Miss Aysie was an incredibly beautiful woman and she had a very handsome boyfriend who had a lovely car. I was pretty frightened of her. I thought she wanted to kill me. She used to tell Mother Connie that maybe she gave me too much of my own way, which was not true because my mother was strict with me. She wanted me to grow up into a decent, respectable lady and always trust in God, she worried that without God I would be just a hopeless cripple.

Chapter One

We had a Scotty dog called Crackers; he was white and fluffy and looked after Mother Connie and all the rest of us. If any bad person came to the door, he would have a go at their trousers at the doorstep and bite off their flesh with his mouth and they would run off like rabbits. We all adored and loved him with all our hearts.

Mother Connie used to take me for walks, just the two of us. Even though we had an enormous backyard and a very big nursery where we had every kind of toy, she just did not think that was enough for me. Sometimes if either of us got tired from the walks we would take the bus back home. I always thought how very fortunate I was to have such a wonderful and loving mother.

On one of our long walks when I got tired, we decided to take the bus back. When we were ready to get off Mother Connie let me off first, but before she got off properly the bus driver started to move. This made Mother Connie fall right on to the road. I was absolutely furious. I shouted out so a couple of men came to lift her up. Then I faced the bus driver and I called him a stupid man to his face. He nearly killed my mother and did not even bother to get her up.

The love I had for Mother Connie had just brought all the rage out of me. To see her hurt or in any sort of pain or discomfort was too much for me to deal with. Still, Mother Connie remained composed and did not get upset at all. I think my shouting at the driver made up for it.

By this time, I was going to school in Manchester. I was always known as "the brown-skin girl" as I was the only person of that colour. I never saw any black person in my life, and I was the only brown person that I knew. When I look around the only brown person, I could see was myself. When I did see a black man for the first time, I was terrified – I ran like billy-o. There was a very rich girl who went to school with me; her mother used to bring her dinner every day – and ME! One day the girl asked her mother why she brought dinner for me too and her mother responded, "Because she's family". I honestly believe she was the sister of the woman who gave birth to me. I just know she was.

Around the same time when I used to go to church, there was a Jewish man who used to run the sweet shop. When I went in to buy chocolate peanuts I would give him a penny and slide it back and give it again and slide it back. I used to get about six bags of peanuts for one penny! But when the others saw it, they decided to do the same, but he would shout, "Where's your penny? Where's your penny?" I realised he must have known the woman who gave birth to me too. And then the same when I went in the Jewish cake shop, the lady used to give me the cake and put the money back in the bag. I must have had a lot of family in the Jewish community – pity I do not know them now!

When I was 14, Mother Connie booked me into hospital to have an operation on my legs as one had grown shorter than the other from when I was tied up as a child by my natural mother. The doctors did their best and they got a little better, but never became right and I still could not walk as normally as other people until I was 16.

Mother Connie had bad asthma. One day when I was 16 she told me she had to go to get some help as her sickness was getting worse by the day, which meant that she had to give up the orphanage and move to a nunnery. She gave me the address of where she would be staying; it was not too far from the orphanage and she told me I could visit her every day. Knowing that she was ill and may be going away, she had bought me a beautiful black patent suitcase and filled it with new clothes, photographs of the two of us from when I was small and coming-up a teenager, and a good bit of money. It was my favourite thing which I treasured very much.

When I went to the home for the first time, I met the nuns. They just slammed the door in my face and threatened me that I should never come back. I was very sad; I was devastated. Only 16 years old and I did not know what to do.

Now I look back I guess they prevented me from seeing her because they did not want me in her will. Her father had given her lots of beautiful things; gold crosses with all different valuable stones such as rubies and emeralds which decorated the chapel at the orphanage. She never married and as I was her only daughter, biological or not, they were worried about me getting everything. I wish I had thought of going to the police for help.

All I wanted to do was to visit her every day, but I could not because the nuns prevented me. I know she would have missed me very much because we were both so close. I did not know if I would ever see her again. Each time I thought about Mother Connie all I could remember was how good she was to me and how I loved and missed her so much. I had so much I wanted to say but no time left, and I wondered whether I would ever see her again. I never did.

It was at this time that I was walking down the street in Manchester and about three women came up to me and said, "You are Rose Rueben's daughter" and I said, "Who is Rose Rueben?" They explained to me that they lived each side of where she lived and that I looked "exactly like her but much younger and prettier". We had a lengthy conversation and they told me everything they knew about when I was brought from the hospital by the woman who gave birth to me. As I mentioned at the beginning, they told me how I was tied up in the attic and that they were the women who had got on to the welfare and saved my life. They would ask how Rose Rueben's daughter was and she'd say "Oh she's sleeping", but when they would walk round the back they would hear me screaming and crying. They also told me what they knew about the man I think is my father. Rose Rueben rented a room in her house to a lodger, he was an African man from Liberia and the women said he always looked so smart, had very white clean shirts, you could see yourself in his shoes they were so clean and he often helped out Rose with her sheets and shirts and everything. I expect they had other lodgers there, but I can see why she took a shine to him. I was quite shocked and was not sure whether to believe them but then I realised every word they told me was true. According to what I had heard the woman who gave birth to me, her husband and her other daughter went to Canada. They were in the garment business and got extraordinarily rich in Canada – they never got into trouble for what they did to me.

Chapter One

After Mother Connie gave up the orphanage, I was then put in a home run by NUNS! They ruled with an iron rod and I always wondered how they became nuns and yet could be so cruel.

One day when I was standing in the laundry, singing, the sister came up behind me and struck me so hard on my right eye it felt like she struck me with an iron rod. I saw stars. It was so hard I thought that my eye was crushed and had dropped out. As I dropped down, I grabbed her habit and brought her down to the floor with me. She immediately told me to leave! I had nowhere to go but luckily, I had a friend in the nunnery whose name was Ella. She was such a lovely girl. She gave me the address of her father and a letter to give to him explaining that I had nowhere to go and needed somewhere to live. I felt so much better – what a thing when you have no relatives in the entire world. Without Ella I do not know what I would have done.

One day when I was getting the train from Manchester to Liverpool to visit some friends I took my beautiful patent suitcase, full up of beautiful things with me to show them, but when I went to get off the train at Liverpool I couldn't find my suitcase! The train driver was called, and we realised that it must have been stolen by a blinking thief! The train driver was gobsmacked that no one had seen such a beautiful suitcase being stolen; he was so apologetic. Unfortunately, this means that I have no photos of Mother Connie or myself when I was young. It was completely heart-breaking for me.

Chapter Two

Marriage

When I was 17, I met a man in Manchester named Edger who was in the RAF. We met at a protest meeting about women's rights and how they should be treated properly, like human beings, and have equal rights with men. We used to go out in Manchester together; we went to dances, to the pictures, bowling and many other things and we fell in love, naturally. We got married. After a few years my husband wanted us to move back to Jamaica, but bearing in mind he was in the forces he therefore could not just discharge himself from the RAF without permission, therefore he decided to send me on my own to meet his brother in Jamaica. Before I was due to sail, my husband said that he wanted to get my birth certificate for me from the woman who gave birth to me. I will never know how he managed to do that! All he told me was that she never even bothered to ask how I was, even though she tied me to a chair for two years so I could not move! She also lied to him that my father was a white

Chapter Two

Jewish Englishman. How could I have brown skin and both my mother and 'father' be white Jewish!? Another surprise from the birth certificate was that Dorothy was not my name! My birth name was Nancy Lily Reuben which remained the case for a good few years before it was changed by deed poll – I did not want to look at my birth certificate from that woman at that time. Everyone continued to call me Dorothy.

Having obtained my birth certificate my husband decided to send me to his home in Jamaica while he stayed in England. He wrote to his brother and told him to meet me at the wharf where the ship landed. I had never been on a ship before you see, and I was very seasick; it was terrible. I do not really know how long it took but I was glad when we landed. The ship arrived a full day earlier than expected and there was no one to meet me; I might say I was pretty worried. Naturally, I had luggage, a great big case. A water policeman came to me and I explained we should have landed the next day and I gave him my brother-in-law's address. He said to me, "Don't worry, I will take you home to my wife. We will leave instructions to your brother-in-law where to pick you up. My wife will love you". He was very certain his wife was going to love me. I suppose he loved me as well but did not want to tell me! But it gave me a nice feeling and it made me feel so settled and happy.

The policeman's wife really liked me; she wished I was staying for good and I had such a lovely time! It is a pity they told my brother-in-law I had arrived. I was taken around to all their friends to meet them even though I was only staying one night. But my brother-in-law came to pick me up the very next day, bright and early. Pity he did not leave it for a week, although he was a nice man too.

Edger's brother was a very rich man and had a beautiful big house with acres of land. His wife was a very nice lady and they had five children – what a nice family. I stayed there a long time until my husband arrived. When my husband came, I heard his brother say to him, "You have a lovely wife, everyone likes her. You must settle down and get a proper job to look after your wife". I thought there was something very wrong as his brother's voice sounded very stern and he mentioned something about my husband's old ways – I did not know what he had been up to, little did I know then he was such a bad gambler!

We moved to Edger's father's home as we needed a place to live together and Edger needed to introduce me to his father. Edger's father was a very nice man. The first time I met him I overheard him call Edger back and say to him, "Behave yourself, stop this nonsense you're doing". He spoke very firmly to his son every time as he knew he was a gambler and continuously told him to get a proper job to look after me. Apparently, Edger used to gamble all the time, if you ask me. From when he was young, I suppose his school friends gambled. This made me more worried each time I overheard these conversations.

Another man who was worried about me was the local minister of the church. When I first went to the church and met him, he so liked me and he said to Edger, "What a nice wife you have, but we have to give her a dog to protect her

Chapter Two

when she's walking around, as some of these men aren't very nice". So, he gave me a big dog to protect me when I went anywhere in Jamaica.

Edger had three sisters living with his father and they did not like me at all, which worried me especially as his father was then getting on in age and was not very well either. I knew that if his father died, they would certainly get us both out. I was very different to them in every conceivable way. I was like a different creature coming into the family. I felt very uncomfortable around them and their actions towards me were unkind. Talk about actions speak louder than words, you can say that again. Once I was coming home, and the dog ran to me so fast he nearly dropped me on the floor. I do not think they liked the dog either, as it always looked forward to seeing me much more than it did them. The sisters told us that they did not want us living with them, so Edger and I decided to move out. Edger was extremely proud of me. I once overheard him saying to a woman, "You couldn't kiss the bottom of my wife's shoes". I could not believe it as I had never heard that saying before. It is a shame I had to leave him, but I will get to that in a bit.

We rented an apartment, still in the city but further away from his father and the sisters. It was around this time that I found out for myself that Edger was a gambler, but not just a little bit of a gambler, a hell of a lot of a gambler! This frightened me, having a man who is a gambler is bound to frighten anyone. It made our relationship quite rocky but when I learnt how to keep my head in the sand it made things a bit better.

Edger opened a shop where he sold beautiful crystals and ornaments. He left me to run it whilst he went off and, I assume, gambled. He was definitely showing off selling such beautiful things, and as I was new, and people found me pretty, he knew they would sell. It was very dangerous to run a shop and any shop had to have security, which ours did not, but luckily there was always a kind man sitting on the step singing who kept me safe from thieves. I remember always thinking to myself what a lovely voice he had. He looked after me and would always say to his friend, "She looks like a doll. Just like a doll". He would stay on the step with his friends and keep me company, and whenever he saw my husband, he would act like he was not there, stop singing and just continue talking to his friends.

As predicted the shop did not last long because of my husband's gambling. I was soon to find out that Edger continuously was using the profit we made to gamble, and this made me disgusted with him; any love I had felt for him had long gone. Talk about irritating, what a stupid man, you could never get on with a man; like that. He did not learn his lesson as he then got a job as a salesman but never came home and was often out all-night, gambling. I did not see any money at all and was not able to even buy groceries.

One day a Syrian man came to the house. He asked if I was Edger's wife and I confirmed I was. He then told me that my husband was a good worker; he sold a lot of goods, but the money always seemed to disappear – which was obviously something that I already knew! He asked me if my husband had a gambling problem, I told him that he did, and the man said he was sorry, but he would have to put my husband in prison because he owed him a lot of money. I was worried about him going to prison and so I told him I would give him his brother's address because he was a very wealthy man and I knew his brother would pay his debt. Whether it was the best thing for Edger or not, his brother paid his debt which meant that he did not go to jail, but it also meant that Edger did not learn his lesson!

None of this stopped Edger from gambling and even though he did not go to jail he was sacked as he was not to be trusted anymore. Edger then got a job as an overseer, managing a very large plantation and they gave him a lovely big house as well. Unfortunately, the police in that part of Jamaica were not to be trusted. Every night I heard them trying to break down my front door as they knew Edger was a gambler and would not be in. I can only imagine what they kept bashing down my door for! The police in Jamaica never give up! I was terrified and so I asked my maid and her partner to stay with me every night. I was very grateful that I had them to protect me as you never know what would have happened otherwise to a young girl on her own in the middle of nowhere, in a country where the police can do what they want and get away with it.

Edger would be away for weeks at a time and come back often wearing the same clothes! It was around this time I was in a shop and a drunk man, who wanted the bottle out of my hand, ran after me and started kicking me. When I got home, we had to call the doctor and that was the first I knew that I was carrying a baby as the doctor said "You've lost your baby" and my response was, "I didn't know I was having one". So, I never told Edger as he did not even know what happened. As time went by I knew Edger wouldn't be able to keep the job and I kept getting worried because there was no money for food whatsoever. I think my maid must have had a word with the grocery man, who I then found out was called Henry, as he kept sending me my usual grocery order knowing that I couldn't pay for it. Not only that, he would include a packet in the groceries with money to pay the maid, which Edger would never ever have thought of. Henry would come and see me to check that I was OK as he knew all I had been through, including losing a child. He was the perfect gentleman.

One day Henry told me to pack my clothes and stay at my maid's house until he could collect me and take me to his auntie. I felt marvellous; I could not have wished for a better outcome. Edger wasn't around as usual, so I packed my clothes in a great big suitcase, everything I had, so that he would know straight away when he walked in the door that I had left as you couldn't miss the great big suitcase. I heard months later that Edger was going from door to door asking people if they had seen me. Shows how long he was away for. It took a very long time to get to Henry's auntie's house, about half a day it took. When I got to Henry's auntie's house I felt so relieved and safe away from Edger and his problems, as I knew he would never change and would never be able to care about anything other than gambling. Henry's

Chapter Two

auntie lived in a very posh place in Jamaica and the area was full of rich people. I stayed there a long time and was treated like one of their own; everything they did they wanted to include me which made me feel right at home. The plan was to stay there until I could book a passage to England by ship. Even though the ship was free, I needed money for when I landed.

At this time, I had become friendly with a young lady called Elsie who had a little daughter. Elsie's husband found her messing about with another man and decided to take Elsie to court to fight for custody of the daughter. She asked me to accompany her to the court for moral support. The judge asked her who I was and she said, "She's an English lady. I think she'll be going back to England in a few years and she's parted from her husband". The judge obviously took a fancy to me and then tried to organise a meeting where he would pick me up in his car in the evening to do God knows what with me! What do you think he wanted to pick me up in his car for?! Saucy devil! I just do not do things like that, but some people they are like that you know; they would jump in a car with anyone, but I was not brought up like that. The blinking idiot. The judge got so annoyed when he came to pick me up and I was not there. Elsie told me he waited there for ages. I did not go to any of the other court appointments after that and I think that was why she lost the case.

Henry came to see me every week without fail with money and lots of groceries. As I have said before, he was a perfect gentleman. If I would have ever met a man like Henry, I would have never married a man like Edger.

I have been very lucky in my life and I have met quite a few gentlemen, even in Jamaica, as well as in England. I saved all the money from Henry for my new life in England.

I forgot to mention that whilst I was living on the plantation, a friendly man I knew had given me the address of his sister in London and told me that if I ever went to London, I should stay with her. When I eventually got to England, I went to see his sister and she said I could stay with her for board and keep. She knew about a job at the OXO company, and luckily whilst I'd been in Jamaica I'd learnt how to type, so I then got a job there in the day and went to night school to brush up on my English and typing skills. The lady I stayed with, the friendly man's sister, was very mean and took practically every penny I earned whilst I worked all day. Whilst working at the OXO company I heard from a colleague that our manager had asked her if she minded sitting next to a coloured woman. I thought he had a flipping cheek, and this really upset and shocked me! If he had said it to her, he must have said it to all of them in the office.

About the same time, I met a young, tall and handsome chap called Herman on my way to work one day who lived in the same flat as I did, but on the top floor. He asked what I was doing living with 'that woman' and where I knew her from because she had a reputation for meanness. I told him that I had just arrived in London and did not know anyone else so naturally had to stay there until I got on my feet. He offered to walk me around London to look for another job after I explained what had happened at work. He took me to the Labour Exchange and when we got there, the woman asked me what work I was looking for, I said typing and her reply was, "We don't take coloured girls in offices in London". I was shocked and stormed out of there very quickly. If I would have had something, I'd have thrown it in her face, but I did not tell Herman what she said as I thought he might not be as restrained! I just told him I did not like that woman and that I would like to go to a secretarial agency.

The next day he took me to a secretarial agency. I explained to them what had happened at the OXO company and at the Labour Exchange the day before and they were shocked. They found me a typing job straight away at The British Museum. Coincidentally I was on holiday the following week for two weeks, so they advised me that it would be best to give my two weeks' notice as soon as I went on holiday. This would mean that I could give my notice by phone and at the same time, let him know how discriminated against I felt. This was all happening at a time when there were a lot of national discussions about racism and equal rights. When I phoned him to give my notice, he was furious, and he made out that I owed him one having employed me. I told him, "What the heck have you done for me? You have not done anything for me. I have worked hard, and you can get lost. They should find you and take you away for being a racist", which made me feel marvellous and as if I'd won a big fight.

Herman and I made the most of the two weeks. We had lovely time. He took me around everywhere; to lots of speeches about women's rights, to the pictures, we went dancing at The Lyceum Ballroom, out for Chinese food and we hired a car for the day and went to the country. I do not know how we fitted it all in. One time when we went dancing at The Lyceum I was in the ladies' and a woman came up to me and asked, "Are you accompanied?" I then realised she was hitting on me which surprised me a bit at how brazen she was, as I didn't know much about that then. When I told Herman he nearly died with laughter. Nowadays things are different.

Herman had been sent to grow up at his uncle's in Jamaica when he was little. They adored him and had brought him up very well. His brother lived in America and was also a lovely man, with a beautiful daughter who came to stay with us when she was on holiday. However, his sister was a different kettle of fish; she was nothing more than a thief! One time she stole a gold earring from me – always looking for something for nothing that one!

Herman loved going to the dog races. One day he took me. That was the only time I would go with him as I am not keen on gambling as you might imagine, because of Edger. Every dog I chose won right out. I tell you; the amount of money was a heck of a lot. We came out with a bag full of money! We agreed to put it towards our wedding one day. I would not go back again to the dogs though, no way.

Unfortunately I lived with that horrible woman for quite some time but after a few years, as Herman and I were so happy together, he said to me, "I think it's about time we got together", by which he meant that we should live together. Herman found a beautiful flat for us to move into and this meant that we could start saving our money to get married. After a few years, as we were so happy together, Herman and I got married. We had a big wedding and a big party afterwards at our local church and lots of people came, lots of people I did not even know to be honest! We received beautiful presents and I wore my dream white wedding dress with a big veil. We had organised a professional photographer who had been in business for years. When we went to collect the photos from his shop we noticed they were a bit strange as one of my hands seemed to be stretched out in front of me in a very awkward position, and was jet black in comparison to the white dress and my light brown skin. At that time no one, including me, knew that I had healing hands – which now seems very strange that that is what stood out in the photo considering what I know my hands can do now! But we will get back to that later… The photos looked very, very odd! He said he would put it right and we should call back in a couple of weeks and we paid him there and then. When we went back the man and his business had completely disappeared; the people next door said he had gone. We were very upset but there was nothing we could do and so we sadly did not have any photos of our wedding.

Herman and I had a few very happy years together, in which time we moved into a couple of different flats and then he tried to organise us a house. When we visited the house, I thought it was beautiful; it had everything we wanted, even a place to park a car. When we got inside it was absolutely beautiful and the woman who owned the house was so nice. The things she gave us on our visit were too good to be true and it would have been marvellous, but I could not explain the feeling it gave me. When we left my husband said to me, "You don't seem very happy, what is wrong?" I told him something was not right, it bothered me, and I could not put my finger on it. My instinct told me that we should not move into that house even though I could not put my finger on why. When we spoke to his solicitor Herman said, "My wife keeps telling me we shouldn't buy the house" so his solicitor looked into it and realised that all of the drains were faulty, the whole house had to be dug up and we would have had to pay for it all. It would have cost us a small fortune. After that Herman's solicitor told him to "Always listen to your wife" – thank goodness we listened to my instincts. But little did he or I know I was going to lose him.

Herman and I used to go everywhere together. Some of the places he would take me to I would wonder how the heck he knew about them. He was not what you would call a drinker, nor was I, but he would take me to lovely pubs just to show me and we'd have a drink and just spend time together. Whenever there was anything going on that he heard about, read about, or thought I would be interested in he would take me. He had lots of friends and loved football. I would watch the football with him on the telly, but he did not want to go and watch it as it was too much time spent away from me. He wanted to take me to America for a holiday, but in those days that was so unusual and expensive I thought it was a bit too far. To tell you the truth, I was not thinking about children then; if I said I was I would be lying. Following the miscarriage when I was assaulted badly in Jamaica I was scared to think about children as I was not sure I would be able to carry a child after that, and it worried Herman too. I am sure we would have gotten to that later. However, after a few years Herman became very ill very suddenly. We did not know what was wrong, but as soon as the doctor was called, he sent him straight to hospital. Herman was diagnosed with mumps and was sent to a specialist hospital outside of London, which meant I could only visit him once a week. He was in there a long time, months, in which time I was working during the day at The British Museum and sometimes I would do night shifts at the secretarial agencies as I was missing Herman's wage. I stupidly did not think to contact the railway company that he worked for as they probably would have helped me financially, silly me. During this time, every morning on my way to work a very tall, handsome man always tilted his hat and said "good morning" to me. When I bumped into him one evening after a night shift, he was surprised to see me as he only ever saw me in the morning. We got talking and I explained that my husband was very ill. He then offered to buy me a beautiful house and all the furniture in it. He said everything would be in my name and I would be safe and happy. I could see he was a married man. I did not have to think about it very long as the way I was brought up taught me that married men should stick to their wives. No way did I want to be a kept woman. I saw him after that driving his beautiful car. He wanted to give me a lift but again I didn't want to get into a man's car because you know, when a man wants you to get in his car and he thinks a lot of you, you know what he's looking for.

After months I received a letter one day – as it was very difficult to get a phone call in those days – from the hospital telling me that Herman had died. I visited him in the morgue. I would not believe it until I saw him with my own eyes. The funeral was near to our home in Manor House, but as Herman's family were all in America and Jamaica it was just him and I. I would not like to tell you I was upset; I thought my life was going to end. I just did not know what to do. I was broken-hearted knowing I would never find anyone like him again.

After Herman's death I moved to a flat on Clissold Crescent. A man called Jim used to live near me; him and his mother living together, he was part of a local family that I knew. After Herman's death I once got talking to his mother, well his mother got talking to me. During our conversation she asked me all sorts of questions about where I worked, how I managed to furnish my flat myself and lots of questions about my financial situation. In retrospect I can now see why she was asking. After this Jim kept asking me if he could clean my windows or help me with the shopping or anything. He knew that I had just lost my husband from his mother and it became obvious that he wanted more from me. After that I stupidly married him which I should not have done but I was vulnerable and heartbroken, and it clouded my judgement. Jim and his mother were sort of lacking intelligence and education, and I think you have got to be very careful of people like that as half the time they do not realise what they are doing. I found out quite quickly that I had made a terrible mistake. He was with me for my money as he was up to his neck in debt and he was also vicious. He never wanted me to go anywhere apart from work, he was obviously scared of losing me – but only from a financial point of view. From early on he would regularly give me a good clout, and it got worse. At this time, I realised that I needed help and went to a solicitor close to my work. He was marvellous. He helped me take Jim to court on account of his violent behaviour towards me. The result was that he was put on probation and even the judge told him, "Find somebody your own size to hit rather than that lovely lady". Even after we were married Jim did not stay at my flat; he would go and stay at a friend's house to gamble – which is why he was so full up of debt. I realised quickly that he was seeing another woman who lived at his friend's where he gambled. I think that she was much more into sex with Jim than I was, considering I did not even like him. To tell you the truth I could not wait to get away from him; living with this man would drive anybody up the wall. I hired a private detective to prove that Jim was being unfaithful. Once we found where he gambled and that this woman was living there we sat in the detective's car and waited for hours from the morning and all afternoon. When eventually Jim came out the detective turned the car right in front of him, so Jim saw that I had seen him. When he came home, he was furious; he tried to grab hold of me, I was screaming, and the woman downstairs called the police. When they arrived, the policeman gave him two options, either "I'll lock you up or you clear off" – luckily for me Jim chose to clear off! And I thought "how good". The lawyer told me to get the divorce going as soon as possible. The only time I ever saw Jim after that was at court. I was just so happy to clean my hands of him! He was a bit more like an animal than a man, he did not have any intelligence, he could not even read or write. That was one episode of my life that I realised dealing with people who are not very intelligent is the worst thing you can do. And it definitely taught me a lesson.

I stayed in the flat in Clissold Crescent in Stoke Newington, it was a first floor one-bedroom flat and I had my own kitchen and living area but I shared a bathroom. At one stage we had some awful people living in the building; on the ground floor there was a woman who claimed she was a dressmaker, but also I'm pretty sure was a prostitute as there were always lots of different men sitting in the passage outside her flat when I arrived home from work. I would have to walk past all these nasty men to go up the stairs to my flat. I spoke to her about it and they stopped hanging around the passage. She must have moved her waiting room to her sitting room! On the top floor there were two nurses; one was a lovely Irish lady and the other was a dreadful Jamaican woman who the Irish lady told me was an illegal immigrant. I felt sorry for the Irish lady as she was so nice and came to warn me before she moved out that the other nurse could be a very nasty piece of work! This I found out for myself soon enough… One day I was in my flat in the kitchen and all I could hear was someone shouting and banging at my door. I was wondering what on earth could be happening, so I opened the door to find out and there she was standing at my door. Her face was full of anger and there was hate in her eyes! I had been combing my long, thick hair so it was down. Before I knew it she had my hair wrapped around her fist and was pulling it hard. She had the strength of an ox, but my hair also had its own strength to withstand the force. Luckily, she was unable to pull it out. She had hardly any hair on her head, may I add, and I think she probably wanted my hair out, so I looked like her. I struggled with her and although she was a slim girl, she had a mighty strength. However, I was able to gather my own strength from within to knee her. After that one of my neighbours called out, and she finally let go and walked off as though nothing had happened. Soon after that she disappeared without a trace. She never told me why she came and attacked me but I am assuming she thought that I had alerted the authorities on her as that must be why she left; although it was probably the Irish lady who had reported her.

Her flat did not stay empty for long. An Indian man and a Chinese man moved in. I do not know the Indian man's name, but he was a polite man and very gentle. The Chinese man however, seemed a bit of a reckless man who never seemed to go to work. Unfortunately, the Indian man moved out quite quickly and I eventually realised why. I had locks on my lounge door and one on the kitchen door which I locked every night and obviously when I went to work. All of a sudden, the main lock stopped working properly which I found when I would try and lock everything before leaving in the morning. it was as though someone had tampered with them. Early one Saturday morning the telephone rang and the person on the other end asked for Tan. "Sorry", I replied, "You've got the wrong number". The person insisted that they had called the correct number and that it was the number on all of "Tan's business papers". What a nerve! The penny clicked and I realised the Chinese man had been tampering with my locks, letting himself in whilst I wasn't there to use my telephone as if it was his and, even more cheekily, had been stealing my tea bags and using my coffee.

I was fortunate to get on with another of my neighbours, Ernest, and I informed him of what had been happening. He came right over and assessed the locks showing me how Tan had broken it so that I could not lock them properly. Ernest fixed the locks, he also put a big padlock on the kitchen door so when I went to bed or left for work, I locked and padlocked everything, so the worthless scumbag couldn't get to use my things anymore.

Sometime after I had been doing this Tan had the cheek to come down and ask me if he could borrow a jar of coffee. He did not have any shame! I said, "Why, can't you get to help yourself anymore?" No wonder the lovely Indian man moved out; Tan must have been stealing all his things too! I had a cat in my flat and I think Tan thought, if he got a dog, we would have a love of animals in common and I would become even more friendly towards him. Tan got himself an Alsatian dog, but he could not look after himself let alone the dog! He locked it up in a room downstairs with no food and I could hear it crying. As it got to night-time, you could smell he was doing his business in the room, so I got on to the police right away. The policeman gave Tan a right talking to and threatened him with prosecution. Thankfully, the policeman then took the dog away. I was very happy because I knew it would soon get a good meal and be given to someone who would look after him well.

I had another incident in that flat with a police sergeant. One day my doorbell went, so I asked the policeman what he wanted, and he replied that he had something very important to talk to me about. When I moved to Stoke Newington, my neighbours had warned me that the Stoke Newington Police could not be trusted. I opened the door and left it wide open so that people coming up and down the stairs could see inside, just in case. The policeman came in and asked me if I had a lager for him to drink! I was shocked but I got him one out of the fridge and once he had drunk that he had the cheek to ask for another one. I said, "Look, I don't run a café here. What is it that you want? You said you had something important to talk to me about". Would you believe it, he then asked if he could have sex with me! "I'm a civil servant, I'm not a prostitute, what do you think I am?" I asked him. He said, "I did meet a lady like you, who was English and African, and we had marvellous sex". I said, "Well what you should do is go back and finish your sex with her as you're not getting nothing from me". He wasn't very happy when he left I'll tell you that, he even came back the next day cursing me like there was no tomorrow because I didn't give him sex, although in the house where I lived there was a woman downstairs whom we all knew offered herself for money – and we all know she was a woman of reputation that enjoyed the company of men for money. I called two friends of mine who lived on the street to explain that he was downstairs cursing me and they came straight over. As soon as he heard them arrive, "Hi Dorothy, how are you?" he was out the door. Asking me for sex just because he is a policeman – I think that's disgusting, don't you?! I think that's more than disgusting!

Around this time, I started spending much more time with an old friend of mine whom I had known for years, Baboni Brown, who was from Sierra Leone. We both lived on parallel roads just off Church Street. Every day I would wake up, cook breakfast for the both of us, and by the time I got home from work he would be at my doorstep ready for dinner. He was a very clever, intelligent man and was very kind to me even though others knew him as a mean man. I think he was quite lonely as he used to have tenants but did not have any anymore. Even though he was about 20 years older than me we got on very well and our friendship developed. I would learn a lot from him especially about Africa and he would always book us two tickets to any educational film; he never asked me if I wanted to go, he just presumed – his brain never stopped. I did find out that he was a Mason, but that is all I could get out of him about that. I remember how beautiful his clothes were, he dressed immaculately with smart suits and watches, I would always be proud to be seen with him.

Chapter Three

Healing

In 1983 a very strange thing happened – to say the least. I was in my bedroom wide awake at 3 o'clock in the morning and I was trying to get up to go to the bathroom but my leg (the one that was tied up when I was a child) wouldn't bend and I was in a lot of pain with it. As I was holding it to try and bend it, I saw a movement next to my window. When I looked, I saw the figure of a young man. He said to me, "Heal your own knee", and I said to him, "Heal my own knee? How in the world can I do that?" His response was, "You have healing hands. Put both hands on your knee". He then walked across the room, past me, straight through the closed door. It was only then that I realised it was Jesus Christ, the Son of God. I put both hands on my knee and it bent immediately! I went downstairs, upstairs, downstairs, upstairs, downstairs, and upstairs in celebration and shock that I could easily bend my knee after all those years. Ever since my knee was tied up when I was a little baby my leg had always been stiff, and suddenly I was able to walk up and down the stairs with no bother! I never slept again that night, I was completely overwhelmed and excited, nervous, wanting to tell the entire world and then the next second worrying whether people would believe me. That is why I wrote this book, to tell the entire world! I eventually decided that if people did not believe me it was bad luck for them; that would be their loss. It might sound silly, but I just knew that I could heal every disease that came to me, chronic or otherwise. Without having any experience yet, I just knew that the more chronic the disease the longer it would take. Only Jesus Christ himself could heal chronic diseases in a minute, but I did truly know that I could heal it as long as I was given the full time that it needed in order to heal the disease. So many people have asked me to tell them why I think Jesus Christ chose me, but I do not know what to tell them you see. I know Mother Connie told me I was going to do wonderful things with my hands, and I'd had big hands since I was a child so it makes sense to me now, but I couldn't tell you why I was given this gift. I've thought about it a lot and I think God would only choose someone who God thought was capable of doing the job, not just anyone would be able to take it – you need patience, kindness, understanding and strength, both mental and physical, and have I got that! I think all the strength bestowed upon me made me think that I could go on healing people without a break, but I've realised from the years I've been healing and through the confidence that I've gained, that I was certainly doing over the hours in healing people. I think cancer should be about one and a half hours each day in healing time and arthritis should be one hour a week but I was giving three hours for cancer healing to patients and two hours for arthritis which was far too long. I was just overdoing it, as I do everything!

It was Sunday the next day, so I was at church as usual. I was having a chat with some friends who were there explaining the life-changing incident that had occurred the night before; everyone was very interested as you can imagine. However, the actual church minister seemed very displeased. He was saying how he usually recommended using oils to heal these illnesses or some other rubbish, and the curate responded in front of everyone, "Well you never healed anyone have you?", which made me laugh! He was trying to make out like he was a healer himself when we all knew that his only talent was drinking gin! Afterwards a lady called Brenda King came up to me as she had overheard our conversation. I had not realised that she had cancer before then; she had it all over her, she could not eat, she could not sleep; she was in a dreadful state and in a huge amount of pain. I arranged for her to come to my house a couple of days later with her husband and, it was very clear to me when I looked at her just how ill she was. I instructed her husband to go in the kitchen and get a great big basin before we started. I do not know how I knew I would need the basin, but I just knew it was essential. I also do not know how I knew what to do but it just came to me. It sounds unbelievable but I have always felt guided by Jesus Christ when I am healing. It comes naturally. Her first session lasted many hours and after a few hours she started vomiting and vomiting again into the basin. She must have been vomiting in that basin for about an hour. I've seen over the years that when I'm healing the pain initially gets worse before it gets better, and with Brenda, because she had so much cancer in her it's as if I had to get rid of the initial layer of cancer before treating the really deep cancer in her bones and her organs. I took her every day after that until the pain of the cancer was subsiding after a good few weeks, at which point I took her twice a week which meant I could take on other patients.

Brenda was a lovely person who I still remember very fondly. I found it was very easy to heal her because she was very thin, and I could see she was getting better each time she came. She was an assistant headmistress and her husband was a painter of pictures even though he never seemed to sell any! After a while when I'd taken the cancer from Brenda and she was 'better' she told me her and her husband had booked a holiday in Italy. When I asked her how long she was going away for, she said five weeks. My response was, "Brenda are you going out of your mind to go on your holiday right now after you have just been healed? Please, do not take any chances, cancer weakens the entire system, there is your heart, and every part of your body. You must halve your holiday". She could see I was very worried, and asked me to go on holiday with them, which was silly really because you can't just take someone on holiday when you have not booked for them can you? I said I could not go but that she really should halve her holiday if she was to get fully better and strengthen her body.

They both did go and she sent me a beautiful card, which I kept, and in it she wrote how well she was, how she was eating really well and didn't have any pain, what a lovely time they were having and how she was looking forward to seeing me when they got home – she thought she was all right you see. Sadly, the next time I saw Brenda's husband he told me she had died just as they were about to leave Italy. They were packing up the car when she said to him, "I'm so sorry I didn't do what Dorothy said". He said, "What are you worried about? We're going home now", and she said, "That's the trouble" and she slumped in the car. He had to take her body to the Italian police station where he was told to leave the body and to come and collect her in about seven weeks. When he went back to Italy to collect Brenda's body, they told him to sit down and have a cup of tea. Seven doctors came to discuss with him his wife's body, and what they had found. They said to him, "You told the police your wife had cancer all over her body. What sort of doctors do you have in England because she did not have a trace of cancer in her system? She died of a heart attack".

If she had listened to me and halved her holiday she'd have been back and if only the heart attack hadn't killed her, I would have started working on her heart, and I bet my bottom dollar I would've healed her. Some people do not listen but what can you do?

I was finding my feet with the whole thing and I bought myself a medical book to help me understand exactly where best to put my hands during the healing appointments depending on the illness. I had one or two patients at that time including Paul who I had also met at the church. He had Parkinson's disease. After a couple of sessions, in which time his shaking stopped completely, Paul said to me, "I feel very embarrassed because I haven't got anything to give you". I told him not to worry about payment and to worry about getting better. However, I don't know if it was due to him being embarrassed but he stopped coming after a while which I was very sorry about as he was a such a nice man, but the reality is that Paul got better and just carried on with his life. The reality is that Paul had no money, so he thought it best to disappear without making any financial contribution to me.

I went to see Diane Abbott, the MP of Hackney, to tell her I had a powerful gift of healing and could save many lives so that she could use this information and give it to her constituents. She rushed me out of her office and shouted, "I'm not interested" about five times, shooing me out as if I was a dog. I was completely flabbergasted. What in the world is she doing as an MP if she will not try and help her constituents' health?

I met a lady called Doris on the bus on my way to work one day. She worked at Covent Garden, and we became great friends. We always met on the bus every day after that and we loved each other's company. One day I asked her if she believed in God, she said of course she did and then she asked me if I had ever seen a vision. I was very surprised as it seems like such a strange thing to ask someone out-of-the-blue, and I explained about my vision of Jesus Christ and my healing hands. She asked if I had prayed for healing hands as she had been

Chapter Three

praying for healing hands all of her adult life. I said, "If I told you I did, I'd be telling lies", even though I had enormous hands! She then told me she had cancer in one of her breasts and she thought she was getting it in the other one. I told her she should come to me for healing and she did for a while in which time I healed the first breast of cancer, but then I think it started to come in the other one more rapidly. For some reason she stopped coming. Her daughter-in-law Sylvia, who had multiple sclerosis, also started coming to me for healing every day. I would always ask her why she did not bring Doris, but Sylvia would tell me that Doris was getting better every time. I later found out from Doris's husband that in actual fact Doris was getting worse and was too ill to come and see me. Why she never told me I've no idea because I would have gone up there all the time. I suppose she thought that because I had other patients, I would not have come but I would have done. I would have got her back on her feet! If you asked me, Sylvia wanted Doris out of the way. What a wicked thing to do! She could not care less for anyone but herself. I was very upset. I would not put my hand back on her, no way! Then she had the cheek to tell me that she had been to a help group with 12 other multiple sclerosis sufferers and hadn't even told them about me – as long as she was getting better, she couldn't give a hoot! She was still running her business but pretending to the authorities she was still ill, even though I had healed her. When I moved, I did not tell her my new address and I would never have anything more to do with her.

During one of my healing sessions with Sylvia the minister at St Mary's Church decided to visit me. While I went to make a cup of tea, he told Sylvia that I would not be able to heal her. I think he was jealous because I had healed Brenda and because he could not heal anything himself and he did not like that I could. When I told the other people in the church they said, "What a pity you didn't give him a glass of a gin rather than a cup of tea, he would've been all right then!", as he drank like a fish you know! When I saw him next, I told him, "Never ever come to my home again to insult people". He is not the first minister who disliked me for what I could do but as my Mother Connie told me, "Don't worry over anything you can't do anything about". She always reminded me of that.

All of a sudden Baboni had a stroke. Luckily, he was taken to hospital and when I visited, I tried my best to help him with my healing hands – but heartbreakingly at that point I hadn't quite worked out where best to put my hands when healing every disease. When I visited him, he gave me his keys and told me to move in and look after his house whilst he was in hospital. He told me that there was money in the wardrobe that I could use whenever I wanted. Coincidentally, at the same time the landlord of my flat spoke to me about whether I would like to move out because they wanted to up the rent by renting it out to someone new. They didn't know I was moving out anyway so by a stroke of luck they paid me £6000 to move out, which in those days was enough to buy a house and furniture! I put it straight in the bank and moved into Baboni's.

Chapter Three

Whilst I was living at Baboni's house I was on the bus one day when a plant pot suddenly appeared in my face. I asked the woman holding it, "What the heck are you playing at? Your plant's sticking in my face", and she apologised and explained that she had been wanting to talk to me. I asked her what she wanted and she said, "I felt your power", so I asked her what she meant by that and she said she knew I had very strong power as she was a spiritualist, and she knew that I could heal. Her instincts had told her that I was a healer and she asked if I could heal her shoulder. Her name was Sandra and she then came over for healing and brought with her the alphabet on different pieces of paper, A–Z. She asked me to give her a small glass and she arranged the alphabet all around the table with the glass in the middle, and she kept her hand on the glass which kept moving to different letters. I had never, ever seen anything like this before and to tell you the truth it was a bit frightening. When she had finished, she put all of the letters that the glass had indicated next to each other and asked me, "Who is Rose Rueben?" For a second or two I did not even know who Rose Rueben was and then I realised and said, "Oh that's the woman who gave birth to me". What a woman, waiting until she is dead to say sorry! She had not even asked how I was when my husband had visited her. That is just to show you that people should do things they would like to be done unto themselves; she would not have liked herself as a baby to be tied up!

Herman and I both banked at Barclays Bank, Stamford Hill and I had a deposit account as far back as 1965.

One day as I looked at my statement of account my eyes spied £2 taken out continuously all the way down the page, which equalled to £12 taken out on each and every page. I was quite astonished, £12 on each page! I had never taken out £2 at a time so I asked the staff at the counter who had been taking money out from my deposit account but none of them could make out the signature. They told me to come back in a couple of weeks while they investigated it. When I went back they told me that the assistant manager had been found stealing and he had been given the sack. I asked, "Who is going to give my money back?" and all I got was silence. Naturally, I left that bank and went to the NatWest Bank branch at Dalston. I thought the bank should have been responsible for my money and pay it all back to me, but I got nothing. As a result, I have never banked with Barclays Bank ever since then.

Baboni and I had spoken about marrying each other, but unfortunately he never came out of hospital and he died. I missed his company very much. I'd have been better off marrying him instead of that nutcase I did marry, but as Mother Connie said, "Whatever you do, don't worry about things you can't do anything about; you just have to accept it". After speaking to my solicitor, it transpired that Baboni had a daughter in Sierra Leone. She hated her father but as soon as she heard he had died she was after his money. The court then took over, sold the house and they told me that Baboni had left me some money so I should find myself a flat which would be mine as long as I needed it. The agreement was that the flat would be in Baboni's daughter's name so that when I go, she would take it over. In the meantime she is supposed to be paying a monthly fee but, due to the fact that I don't think she's alive, as I haven't heard from her since 1989 (I think very much she passed away during the Ebola crisis), and I've paid every penny towards the flat, I will just ask the judge for it to be put under my name. I'll ask him to add an extra 80 years on the lease at the same time! Incidentally I know for certain that the solicitor, who is still my solicitor, didn't want me to write this book, but the thing is I wrote it to help people and to save lives.

In 1989 I found the flat that I am living in now, still in Stoke Newington. It's quite a small flat and quite contained but I can fit my treadmill in it, which is very important to me – and I still go on it twice a day without fail! At first it was not too bad. The lady who lived above me (No. 3) was very nice and we got on very well together. Her husband had owned the whole building but had died by the time I moved in. Whilst he was still alive, they had decided to make the building into flats and she had a lovely flat. However, she did not have a television so if there was anything on she wanted to see, she used to ask me if she could come down to my flat and watch it. I was always glad to see her because she was a very nice lady and I told her she could always come down and see anything she liked. Unfortunately, a few years after I moved in that lady died and I was very sorry when she did. I was also worried about who might come in her place.

I was quite right to worry. In 1996 a millionaire man who had a house further down bought his daughter the flat above me and the one next to it. He was a very rich man, the type of man who gets away with anything. His daughter moved in and started running a full-blown industrial laundry business which uses dangerous chemicals and the noise of the machines was terrible; they would run them practically all night and it would wake me up. This, would you believe it, went on for 18 years. When she had finished with the chemicals she used to put them underneath my window, the very one I would open for air, and I think she was either trying to make me ill or kill me as we have great big bins in the car park which she could've put them in. The chemicals have seeped down from the flat upstairs through my wall into the cupboard. I have had to throw out four big bags of clothing, handbags and a duvet because they were covered with sticky chemicals, and also, I threw out a beautiful carpet. They were not even satisfied with the two flats. She wanted my flat as well; talk about greedy is not the word! She sent a man to me to ask me if I would sell the flat but when I told my solicitor how much they had offered, he said it was worth double that! What I did not tell him was the man she sent offered to "take me away for the weekend". He must've thought that was marvellous to me, but I said, "No way, this flat is not for sale, and nothing in it neither. I have called the council so many times to complain about her laundry business and all they do is fob me off! The council eventually sent someone to investigate and I stood at my door whilst he went to speak to my neighbour. She did not let him in, she stood at the door and I heard her tell him they had gotten permission from the police to run the laundry. Apparently, they were paying Stoke Newington Police (the sergeant) to run the laundry. When the man from the council came down the stairs from his investigation, he tried to hide his face from me and rushed out.

The neighbours at No. 3, after a few years, started a family. First a boy, then twins. After a couple of years, the twins started walking and every morning I would hear crying and screaming. It just made me remember my childhood and wonder what could be happening to those small twins. It worried me one day when the mother and twins were coming in and I saw the mother hitting one of the twins on her legs. The child started screaming and crying. I then realised that it was all about the little child not walking the way she liked so she beat her for it. The beating went on and on. After this incident I rang Social Services and reported it, but nothing happened; she was still screaming every morning. I wondered when this woman would ever stop what she was doing to her child.

When she moved in, she started setting up the laundry business and got a man over who started pulling all the pipes out. All of a sudden, the water started to pour in my bedroom! I tried very hard to get in touch with the lady in the flat upstairs but there was nobody up there. Luckily, I saw a man coming in the same day with his tools and I was so desperate to stop the water running in all different places in my room, causing a lake, so I asked him to take a look. He got quite a shock when he saw my bedroom. He said, "She tells so many lies, I'm sick and tired of her.

What has happened to your room is absolutely terrible. I will tell her about the water and then I'm not coming back – she'll have to get someone else". I told my solicitor and he sorted it out with the insurance company but in the meantime, I had to sleep in the living room for six months because my bedroom had to dry. What a palaver! She caused one palaver after another.

Eventually after 18 years she divorced her husband and moved to America. Unfortunately for me she moved another woman in who runs the business and her husband runs a factory in there as well, so I not only have the dangerous chemical laundry, I have the factory as well. One day I came home with the Dial a Ride man from shopping and caught them delivering all the bits and pieces, trying to sneak them in. They had all been left in the passage; I could not even get to my flat. So, we have all business up here; it seems as if I have been living in a factory and a laundry from 1996, and so it goes on. I believe that the former neighbour who went to America deliberately made sure she put a lady in the flat who was just as bad as she was. This woman has one son and he is very much out of control. I think he has got something wrong with him as he never seems to grow or go out anywhere, not even to school. He purposely scrapes all the furniture along the floor constantly and, as he never goes outside, I think he has outside toys inside which make a hell of a racket. He never seems to stop! His mother must be hard of hearing, otherwise it would drive her mad living in the flat with all the noise! It is a good job the government has made noise pollution a criminal offence.

I am thinking of taking the parents to court to get some peace and quiet – but it will not make a difference to them; they get away with anything.

Throughout this whole period, I have written to many MPs; firstly, I wrote to Ken Livingston who was the Mayor of London, he is one of the most honest Labour MPs I have ever come across, he is a good man! He told me to write to my local MP, Diane Abbott, to explain everything and she should be able to stop it. I did this but I never did get a response and as nothing changed whatsoever, I assume she did nothing about it anyway. Some time later I was shocked to discover she decided to stand for leadership of the Labour Party, I could not think of anyone less equipped to lead the Labour Party, fortunately her bid to become leader was unsuccessful. I have also written to many different MPs about having powerful healing hands so I could reach more people and save more lives, as I can heal cancer, arthritis, and all sorts of diseases. The only replies I received back were from Conservative MPs. I certainly would only vote Conservative.

The trouble with my neighbours seems to be never-ending. There have been many different incidents; one time large wooden boards appeared outside in the passage on my side of the wall with my flat number on it so my friends in the block kept asking what they were for, but I had no idea. I think the woman who owned the flat above with the laundry business knew that her chemicals would seep into my flat and ruin some of my things, so she convinced Marcus King (the building manager) that she would pay him a lot of money to get me out. I think they were waiting for me to go shopping so they could block me out of my flat using the boards. What an unprofessional thing to do as the building manager! I told my solicitor and he could not believe it; he assured me no one could get me out of my flat without going to court. Another time that she tried to get me out was by saying there was a strong smell of gas coming from my flat. She was obviously worried that her dangerous chemicals would blow her sky high, but I would not open the door to her as I could not smell any gas. She called the police. They were very quick to come over and when I opened the door to them one of them held my arm behind my back before I knew it, but the sergeant with him told him to "Take your hand off her back". I opened the windows at their request, even though I could not smell any gas, and they went away. This continued over a number of years, every now and again one of the ladies in the flat upstairs or the police would come around to make me open my windows. I'd do so, and they would go away. Eventually British Gas came and found that there was actually a gas leak the whole time but in the meter cupboard in the entrance passage and not my flat. I asked him to "Go upstairs and tell that nitwit", so he did. Can you believe they did not come immediately considering how dangerous gas is! I have also had flat No. 3 using my address to receive post. Once I received a notice from the leaseholder saying something to do with me moving out of my flat! They thought I had got married as I had in fact changed my name back by deed poll to Rodgers, the name my Mother Connie gave me. But as my name was different on the lease they were trying to get me out. What it had to do with them I have no idea. It got me so panicked that I sent it back instead of giving it to my solicitor. When I spoke to him about it he said I should have given it to him instead of sending it back, but he sent them a strongly-worded email telling them that you just can't do things like that and no way could they get a person out of their home without going to court. I must say I felt very much more relaxed after that.

I had a friend called Mrs Paula Scarf who lived in my building; we got on very well. About 18 years ago Paula had a stroke and the doctor asked her who her next-of-kin was. This shook her up and she told me about her health scare as she knew I had healing hands. She knew she had many blood clots from the stroke. Luckily she knew where they were, so I got rid of them one by one over ten months and she was clear of clots. When her husband died of cancer, she allowed a man called Ellis to rent her second bedroom as she was terrified to live alone. She always asked me how I managed living on my own, but to tell you the truth it did not worry me at all. I always felt someone was with me anyway; my guardian angel. Ellis drank like a fish. Paula tried to get on with him and naturally he was glad for the room that she let him stay in. One day she said to me, "When I die, make sure my flat does not go to Ellis's family. I want it to go to my cousin in Belgium".

ANNOUNCEMENT: To Mrs Paula Scarf's cousin in Belgium, Paula passed away and I would like you to contact me because she left her flat to you. Please ring the bell of flat No. 1.

The doctor had told Ellis many times that he would not be living long and in fact he passed away the week after Paula died. The flat was left empty then, but since, it seems to have been sold and someone is living there.

Where I am still living now, a lady called Joyce moved into the flat next to mine. We soon became very good friends and we used to go around to each other's flats every week for tea and cakes and we would talk for the whole afternoon. Joyce would tell me so many interesting things, all about her late husband who was a colonel in the army and she also told me that she was very afraid of her own daughter. She knew she was very greedy for money and of course Joyce was quite well off as her husband had left all the money to her. She had even bought her flat with cash! We were both very happy with our friendship and having our flats so close together. It never came up in conversation, and sometimes I do not bring it up as I don't know how people are going to take it, but I had never mentioned to her that I was a healer and I could heal chronic diseases.

One day Joyce mentioned to me that she had difficulty breathing and felt that she was not very well. She went to hospital with her son and the doctors told her that she had cancer. That was when I told her about my healing hands. I told her, "I didn't tell you as I didn't know how you'd take it, but I have got healing hands and I've already healed a lot of people". When I put them on her lungs at the back, she said she could feel my hands and how fantastic it felt. Joyce offered to pay me, but I was having none of it; I just wanted her to get better as she was my friend. Her son lived nearby, and I met him when he came to pick her up one time, and her daughter lived in France. Joyce told me she was hoping her daughter would stay in France, but she would not as there was money involved and she was greedy for money. Her daughter came over straight away but neither the son nor the daughter liked the fact that I had healing hands – the more Joyce told them how much she loved having my healing hands on her, the more they didn't like it! Nor the nurse from Barbados! I could see it in her daughter's eyes how she wanted me to clear off, but I would not as I had promised Joyce I would be there every day. I went to Joyce's every day to treat her and was careful to arrive before the daughter did. One day I went over as normal and Joyce was sitting up in bed, but when I asked her if she was OK I did not receive a response. After feeling her hand, I realised she was dead as a door nail and straight away asked the daughter what was going on. Her response was, "Well I asked the doctor to give her an injection". I could not believe it and there was nothing I could do. I could not tell the police; they would not believe me anyway – especially not Stoke Newington police. She had asked the doctor to give her own mother an injection which obviously killed her immediately and had then sat her up in bed as if she was alive! What lies she told the doctor, no one will ever know. I wondered how much she paid him to do it. What a wicked thing to do to your own mother. Her mother was right to be terrified of her; she knew her daughter would try to kill her, and she did. She made a good job of it and all! I told her, "They have a saying, what goes around comes around"; she knew what

I meant, and I was so disgusted I left. After I came back home from Joyce's flat I did not know where to turn – I would miss my friend so much. One does not know where to complain because nobody will take any notice. I just sat at my open window. When later on I saw them leave Joyce's flat with her coffin, her daughter saw me looking through the window, she smiled and even waved her hand at me... I just shut my window and thought "My God that woman's got no shame whatsoever". She was happy as a lark! Her own mother – I might tell you I was very upset. I prayed that Joyce would rest in peace. It is a pity as the doctors should never have touched her; the cancer had gone, and they had no right to do what they did.

I always think when you do something evil like that you always get something back worse. You get back what you give; when you do good, you get good. What we have to put up with sometimes and keep quiet is so sad. Joyce could have been alive today living happily, as I have healed people much sicker than she had been. I really missed her.

It makes me so sad that so many people say they are faith healers yet they have not a clue how to heal. I know I can heal cancer, arthritis, heart problems, psoriasis and all sorts of other diseases which can all be proven through all of the people I've healed. I very much wish I had seen the vision before Herman died. I could have healed him and Baboni.

I have healed many different people along the way, including one woman and her two daughters who all had sickle cell disease. A young lad came to me in a wheelchair who could not walk or talk as he had a cancerous tumour in his brain. He was only 18. To say thank you for healing him he sent me a beautiful framed poem which I still have on my wall to this day. Since I healed him, he walks, talks and drives a car. He also got married and has a daughter so I am very happy that I was able to help him. I asked him if he told other people about me and he said he did but they did not believe him.

There was a man called Emmanuel who came to fix my telly. He was from Malta but lived in London with his wife. Whilst he was working on my telly, he mentioned that he had a very stiff and painful neck. I told him, "You sit down, and I can heal it in 15 minutes", and I did! He was so impressed he then asked me if I could heal his baby who had been born with one ear. I agreed and for three hours each week he brought his baby over and I kept my hand on the baby's ear. I could see the ear forming slowly over a number of months. Emmanuel could also see it, but his wife could not at first – until it was fully formed and then she invited me for dinner to say thank you. Over dinner Emmanuel and his wife told me about her father and his brother who were both living in Malta. Her father had two very swollen legs and could barely walk, and his brother had been in a terrible accident and had all sorts of things wrong with him since; difficulty breathing, difficulty walking around; he was in a very bad way. I went to Malta and started work on the brother first. I kept my hand on him for days and nights, even whilst he was asleep in bed with his wife. After a number of days his breathing had improved, and he was feeling absolutely marvellous. He then asked me if I could heal his brother who had a trapped nerve, so I healed him also. I then met Emmanuel's wife's father and worked on his swollen legs. What a dreadful thing. I could feel how much pain he was in! When I am healing, I can feel any pain that my patients are experiencing in my hands; luckily, it goes away once I have finished. I worked on it all day but could only fix one of his legs as it was so bad. Whilst I was in Malta, I did a lot of healing. There was a man who had cancer in his back and could not bend over. I worked on him for a whole day and at the end of the day he bent over and was so amazed he brought out a big wad of cash to pay me, but I refused it. "I don't want your money, you keep your money", I said. At the time they had a dreadful Prime Minister who was stealing money from people left, right and centre. Some people were paying everything they earned. A lot of English people had flats who just sold up and left, which made things much worse. One day ten people came over asking for me to put my hand on their heads for an hour each because they were all suffering from nerves and anxiety due to the situation in the country. I worked solidly for ten hours – oh my God talk about tired. I also met a lady who desperately wanted a baby but kept miscarrying every time she got pregnant. She became pregnant just before I left, so I regularly kept my hands on her tummy to help her and when I was back in England, I received a letter telling me that she had had a healthy baby – all because of the power in my hands. By the time I left I could not count how many houses I had visited in Malta, all wanting my hands on them. I never took a penny! A friend of mine said I needed to see a psychiatrist after that trip as I had turned down so much money, not taking a penny. They were so in need because of the economic situation in their country. You cannot take money from people when they are in need; that is terrible!

You certainly need to have a lot of patience to do healing. It is not a quick fix, and healing, depending on what you suffer from, can take quite a few months; whereas if a pain or an illness is caught straight away it can be healed very, very quickly. One young chap came to me once saying he could not sleep. He had pains on each side of his neck, so I put my hands on it and the next minute it was gone. I always say my healing is slow, sound, and permanent – and it is. You also get so many enemies; that's why the doctors and the MacMillan nurses don't like me, and that's why the church ministers don't like me.

In 1993 I then healed a policeman, Christian Luke Barker from Hertfordshire who had been given six months to live. Christian was diagnosed with a cancerous tumour in his brain and also complained that he had dreadful pains in his stomach. I then discovered he had MRSA in his large intestines which took me about five weeks to get rid of, having my hands on his head for three hours every week. It took ten months to heal the cancerous tumour in his head and as a result, miraculously, he is still alive today – 25 years later! Christian was over the moon and told lots of his friends, so I then healed one or two of them of various illnesses, and Christian told me that they all meet up for a drink regularly to celebrate their good health as a result of my healing hands.

I later healed his mother and father who both had arthritis. His mother also had two bad ankles and something wrong with her spine. He has a very nice family. His mother was a very helpful lady, always offering to do ironing and such like. I took her up for treatment for two hours a week and it took a few months, but after a while she was as right as rain.

I also healed his sister who had a serious swallowing problem. She had been told she would have to have an operation, but that it was a very serious operation so instead she came to me. I held her neck for hours and hours on end and straight away she was able to swallow! No need for an operation! I then healed his two young nephews who had asthma. They came to me week after week and they were lovely, well-behaved boys.

I am a very good friend with him and his wife and I still go and visit them sometimes at their lovely house in the countryside in Essex, and it is always very enjoyable. He also invited me to his second wedding with his lovely wife, Wendy, and even mentioned me in his speech, saying, "If it wasn't for Dorothy, I'd be six feet under". I went to his retirement party in a big countryside manor which was a very nice weekend too. It makes a difference when you live on your own and do not go out often and have no relatives like sisters, brothers or such like.

I healed another policeman, Stuart, who I met through Christian. He had bowel cancer. Both of them wrote to the Royal Marsden (the cancer hospital) asking them if they could walk me around the ward to see if I could help anyone who wanted to be healed. The doctors cannot heal everyone by their means. There are numerous diseases that cannot be healed as there is no medical cure yet. I think they should take all the help they can get, especially when they know and have heard of someone who can heal cancer. I suppose their disbelief in my form of healing is why they never answered the two letters that Stuart and Christian sent.

Only a few years ago I heard Prince Charles say on the television that if anyone knew of any healers who could heal cancer, he would like to know them or meet them. I wrote three letters to Prince Charles at different addresses, but I honestly don't think he saw them, as the same receiver of my letters kept replying to my letters but I never heard anything from the prince at all.

I have had many invitations to go abroad to heal: America, Malta, Paris, Nigeria, Turkey, Greece and many others. One time when I was invited to America, I was in the post office and told them about my invitation. They told to be very careful because of my birth certificate. Apparently, they said the Americans would think I was a liar because I am brown skinned, but according to my birth certificate I am fully English, and they said I could be put in jail. Well that frightened me like billy-o and stopped me going to America. I just for some reason do not like leaving England. Maybe I am too comfortable in my little corner of good old England. I feel very uncomfortable when people are talking in another language which I can't understand and I think in England it is very rude for people to talk in another language, especially when you engage them in a conversation, because not everyone can understand them; but then again, maybe it's because their English isn't very good but I am not lazy in trying to understand other languages. The problem is that all nations live in England and I can't speak all the languages of these nationalities. I always think people should stick to the language of the country in which they reside. I am very happy that the government have brought in a rule that states everyone has to pass an English test when moving to England. I have not been on holiday for many years. What a thing when you have no relatives in the whole wide world. As I've been on my own for many years I'm a very independent woman and often spend Christmas on my own as I actually enjoy my own company; but it does not mean that I decline invitations, as long as the company is of intellect and can hold an intelligent conversation. In fact, I always feel as if there is someone with me – my guardian angel.

One young woman came for healing with her boyfriend; a very nice man. She had cancer in her bowels and bladder, and I put my hands on her for three hours. After the treatment she was in a very bad way as she was so full up of cancer and it is painful to begin with before it gets better. As soon as she left with her boyfriend out of the door, she shouted to him, "How dare you take me to the brown-skinned woman, and even have her put her hands on me!" I did not hear her boyfriend answer her, but I knew he was very embarrassed because he telephoned me later and apologised. I told him not to worry as it was not his fault.

Another man named Stephen came to me for healing as he had a tumour in the brain. When I put my hand on his head, I felt something like plastic and asked him what in the world did he have on his head? He said that the doctor was experimenting on him by trying to take the cancerous tumour out of his head using a needle. I told him I had never heard of such a thing and the sooner he asked the doctor to take whatever he had put in his head out of his head, the better he would be. I was quite surprised he had that thing put in there when I could have healed him. When he asked the doctor to take it out, he did not; he said he wanted to leave it in there a bit longer. The doctor wanted to be rich and famous whilst the poor man with five young children was slowly dying. I just could not understand why a doctor could be so callous just for himself. Stephen unfortunately died because of this experiment when I could have healed him. Having something plastic in somebody's brain – I have never heard of such a dreadful thing to happen.

I have experienced quite a few people trying to take advantage of my healing abilities, trying to get something for nothing. One day a man came to my door and asked me if I was a healer. I told him that I have healing hands and he asked if he could be my partner in healing, I then asked him what kind of healer he was, to which he replied that he was a spiritual healer. I told him that I didn't know anything about spiritual healing and can't understand why he thought there was a link between us – according to what I hear from a spiritualist, they can't heal at all, they just listen to dead spirits. Straightaway he asked me to heal his arm and hand, which was a bit of a signal that really this had all been his way of getting something for nothing. He had hours of healing, but he did not give me a penny like some others do. I think when you are not well known they think they can come for nothing or very little. Some came for months and never gave me a penny, and still expecting to get dinner every time. Talk about taking liberties! This time it'll be different because people who want healing will have to pay me more money as I'll be having people keeping me safe, looking after me and being present whilst I'm healing at all times once this book is out; and I shall have to pay them as they won't be wanting to come and do that for nothing.

There are many examples of people taking liberties throughout my healing experiences. Stuart, Christian's friend, told me that I was taking peanuts. I did nearly all his family and I got less than peanuts, but I did not mind. I have never demanded more. Another man who had a brain tumour, who was recommended to come to me by Christian Luke Barker's first wife, had the cheek to tell me he was not putting a penny down on the table. I honestly think they would make an angel swear these people! I told him not to come back. The sauce of them! Another man came to me with a bad back. On his last visit we agreed that he was better, and I then went to make a cup of tea. When I got back to the living room, he was pretending to be fast asleep. I then woke him up and told him to go home. He had the cheek to say he thought I would allow him to stay the night. I told him that I did not do bed and breakfast. He did not look very pleased, but that was his problem. The cheek of the living devil! When you are a single woman people think they can take liberties as there is no man around.

During the time that I was healing Christian, a man came to fix the telly and saw me with both my hands on Christian's head. The next time he came he asked me if I was a healer and I explained that Christian had a cancerous tumour in his brain which I was healing. He wanted me to heal his hay fever and also wanted me to marry him! But I could see there was more to it than met the eye – some men think they are God's gift to women. I think he was looking to see if I had money, which I did not. He must have thought being a healer would mean that I was rich. Little did he know that I was very poor indeed, as most people did not give me a penny for my healing, and those who did gave me peanuts.

A woman came to me from Milton Keynes and explained to me that her mother, June, was in a hospice with a brain tumour. I agreed to visit her mother and she drove me to see her. I had not been in her car more than two seconds when she told me she wanted to write a book about my healing hands, and she knew it would be a best seller! I was flabbergasted; she had not even asked me if she could write a book about me, she just assumed that she could. She said she did not care about the money and wanted to write the book anyway, as if I believed that she was not doing it for the money. I never really answered this conversation, I just laughed to myself and thought it was a load of nonsense. I started visiting June in the hospice regularly and as soon as they saw she was starting to get better they allowed her to go home, so I continued to visit her at her home, even staying there a couple of days to intensively heal her before I went home. The number of hours I gave her was enormous. I do not think anyone of them appreciated it, only June and her husband, as June's children thought I was after their father for some reason. I have never heard of such a load of nonsense. Whilst June was at home a carer would come and look after her, bathe her and get her dressed and so forth. June told me one day that when the carer had been there, June had fallen over and knocked her head really hard on the bath. I don't know what the carer was doing to allow that to happen but it worried me that just as June's brain was getting better she had to go and give it a good knock on the enamel bath! I don't think she ever got quite right after that. One day, when I had my hands on June, healing her, her son came in the room and started shouting at me. I do not know what for. I did not answer, I just thought what a pathetic man and that he had such a cheek considering all of the hard work I put in. When he left, June apologised and said, "I'm so sorry, please forgive him". I was so glad to get away from there. It is amazing what a healer has to put up with. I do not think any other healer would have to put up with what I did, and it certainly taught me a lesson.

 After a meeting at the church which I attend on Albion Road, the minister told me they had chosen me to go for a week to a Healing Ministry in Derby. The woman who was usually sent every year was not at all happy that they had chosen me. I asked another lady why she wasn't nice to me after that and the lady said to me, "Well she's always pretended she's a healer and now they've found a genuine healer and they're sending you in her place; of course she's not happy!"

When we arrived in Derby at the first meeting, we were asked to share our experiences with all present. Each one of us had to tell all of our experiences with the Lord Jesus Christ. I told them about seeing the vision and the Lord God blessing me with healing hands. Everybody was very interested, especially a couple of women who came to me for help. I asked them what was wrong and they said it was something to do with one of the ladies, Joan. There was something wrong with her muscles. I sort of knew right away that Joan had muscular dystrophy all over her body.

When Joan came up to my hotel room for healing, for some reason I grabbed hold of her neck. I suppose to me her head did not look straight. I pulled her neck in an upward position and I heard something crack. In shock she said, "You have just put my head in the right position". I then told her I would do the healing from her feet, I do not know why, but we got started right away.

Joan told me she had met five healers where she lived, including herself, as she said she was also a healer. I asked her why she did not try to heal herself and she said, "Please don't let that put you off, none of the healers including myself are as powerful as you are". She then asked if she could invite me to her home for a week. I of course knew what she wanted; she was in a terrible condition and she wanted me to stay with her so she would heal fast.

I was hesitant at first because I had to return to my office and I knew she was a very mean person, the type who wants something for nothing, but I eventually went. When I got to her house, I put my hands all over her for the most part of the week. Joan was a very wealthy retired teacher; her husband was a solicitor and they lived in a private street in Buckinghamshire.

While I was there, she introduced me to two people, both of them were very ill. One had arthritis so bad, her whole body was riddled with the disease to the point that her knuckles had been taken out of her hands. I was only with her for two hours. I went to visit her because I felt so sorry for her – the poor lady should have had me for 12 months and if she had, I could have healed her knuckles too. When Joan came to pick me up, the lady asked Joan if she could bring me every week. Joan smiled and told her that I live in London. Joan never once told her she herself was very ill and that she had invited me to stay with her for one week; she did not offer to bring me back during that week either. She was hiding her illness.

I went straight back to the office when I got back to London. On my first day back, Joan telephoned me asking if I could come to her flat in London off Baker Street, York Way. She also asked me if it was possible, I could come every evening after I leave the office. I said certainly not, but I went that evening. I stayed with her for six hours. She begged me to come again, I guess my healing was working on her. It is a very good thing I was not greedy for money, even after all those hours she only gave me peanuts. After weeks of going up and down from her flat

Chapter Three

she told me she was better and thanked me. I told her I thought she needed more hands on her arm where she had a splint, but as she said she was better I thought it saved me ever going back to her again. She of course knew better than me. However, a few months after, I got a letter from Joan asking me if she could invite me for another week to Buckinghamshire. I had a word with my minister and told him all about Joan with her muscular dystrophy and he told me she was just using me for her own ends. I never went back.

Not only did the Lord give me healing hands, he also gave me a gift of profiling. I think it goes with the healing that I can sort of read people sometimes.

I had a friend who rented out flats. I got her a tenant once and told her she would not have to worry about him because he was very honest and reliable, and he was. My friend was so impressed with my profiling powers. She then asked me if I could help her profile a woman who wanted one of her flats before she moved in, as she was very unsure about whether to trust her. After inviting her for tea I told my friend not to ever allow her to owe even one week's rent because she looked a bit dodgy to me. Whilst she was living there and she was paying her rent and not asking any favours it would be fine, but as soon as she started asking for favours, not to trust her. And that is that.

A friend of mine a few years ago asked me to meet her new boyfriend as they were supposed to be getting engaged. When her boyfriend came to see me, he brought three large bottles of strong drink which I do not drink. I could see he was trying to sweeten me up and I knew he was driving so I just gave him coffee and put the alcohol away in the cupboard. We had a long talk together during which I asked lots of questions and formed my opinion. After having met him I asked my friend Lucy if she wanted the truth or a pack of lies. She said she wanted the truth, so I told her my honest opinion was that he was a liar and she walked straight out, very annoyed. About three months afterwards she came back and told me I was right. Of course I was. However, I am not always right; we all make mistakes.

Chapter Four

At the flat where I am living now and have been since 1989 having moved out of Baboni's, Mr Alroy was the agent running the flats. He was hard working, very trustworthy, very nice and never stole any money or a thing. Unfortunately, a company called Marcus King then took over the flats, and the man who ran the company, whom we all referred to as Marcus King, was a dreadful man. He was greedy and I soon realised that he was charging me much more money for maintenance than anyone else. Even my friend in the two-bedroom flat said they never paid what he was charging me, nowhere near that sort of money. My maintenance bills kept increasing in large amounts even though I knew I did not owe them anything. He also changed the building insurance to his own name so that he was pocketing all of the insurance money. I told my solicitor and he wrote to the agent asking them to explain the bill but they did not reply. Dealing with these type of people is not easy; they are greedy, dishonest and very hard to understand. With all the money he stole he bought himself a Jaguar car. Over the years he has stolen thousands of pounds sterling from me and I hope I can get all my money back one day.

One week before Christmas 2010, I heard a very loud knocking on the window at night, where the lawn is. I opened the double glazing and asked this very tall man, who must have been about seven feet tall what he wanted. To my surprise he asked me if he could come in and show me something. I told him to clear off. I was not interested in what he had to show me, and I thought that was it. The very next second, he was in the building knocking outside my front door. Now to me that seemed very strange. How could he get into the premises so fast? I asked who was there and he repeated what he said at the window. I told him I would call the police if he did not leave and he could then explain to them what he wanted to show me. He then left. A week after Christmas the same man turned up again, standing at the gate of the lawn, staring at me through my open window while I was feeding the birds bread. I then phoned the police and told them a criminal hitman had been hired by Marcus King and he was trying very hard to get into my flat which was very frightening. Knowing Marcus King, it was then I realised he was either a convicted rapist or trying to kill me off. The policeman told me to telephone them if he came again.

The man came back on 21 January 2011 with another story. He rang my bell this time and said he had a parcel for me. I looked through the spyglass in my door and saw him in uniform. I asked him what the name was on the parcel and he said it did not have a name because they forgot to put it on. He then realised I was not going to open my door and went away, but it was all very disturbing as I wondered when he was going to come back again. I know Marcus King was responsible for this criminal coming to my window. He thought he had frightened me so much that I would pay all the money he had charged me on my maintenance bill. I knew I did not owe him and I found out that he was exploiting money from all of the vulnerable people in the building, such as the sick gentleman who had just lost his wife in another flat, although I was getting the brunt of it as a single woman and was being charged the most. I seemed to be the one hit worst, the money he kept piling on my bill was thousands of pounds. After he hired the hitman on me I told Marcus King I had reported him to the police. He was a man known to the police for his criminality. He then gave the flats over to another company, Brickman Yale. We were all very pleased to see the back of him! Brickman Yale did not stay for too long. They wanted to renovate and develop the whole place which would mean we would have to pay thousands of pounds for it which was very unpopular with everyone, as not everyone has that sort of money. The father of the woman in No. 3, the millionaire, then took over from Brickman Yale. Once he took over, he wanted all our mothers' maiden names and bank account details. I do not know whatever he wanted it for and of course all of us agreed not to give him this information. He simply has not got a clue on how to run a genuine business.

Chapter Five

Shirley Bassey's Sister

A few years ago, whilst out shopping I met Shirley Bassey's sister, Ella. She had a haberdashery shop near Brownswood Road. She noticed that I had a northern accent and was mixed race, as she was, and we got talking. She asked me to come over to her flat and have some tea. I said, "You come over to my flat first for tea and then later on I'll come to yours". To tell you the truth I never liked walking very much because of my right leg that never, ever bent properly ever since I was tied up as a baby. I would still walk but I was never much for it. She came over to mine for tea and told me quite a story about her husband – he did not seem to be a nice character. She was very unhappy and was planning on getting another flat far away from him (which she soon did, not long after we met). I told her I was very sorry to hear that, and she told me she would love to keep in touch with me.

One evening her husband came to my flat. When I saw him, I just thought Ella had sent him with a message, but when I asked him what he wanted he had the audacity to ask me for sex! I told him to get out otherwise I would call the police, he could see I was very serious and left. Cheeky blighter! Because I live on my own some men think I am an easy touch. I let them know I will see them in jail first – some men have no respect. I was brought up by a Christian lady. I do not blame Ella for getting rid of a low-life character like him. Even after that, I was shopping and passing the shop that Ella used to run with him, he called me and had the cheek to ask me if I would go to court with him to give evidence against Ella. He was taking her to court to try to prove to the court that Ella was never faithful in their relationship. He knew her sister was Shirley Bassey and thought he would be able to get some money from going to court and hopefully, winning the divorce case. He wanted me to speak in court to prove that she goes with a lot of men, which was a complete lie, and he said he would give me £80. I told him he did not know me at all. I told him, "You can stick your £80 as I don't do that to friends!" I told him I would go to court with Ella, and not him. I would tell the court just what a dreadful liar he is, what he asked me to say, and how he disgusts me.

Later on, when Ella got in touch with me, I asked her if she would tell her sister about my healing hands, but for some reason she did not want to tell her sister anything about me. I do not know why.

Chapter Six

I once healed a mother and her two children of sickle cell disease. Apparently when she kept going to her church after I had healed her, the pastor asked her why she was looking so well and attending the church so often. She told the pastor about me – he was very interested and kept asking her for my telephone number and my address, but I told her not to give it to him. However, she did give my details to him and he phoned me asking if he could come and see me. When he came, he told me he had never met a healer before and he started to read the Bible, which I had read many times. He said to me he had told his bishop about me; what for I don't know, and I told him I was brought up in the Church of England not Church of God (which is where he was from). He had the cheek to tell me I should change my religion, but I would never do that. I did not take a blind bit of notice of him, but I felt rather suspicious of him – I did not think he was a genuine pastor. He kept coming over regularly to read the Bible and trying and convert me – he should convert himself; I do not know why he was trying to convert me! He once told me that he had told the bishop that I would be coming over and cooking a meal for all of them. I said, "Cook for you lot! I can't even cook for myself", which I can't and what the heck would I be cooking for him for, I didn't even know him? I think he realised he was never going to crack me and after he had been coming for about three months, he asked me if he could stay the weekend. I rushed to the door, opened it, and told him to get out and to not come back. He seemed quite surprised. After another three months he had the cheek to phone me and ask me if he could visit me again. I just put the phone down. That finished with him.

Chapter Seven

Some time ago, *Reader's Digest* kept sending me knitting patterns and over the months they became such a lot. I had not ordered any of them and I simply thought *Reader's Digest* were giving them away free as I do not even knit and was not interested in them. One day at the office I happened to mention it and one girl said I should not kid myself as I would be getting a court order requesting payment. I told her that I didn't order any of them and she said it didn't matter, they would still send the court order – however as I'm someone who can speak up for myself, knows the law, wasn't frightened of them and was ready to give them what they deserved, it would all be OK. I did just that and unbelievably, I did get a court order. I just ignored it. I could not believe these people; they hoped I would get frightened and pay up for something I did not even order.

One day a woman arrived at my flat door. How she got in the main door, I will never know. I asked her what she wanted, and she said she had come from the *Reader's Digest*. I told her that people like them like to blackmail people for money and I told her that I was not paying

Chapter Seven

them one single penny. She asked if I still had the knitting patterns and I told her she was very flippin' lucky I had not thrown them in the bin yet. I also made her aware that I had heard that they do such things often and I had been doing a little investigation. I had found out that they only did it to West Indians. Did they think I was a West Indian? I have no West Indian blood in me at all, but they thought they could blackmail me. I soon let her know I was not someone to be messed about with. I bet the woman was glad to leave!

I met a woman driver from the taxi company that I still use, and after a short time of knowing her, she kept begging me to lend her some money as she wanted to open a shop at the market, and said her husband wouldn't lend it to her. That should have told me something, but I still went ahead and lent a few thousand pounds to her. She paid some of it, but then she stopped and kept on saying that it was my fault for lending her money. It was quite a bit of my savings. Talk about ungrateful! I did not think for one minute she would not pay it all back. She also heard that I had healing hands and had the audacity to ask me if I could give her daughter six month's of treatment, three hours a week. I asked what was wrong with her and she told me it was a mental problem. I told her I do not do mentally ill people as I leave that to the psychiatrists, but I still did. She said she would give me some money for doing that but after six months she still did not give me a penny. I was certain then she would give me all my money back including interest as she kept saying she would, but I then realised what a bully she was and worried I would not get my money back soon, if at all.

I decided to see my solicitor. I should have gone to see him before I lent her my money. However, I did get a receipt from her before I lent her the money so I gave him this. On 19 January 2006 my solicitor took her to court, but she did not turn up. I could see she was a very greedy, grabbing woman. In the end whenever I ordered a computer taxi cab, I asked them not to send me a woman driver so that I would be sure I would never get her again. I still have not got my money, which is a few thousand pounds, but I hope to get it one day as I do have my court receipt. She and her husband are very wealthy and could easily pay the money twice over – they have more than one house; they have many houses which are not even declared. Well the government soon will know and get my money for me.

Chapter Eight

I have never liked Tesco though people say they are cheap. I just have never trusted them. Years ago, I heard they used to take meat off the floor, blowing off the sawdust, claiming the meat was fresh but it was not. The other day someone I know had their purse stolen while shopping in Tesco. She told the manager but they did not want to know. If that happened at Sainsbury's of course, they would find out if it was genuine and they would give her some shopping back and part of what she lost. Tesco I think are very mean – with all the shops they have, they should be ashamed of themselves. They are still looking for more shops and I get tired of hearing their advertisements, every 15 minutes.

A woman I knew, Rose, asked me if I could give her healing sessions. She had psoriasis. I took her for nearly a year, one day a week for three hours. She used to bring me fruit and vegetables, all rotten. She had bought them for herself every week and brought what she had left, knowing full well I would be throwing it away.

Some people think they can get away with anything. On top of that, when she got better, she had the cheek to tell me over the phone, that her own doctor healed her. I told her there was no cure for this disease, and that she was very ungrateful. If she told her doctor, he would have to deny it.

Rose did not like the idea of me being able to heal chronic diseases. After all that, she sent a friend of hers to me who had just come from America. His knees were bad. He came to me for a while and was so happy when I got one of his knees better. Rose could not believe he was better. The man told me that Rose kept phoning him every half hour to ask if it was truly better and if the pain had come back. He told her he was healed and to stop phoning him. He was sick and tired of her behaviour; apparently, she wanted the gift I had.

The gentleman asked me if I would like to go to America with him when he was going back. I said I did not think so, but he said he would pay my passage both ways just in case I did not like it. I was uncertain about the whole thing, so I did not go.

When I received my bank statement, I could not understand why Talk Talk was on it. I had never changed my telephone account as I was using BT. Long ago, I was with One.Tel before they sold out to Talk Talk. I rang BT to ask them what had happened and they said that Talk Talk had told them I wanted to go over to them. I then rang Talk Talk to ask them who gave them permission to take over my telephone and they told me it was a mistake. I just cannot believe what brazen people they are.

I did not want to lose my telephone line so I rang BT to ask them if they could put me back on their books and let me know when so I could cancel Talk Talk. When I got back to BT, I rang my bank and asked them to cancel all monies that Talk Talk demanded. After it was cancelled, I started getting threatening letters and phone calls saying that they were going to send the bailiffs. I then went to see my solicitor who wrote them a letter. I have heard nothing more from them since.

When I had my accident, I was in two different hospitals. BT were billing me as if I was at home so I sent two from the doctors letters to BT. A woman from BT then telephoned me. She said it did not matter, because as soon as I came out of the hospital, I would be telephoning anyway. You see their attitude; they could not care less. They have been billing me for broadband although I have never had broadband, but that does not worry them. The video man that came to fix my television asked if he could buy my video player off me and I sold it to him for peanuts, but I later changed my mind and gave him back his money to which he was not pleased. He was the sort of person that enjoys taking advantage of people all because I bought my laptop from where he worked, so he apparently told BT to sign me up for it. I have never signed for anything, but they still keep giving me big bills. I still do not have broadband which they know, and they get away with it. They get worse and worse. In life you are what you do, in life you are what you experience.

In 1992, a lady, Barbara Morgan, telephoned me and asked if she could come for healing. She had cancer in her stomach. She was so ill that she could not eat.

Barbara told me she was admitted at St Thomas's Hospital, but they discharged her to go home, and when she could eat again, they would operate. I was quite astonished because I knew when she started to eat again she would not need an operation because the cancer would have gone.

Barbara had four sons and one daughter who were very anxious for their mother to get better. She came for healing twice a week, three hours a day. After a few months she started to eat very well. Her four sons and daughter were delighted. Her eldest son however, wanted the doctors to experiment on her. That left me quite puzzled.

Barbara then decided to let the doctors experiment on her. I advised her not to let the doctors touch her as I had healed the cancer by that time, but she still went ahead. I could not stop her. I am just the healer. I felt very sad for the three sons, and her daughter also did not want her to go. Barbara asked me if she could come to me as soon as she came out of hospital. I said to her she could come any time she wanted and that I honestly had a very bad feeling about the experiment. I was really worried.

Once she got to the hospital, she phoned me. I could hear in her voice that she was very frightened. I felt so sorry for her. She asked me if she could come to my house once the experiment was over but her three boys and daughter asked me if they could pick me up and bring me down to the hospital. I agreed and after a short while, the sons came to get me. I myself was very nervous because I had an idea the doctors were doing things, they had no right to be doing.

Chapter Eight

When I got to the ward, I saw her daughter by her bed who said my mother had not opened her eyes since she went into theatre, not until I came through the door. What I saw in Barbara's eyes brought me to tears. Her daughter also told me that the doctors asked the eldest son if they could take her back to the theatre, as they had punctured her lungs. They had kept her in the first time for 12 hours and they wanted her for another six hours.

I knew Barbara was dying; the doctors and nurses also knew. They put up a big pretence. There were so many tubes, all over her face, head and body. I knew it was all camouflage. I felt so distressed that they could do that to her. Her daughter and sons were asking the nurses to turn their mother on her side, so I could put my hands on her lungs. The doctors did not want to do anything like that; they knew what they had done already. It made me feel so sick. Who gave them permission to experiment on her like that, when she did not need it? The cancer was only at her stomach and I got it out.

The doctors did not want me anywhere near her. The sons asked them if they could let me be there when they were taking the tubes out of her body. Although they agreed, they took the tubes out at 2 o'clock in the morning and said there was nothing more they could do. It was clear from the time they decided to take it out that they did not want me to be there. If they had called me, I would have been there. Barbara died. She could not have survived what they did to her.

Sometimes I feel so sad that no one listens. I pray and ask God to help me and he always does. I think some of these doctors should be accountable for their actions, for what they do. It is the family who suffer for their consequences.

A woman phoned me for a healing appointment. She told me some story about her husband being a 'top policeman' in some big job, but when she came to see me, she told me a completely different story.

Then she started to run down the President of the United States, Barack Obama. I told her to give him a chance, he had not been in his job long and the other one before him was not as good as he was. I thought he was doing a wonderful job anyway. Talking to someone like her was hopeless. I knew she was a racist.

When I first moved into this flat, the bedroom was so poorly furnished. There were two very small wardrobes – you could not fit very much in them – and there was a long cupboard all across the top of the bed. Naturally, I put lots of clothes in that. One day, as soon as I got out of bed in the morning the cupboard dropped down. If I had been in the bed at the time, it definitively would have killed me instantly. When I got someone in to fix it he was quite surprised. He said, "The person who put that garbage in should have been prosecuted". The cupboard on top of the bed was so dangerous, it was like having chewing gum stuck on the wall to hold it up. That is another gift God gave me, a guardian angel. That episode I am to show you.

I used to visit different churches just to see how ministers would react when I told them I was a healer and could heal chronic diseases. I was quite amazed to see how they turned quite horrible, ready to run me out of the church.

Chapter Eight

I visited the Church of England church in Essex Road, where I saw a man in a wheelchair. I asked him what was wrong, and he told me he had multiple sclerosis. When I told him I could help, he told the woman priest. You could see the hatred in her face once he told her. She ran me out of the church.

You would think ministers in the church would be glad to meet someone who could heal chronic diseases; instead, they dislike me. They cannot heal themselves. The looks I used to get from them are so terrible that I would not be able to describe it. The doctors and nurses did not like me either.

I remember, a lady asked me if I could help her husband, who had a terrible accident with a horse. I used to go to the hospital with this lady at Stanmore Hospital. I told the wife to be very careful and not to let any of them know that I am a healer. After going there a few times, one of her husband's very close friends came to see him and shouted, "My God, you look so good and you're eating! I've never seen you eat before!" I put my fingers to my mouth, trying to tell them to be very careful of what they say.

It frightened me to think of the doctors and nurses knowing I did not want them to know or hear that I am a healer. When they saw him eating (which he could not do before) they were very annoyed. The next time we went, they deliberately put something like a piece of very heavy armour on him so I could not put my hands on him. His wife asked them how long it would be on for and they said it would be on all that day. The armour was from his waist up to his head.

It would have been impossible for me to put my hands on his chest and lungs. They were the two places I needed to put my hands on for his healing. I knew they had done this deliberately. Just how callous can these people be? This of course was just for spite because they saw me doing what they could not do.

They call themselves doctors, nurses, priests and ministers but they are so against people that God has given such a powerful gift to. I wish someone would tell me why all these people are so against genuine healing. It is not all of them. Just some. I have healed so many more people. All these diseases that I have healed and cured can be checked and confirmed; people are more than willing to give testimony.

In 2013, I had an accident. I was changing a very low chair for a higher chair in my bedroom My leg got stuck in the chair and I fell on my back. I was laying there for two days. After two days, the stick I had in the passage, all of a sudden fell in the bedroom with a loud bang. I looked but could not reach it and then it started to move. I grabbed it, banged the telephone above me and the telephone came straight into my hand. There was someone up there who did not want me to die, who to my understanding is the saviour of the world.

I phoned 999 and told them I had an accident and had been on the floor for two days and that I could not move a muscle. They then sent an ambulance. When they came, they took the door off to get to me, but fixed it back immediately. They took me straight to Middlesex Hospital, why so far I'll never know because my nearest hospital was in Hackney, Homerton Hospital.

Chapter Eight

I had a big hole in my back and also in my foot, right at the heel. I was in that hospital for two weeks or just over. I went home still very poorly, with two holes there. A nurse came to see me at home and asked if she could look at my back. She was shocked when she saw the hole and called an ambulance right away. They took me to Homerton Hospital.

While I was at Middlesex, I had to give the keys to my flat to someone to get something to put on my feet. When I got my keys and came back, I was told by some of the people who work at the hospital to get rid of all my furniture, and the wanted to know what I was doing with bread and nuts in my kitchen. I told them that I feed the birds every day, what it had to do with any of them, I will never know. I am beginning to think when you are not well, they take too many liberties, knowing you are weak. I was quite appalled at their behaviour. I could never do without my furniture. It helps me to walk, and I use it to help people who come for healing, when they are unsteady on their feet.

When I was very poorly in hospital, the minister of the church I attended, telephoned asking me if I could give my keys for two hours, to a woman who worked in the hospital, to change my mattress. According to them, it would be better for my back. Though I was very ill, I did not want to give her my keys at all, but then again when you are ill people take liberties. I reluctantly gave in and I am very sorry I did.

She gave me a letter to give to the minister when she came back with my keys. It was sealed. I unsealed it. To my horror all my bank details were in the letter. I asked her who gave her permission to rummage through my private correspondence. She went as red as a beetroot. She had the nerve to ask if I could give her my keys again.

When I had a couple of days left before I went home, this impertinent girl, who rummaged through my correspondence, asked the nurse four times if she could get my keys again to put in the mattress. I told the nurse to tell her to wait until I got home.

When I did get home, I was shocked to find out she had stolen £4000 of my designer clothes which I often give to charity. She also put a glass tumbler underneath my chair in the bedroom where I had the accident and broke a long mirror in the passage, which cost me £140 to buy and get fixed back on the wall. She had piled up another set of clothes, hoping she could get my keys a second time. She had already taken all the best clothes. She was nowhere to be seen. I was so disgusted that someone who worked in a hospital could see that I was very poorly and do such a terrible thing. I could never buy these types of clothes again; they have changed hands and I cannot afford them now.

I reported this theft to the 101 police and they sent somebody down and told me it would be investigated. It turned out to be one of the Stoke Newington police officers that had seen my name and asked the 101 police what my name was doing in their books. They told him about my robbery while I was ill at the hospital. He told them he knew me and asked to take the case over.

I was flabbergasted because I had only seen him once. I think the 101 police should have asked me first before

Chapter Eight

handing the case to him. After all, I had asked them, not the Stoke Newington police. I was warned about them years ago. The policeman still had the nerve to phone and tell me he had taken it over. I was very disappointed. He did nothing at all. I think he wanted to make sure I did not phone the 101 police because of the things he was hiding. You bet my bottom dollar. I lost all my clothes and all that money. He should be ashamed of himself as he was supposed to be keeping the law. Why in the world did he take it away from the 101 police (I would very much like to know)? I still hope the 101 can still take it over.

I wrote a letter to the doctor at the hospital telling her what had happened. She was shocked; it quite surprised her. I think she was very upset for me. I did not quite explain to her what went on with the police. I just told her I should not have given the woman my keys in the first place. Of course, I was very poorly then.

I cannot believe the smooth-talking minister on the other hand, was telling her to find out what I was worth. Talk about putting you off ministers! Any like him are a disgrace to the church. He came to see me, after I was discharged from the hospital as if nothing had happened. I could hardly walk. I still had big holes in my foot and back. The cunning minister suggested I give him my keys, to save me hobbling to the door when he came to visit.

When I realised he was the person who caused all this theft, I got someone to collect the keys from him as I did not trust him. I knew he had made another set of my keys. He once came into my flat without my authority and stole all my hospital appointment letters. I very quickly went to the Yellow Pages, found a locksmith, and changed my lock. What a disappointment for him when he came back to my flat and could not get in!

He still had the nerve to send one of his congregation to see me. When the person came to my door, I just put my head out and saw him kick the main door with his knee. It was locked. I asked him what he wanted and not answering me, he then asked me if I had the code to the premises. I realised he was lost for words, so I quickly gave him the code and shut the door. I had not been in his church long. I am sorry I ever joined that church, but we all make mistakes sometimes.

I cannot understand the Bishop of London talking about David Cameron leaving children hungry, when there are so many free food shops that people can go to pick up food. What in the world is he talking about? It is about time he started to teach his ministers to stop taking people's savings instead. I hear a lot about them every day.

I personally think that David Cameron is the best Prime Minister I have ever known. I think he works very hard and would love to see him win on his own. I would not like to see anyone with him; he is capable of being the Prime Minister in his own right.

Chapter Nine
Malta

An elderly lady asked me if I could go to her house as she had a very bad heart. I told her if she came the next day in the morning I would go to her house with her and stay the whole day. The next morning, as I waited on the veranda, I noticed another lady was with the elderly lady with the bad heart. I asked her about a lady with the bad heart. She told me that Maria, who lived where I was staying, told the elderly lady not to come around at all. I was appalled. I asked Maria what she meant telling the lady not to come and she denied she ever told her such a thing. I did not believe her. I noticed in Malta that they are very spiteful to one another. I was very sad I could not help the lady with the bad heart. I would never go back to Malta; mainly because they do not all speak English.

A business lady in Malta offered to build a beautiful house for me if I decided to stay. I shall never have to do any work, just use my hands. I told her I could never leave England; it is my country and I would miss it very much.

I am an animal lover and I did not like the way they treated cats and dogs in Malta. They left dogs on top of the boiling hot roof tied up, and the beautiful cats running so wild, it certainly made me feel very sad.

A boy where I was staying started hitting a dog very hard for no reason. I was just getting in a car when I heard the dog crying. I jumped out of the car and asked the boy what he was hitting the dog for. He just looked at me, he had no reason to hit the dog. I told him he should not ill-treat animals. I asked if he would like it if someone started hitting him for no reason at all. I could never live in a country like Malta.

Where I was staying, Marie had three children. One could not walk, the other one had difficulties and the third was healthy. The one who could walk would come in and start shouting at his sister in the bed whenever he heard her screaming in pain. I would put my hands on her tummy and after a few minutes she would smile at me. She must have wondered who I was. I would stay with her until she fell asleep. I somehow felt so sorry for her. Marie never told me what was wrong with her.

I went to visit a man who had a bad back. I stayed with him the whole day. When I was about to leave, he handed me a big wad of money, but I refused it because of the Prime Minister in Malta who was stealing all of their monies – so corrupt these politicians.

Chapter Ten

I went to Paris once on a bus trip for a weekend. We got lost and we could not find our destination. We asked quite a lot of French people, but none of them could help. They were not very nice. We eventually came to a hotel where we found an American and he explained where we were and how to find where we wanted to go. We were happy we found him; he was very helpful to us. I would not want to go to Paris again because the people were not friendly.

I am desperately trying not to forget our doctor who retired some time ago. I am stating this on behalf of a lot of her patients, and of course myself; we were all so sorry when she retired.

Her name is:
Dr V. N. Patel
The John Scott Health Centre
Green Lanes
N4 2NU

Dr Patel always had time to listen to everybody no matter who they were. She always gave you a thorough examination, all over the body. She was a dedicated doctor, her patience had no end. We all miss her very much. I am stating in this book to which ever government is in power that she deserves a very high award. We would all be happy to see her get the recognition she deserves for her high quality care and patience.

I joined the Dial a Ride service in 1989. I think on the whole; it is a very good service. When I had my first memorable incident with one of the Dial a Ride drivers, I had known him for a long time. He was always talking about himself. I was never keen on him, but all of a sudden, he started to be extra nice to me. By that time, I had had my accident and was in a wheelchair. This said man heard I was writing a book about my life and told me he would help me to choose a laptop. He suggested I buy an Apple computer. I was not very sure. I had a word with the chap who fixed all the computers in the area and he said I didn't need to buy one as it would be far too expensive and useless to me as I just needed it to write a book about my life. He thought the man was up to something. How right he was.

I found out that the Dial a Ride man wanted me to buy an Apple computer because he had one the same but his had broken down. He was certainly looking for an opportunity and other things as well. He wheeled me all round a part of London, parking his bus at my home and kept me company for half an hour. What for I will never know. Then he had the cheek to phone the Dial a Ride service and ask them if they could pick me up, and take me to Comet, without my consent. The store was closing down. I asked him what he was playing at, asking the Dial a Ride to pick me up, and take me to the Comet store. He replied that I was afraid to spend my money. I told him how I spend my money was none of his business.

I told him I am a respectable lady and do not socialise with married or single men unless they are close friends. Things certainly changed after that; no more wheeling around or keeping me company for half an hour. I think because I was in a wheelchair at that moment, he thought I was an easy prey and the comment he made to me was so disgusting, I will not repeat it. I told the Dial a Ride team that I did not want him coming to pick me up and they stopped sending him.

Whilst going to work every morning at the Civil Service, I would see this very tall, handsome gentleman every morning. He always used to tilt his hat, smile, and say good morning. He seemed such a gentleman. I used to tell my husband Herman about him. He used to say, "Though a lot of people don't know it, there are a lot of nice people about". That is so true. When my Herman got very ill, I used to work late hours at a secretarial agency as I needed the money to buy certain things for my husband.

I happened to see the tall gentleman when I came home late one night. He was surprised to see me at such a late hour and asked me if everything was all right. I told him my husband was very ill in hospital and the doctor told me he may not recover. He said he was very sorry and told me he would buy me a house. He was very serious, but I could not take such an offer because I realised, he had a wife. I think when a man is married, he should be faithful to his wife, though I do understand when some woman takes the easy way out. I of course was brought up very old fashioned.

A long time after my accident I started physiotherapy. The first lady physiotherapist told me I would have to wait before I went on my exercise bicycle, and she was right. The second girl was not very nice. She said it was hard to believe my age and that she was going to bring someone different. Each time she came I told her I would not like that. I told her I am not a puppet show. I could see she was determined to bring different people, so I telephoned her boss and explained to him what she said. He assured me that it would not happen again; I felt relieved. Then she started telling me what I should get rid of, such as my chairs, exercise bicycle and different things.

I do not think that a physiotherapist should tell you, or anybody, what to get rid of in your house. Their job is to help you to get better, but some of them can make you feel worse.

Even though I am a healer, when you fall it is not how or where you fall, but who stretched out a helping hand, and that stretched out hand can come from an unlikely person it could be from a tramp or even a doctor – or should I say the medical people? I would never tell people not to go to the doctors, but make sure you don't go there to be their experiment and make sure they don't cut off your body parts as a quick fix to simply discharge you out of the hospital.

Chapter Ten

When she brought the sitting down bicycle, she told me not to get the one I wanted as it was over £100. All the others I tried moved, that one did not. When I asked her to give me all the details about it, she pretended she knew nothing about where it came from, because she did not want me to get the same type.

I could read her like a book; she was far too spiteful and a real bully. Like the sticks she gave me; she could see I had one heavy stick and she got me two light ones. They were no good for me, but I did not want anything to do with her, it was just a waste of time.

I used to work at the British Museum. After being there a few years, I joined The British Library, the same firm as the British Museum.

There was a woman who worked there, she was a real menace. She caused a lot of young lads and young women to leave their jobs, due to her terrible behaviour. She accused me once of stealing. I could not believe it. We had a squatter at our flats, and he asked me if he could borrow my keys; he claimed he had applied to the housing people for money. I did not like the squatter who seemed a very distasteful character. I simply refused to lend him my keys. When the people from the housing came, they could see he was a squatter, so he found out where I worked and that is why this cheeky woman had accused me of stealing – perhaps he had stolen from her.

The squatter had written a letter of complaint about me to the housing people, he claimed he was a doctor. He gave himself so many honours and letters after his name. Anybody could see they were all made up, but it so impressed the woman at the housing department. That is why she called me and accused me of stealing.

I reported her to the Union, and they were furious. They told her she must apologise, because they knew me to be a very honest woman. How dare she embarrass me in that way? She made sure to telephone me and apologise; she did not want to put it down on paper.

A few years after that they sent her to Boston Spa on quite a big job. She knew then that I was a healer and could really heal. I heard that the same woman had a nervous breakdown. So, she invited me for tea and cakes. Of course, she wanted my hands on her head. She seemed to have a very short memory for accusing me of stealing. I did not even answer her. I was quite shocked that she wanted me to go to Boston Spa for tea and cakes after her disgraceful performance.

Before I joined the British Museum, I worked at the Secretarial. What a lot of experience one has doing agency work, jumping on and off Tube trains to get to the job. One day on the Tube, I saw a young chap put his hand in this girl's pocket and take out her purse. He saw right away I had seen him and gave me dagger looks. He knew I was trying to get her to look at me, but she did not. That may have saved her life. The boy looked very savage. I felt very sorry for the girl but there was nothing I could do. I jolly well wished I could have been of assistance to her, but I guess this is part of inner-city life.

There was once upon a time when I worked in the government department office during my holiday through a job agency. I never went on holiday. The agency told me

Chapter Ten

not to tell them I was not permanent or on holiday. The supervisor there gave me a very hard job with plenty of figures. Fortunately, I was used to doing everything to do with figures. After I finished the two weeks, I heard the supervisor ask for me the following week. I felt so bad because I was only there for two weeks. She did not want the other woman that was there with me. I thought to myself, she will be left with no one. I felt very uneasy, but then again there was nothing I could do. Maybe she did not want the other woman because she did not like figures, but I took whatever was given to me.

Sometimes in life, we find ourselves in very awkward positions and there is not much we can do about it. I think with that kind of job, it is everyone for themselves.

Another time I was collecting my wages from the agency. The woman told me to watch my wages. Before I reached the Tube, my wages had gone. A man had deliberately bumped into me, and of course my wages had disappeared. I went home to a sick husband and no money. I made sure never to go back to that agency again, and always carried a shopping bag instead of a handbag. Of course, when I reported the loss to the policeman he just smiled. It was useless telling him anything at all; to him it seemed like a joke.

I had gone to the British Museum as an agency worker. The lady I worked for asked me if I would like a permanent job. She said I would get paid for holidays, but I said I would think about it. In time I thought it would make sense to be paid for holidays and get a pension, so I took the offer. I stayed for 23 years.

I joined the British Library, which was connected to the Museum, and I healed a few people there. When a certain gentleman asked me to be his secretary at the library, I said no. That was the biggest mistake of my life. I really regretted it as he was a perfect gentleman. I was very annoyed with myself for making such a blunder, and a dreadful decision. After that I just continued until I retired. I suppose we all make dreadful decisions in our lives until it is too late to alter them.

I do think that British Telecom should be watched much more than they are because they get away with so much. For argument's sake the engineers can use your phone anytime they please, giving people big bills. In 2008 and 2009 I found loads of mobile calls on my line, I have never used a mobile on my line. When we investigated, it was the engineer using my phone. When we told British Telecom, they decided to give me some money. They were not surprised when we told them (which implies that they do it all the time).

The gas people need to be monitored much more also, as they are always complaining about my boiler that it is lasting far too long. When they come to check on your boiler they put it so high they hope it will go bust. You have to get someone to turn it down. Their behaviour is terrible. A friend of mine told me the gas people literally tore her boiler right out without her permission and told her to buy a boiler from them; she said it quite distressed her.

I do think a lot of these hairdressers should be monitored, especially Kuntakt hairdresser, in Stoke Newington,

Church Street. When I went there, they were charging me for two tubes of colouring, but I only used one. While I was getting my hair done of the hairdressers told me to take my necklace off, but when I went to collect it, it had disappeared. I never saw it again. The man in charge could not be bothered about anything anyone talks about. That hairdressers is so expensive, but when I complained about how expensive they are, and the loss of my necklace that went missing from the shop, he told me not to come back.

A few years ago, in the early 1990s, a man came to me from Mill Hill, asking me if I could help his son who had a cancerous tumour in his head. He asked me if he could take me to Mill Hill as his son would not go anywhere. I told the father I would, as long as his son behaves himself whilst my hands are on his head. He said he could assure me it would be all right.

I went there a few times, then all of a sudden, he told me God had given him healing hands so he would take over. I thought that was wonderful. He would be able to heal his own son. His wife did not seem very happy, so I asked her why and she said because she did not believe him but could not do anything about it. I told her to give him a chance and see how he gets on.

I heard sometime after that his son died. His wife was devastated and I felt so sorry for her, especially as she had already lost a daughter. They should have made me aware. I suppose he felt very embarrassed.

Sometimes, we have to put our pride in our pockets – he may have thought he had healing hands, but he was mistaken. I felt very sorry for him, I know he loved his son very much, both the mother and father are now separated.

There was a gentleman in Stanmore, who I was helping to get better in September 1995. He had an accident on a motorbike which made his leg disjointed. It was quite a serious accident. He was with his girlfriend when it happened, but he was the only one that got injured. He came to see me in a wheelchair and he was in excruciating pain; it was his leg which was giving him the most pain.

After a couple of sessions with me, I started to realise that his leg had not been treated correctly hence why it was so difficult to heal and causing him such agony. The area felt as though it had not been knitted together properly. I mentioned this to him, and he understood what I was trying to explain to him, but I could not understand what the doctor had, or in his case, had not done correctly.

He returned to me again after seeing the doctor regarding his leg. As I laid my hands over him, I could still sense that the leg was no different from the last time I had seen him. Once again this meant yet another trip to see the doctor. How frustrating this was for the young man, to have such a crippling injury which was not healing the way in which it should, and coupled with trips back and forth to both the doctor and I.

Eventually he stopped coming to see me as it was extremely challenging for me to try and get the wheelchair up the stairs. He asked me if I could come to his home, but it was very awkward for me as he lived quite a distance away. To make matters worse I then discovered that his partner had left him. I could not believe it, as if he had not already been through enough. I felt so sorry for him. However, it all made sense as to why he was no longer coming to see me for treatment. It was because she stopped bringing him. Her behaviour was so wicked and callous, and to add the icing on the cake she had got with another man and was having a baby. I just could not process it all! I wonder if she has heard of the saying 'what goes around comes around'. Her time will come when she least expects it.

I did find out in time that he met someone and found love again. That really made me feel good inside, knowing that he would no longer be alone, and he had the support and love that he deserved. I will certainly continue to pray for him. I tried my best to do what I could do for him, but at least my mind was at rest knowing that he was not alone and unhappy.

The doctors and nurses should be glad that there is someone available to help sick people and people in terrible pain that need alternative healing or natural healing, such as that I do with my hands, and thank them more than send them away. How dare they, they should know that this power only comes from God. I am hoping that someone in the government does something drastic about this, because believe me, it makes healers, I mean genuine ones, quite weary when they know they can do more than what they currently do.

Why in the world should they get spiteful over a person who is trying to do good for all and save people's lives? I am sure if they wanted help, they themselves would be glad to get help from a healer.

I once had a phone call from a man who lived in Ireland, Stuart by name, he asked me if he could come for healing. I asked him what was wrong, and he told me he had skin cancer on both of his legs. I also asked him if he had not visited healers in Ireland. He said he had but none of them could help him.

Stuart told me he went to America where he nearly died. They gave him something to drink which did not help him; it kind of stuck into him. When he returned to Ireland, his daughter told him about me being able to heal cancer.

A friend of her husband (Christian Luke Barker) had six months to live with a tumour in the brain. I healed him in 1993 and he is still alive. Christian today is a living testimony.

He asked me if he could come for healing every day for two weeks because he was on holiday then. We arranged a time and he came with his wife on 13 April 1994.

When I saw the bandage so thick on both of his legs, I told his wife to take off the bandage otherwise I would not be able to see the cancer. They were so shocked, and Stuart told me that none of the healers or doctors had ever told him to remove the bandage. I said to him, "No wonder none of them were able to heal his legs. When you come here, allow your wife to take off the bandage".

Now if you have anything wrong on the arms or legs, you can take off the covering; if it is on the body, you heal over clothes. That is how I do my healing. I gave him hours of healing, because he had just the two weeks and he had to go back to work. He came every day for two weeks. With all my other healing I would get quite exhausted when I had finished, and would you believe, it is all for peanuts.

He asked me if he could come again in six months. I said it would be all right. The poor man had a few frightening experiences, but you could see by the whole session he was quite happy.

People know when they are getting the right treatment. They feel it and know it. All I use are my hands, nothing else, and they are what Jesus Christ blessed me with. What more could a person want?

It went on until he did not need to come anymore. He was better. Now the sad thing about this case is it shows you few people have genuine healing hands. Stuart told me nearly all the healers in Ireland have posh houses, big cars and charge a lot of money, but I on the other hand just take peanuts. He really appreciated me getting my hands on his legs. He asked me if I would ever go to Ireland, but I told him I did not think I had the time. He was sorry. I had healed so many people in the past, I well needed the rest.

In 1993 a young lady, Myrtle, came to me, with two arthritic knees. She was about to have an operation on both of them. She told me that someone gave her my name and phone number. Myrtle asked me if she could come for healing, so we made arrangements. She came every week for two hours. In about seven months her knees got better.

I found out with a lot of people I healed, on the whole, that some of them like to tell other people about their healing but some do not. I think some of them are worried because they might not know who they are telling. Like the loads of letters I sent out to members of parliament and the only MPs who answered were the Tories. That is why I like them. They are the most caring of all of the political parties in Britain.

I healed a lady who came to me from Spain. She had not slept properly for 27 years. I started healing her, with my hands on her head for many months. After she was better, her daughter came to see me and told me they could not find their mother. After they were exhausted from looking for her all day, they decided to go to bed only to find her fast asleep. She had been there all day and night. My hands had healed her after 27 years. I do not think she told anybody when she got back to Spain. I think it was ungrateful of her as there are so many people who have the same problem as she did, and she would have known that. How very sad.

A young African man came to me who had shaking hands, and no one could stop them from shaking. He also had heard how I healed Christian Luke Barker in 1993. He said he had been to many different neurologists. He asked me if could help him. I started putting my hands on his head and his spleen, I do not really know why I put my hands on his spleen, because somehow, I think my hands on his head would have been enough. But whatever comes to me I do. After I healed the shaking hand, the man did not even thank me. Would you believe it? Such people are not worth touching or thinking of. Come to think of it, I had this African man for seven months of treatment and not even a thank you.

To see people on the television so poorly, I wanted to shout out and tell everybody I could heal them, but I know it would make no difference because they would not believe it. After I had the accident, I went to Sainsbury's; the Dial a Ride service used to take me every week. When I told the lady, who sometimes used to take me around, that I could heal cancer, I asked her if she believed me, but she said of course not.

I remember a little boy. His mother asked me if I could heal him. I did not really know what was wrong with him but his mother told me that the doctor told her what he had had no cure, but she still brought him to me, trusting I could heal him.

When we started the healing sessions he did not like my hands, because they are extremely hot for him. But his mother was desperate and believed I could help her son though none of the doctors could do anything for him. The mother said to me she knew I could heal him, as he was so young. We started to bribe him with chocolate for him to stay still and quiet for two hours. He came once a week. After a few months he was as right as rain. His mother said to me she thought he would have to live with what he had for the rest of his life and did not know how to thank me. I told her always say your prayers and thank Jesus Christ the saviour of the world and tell other people in case any of them want help as she did.

It rather amazed me how people would not tell anyone else as long as they were all right and completely better; it just seems to go completely out of their minds. I am so different. If I even knew something and I thought it would benefit anyone else, I would tell as many people as I could.

A young women came to me in 1994 with arthritis in both her knees. She asked me if it would be possible to fit her in for healing, as she realised I had quite a few people I was healing at that time. She was going to have an operation, so I started healing her. It took her about six or seven months.

When she was better, she told me her dog had cancer and asked if it would be possible for me to heal it, as I had a cat myself. I healed her dog in their car; it was quite a big dog. I gave it a few sessions as animals do not take as long to heal as humans. After I healed the dog, I do not know what she told the vet. To me animals are very important. I do not like to see humans or animals in pain.

She also told me that her husband had cancer and I asked her why he does not come for healing. She said, "Dorothy I wish he would come to you, but he's got it in an awkward place. He feels too embarrassed. He told me he would never go to a woman not even a female doctor". I felt very sad for her; she was such a nice lady to be left without a husband. He was such a nice man. The two of them were very happy together and she was going to be left alone. I tried all I could to persuade her to change his mind, but to no avail.

When anyone comes to me for healing, I always say my prayers first, at the beginning of healing. That I find is very important to me.

A husband and wife came to see me; they had problems. The husband suffered with panic attacks; he had been visiting different doctors for years. However, what surprised me is that I thought that panic attacks were easy to cure by the doctors, but I heard it just depends on how severe they are. I gave him two hours once a week. I did not remember to put the date when he started. He put down his address and his telephone number on the table, after around six or seven months with my hands on his head he was completely cured. He used to teach people how to play the piano. His marriage certainly got better after being cured. He did tell people, he told me, and I know he did. He was an extremely nice man and I was happy for him. I could see everything was going right with him and his wife and I certainly thanked God for that. The healing brought them closer together and happier than ever before. What more could anyone wish for? Afterwards they moved to Cornwall.

In 1995 a young chap came to visit me; he had cancer in his leg, stomach, and private parts. I was a bit embarrassed and apprehensive to begin with, but he did not seem the slightest bit embarrassed, but I do not think I would ever do that kind of sensitive healing again. I try my hardest to ensure that anyone coming to me for healing feels at ease and comfortable.

For some reason he did not want his mother to know that he had cancer; maybe he did not want to upset her. He also told me he knew a young teenage boy who had cancer. I told him to tell the boy about my healing so he could also come. He never did tell him about me – I suppose he was full of himself. I do not think he told anyone that I was healing him. He always said, "Oh, once I start getting better, I will start to tell people about you and all you have done for me". He used to always talk about moving to Australia. I could not understand it myself. Born, bred and educated here yet he had no interest in England or the people living here. After I had healed this chap I never heard from him again.

People can be very strange. Even though I can profile people sometimes, it can still be hard to understand the way some people's minds work. God gave me this gift along with my healing. I can sometimes read people, but it is not possible all of the time. Some people are very difficult to read.

I have been able to heal so many diseases and cancer. I have lost count!

I healed a woman a few years ago who told me that she wanted to have a baby. I asked her if she had ever been to the hospital to find out why she could not conceive. They could do internal tests like scans and x-rays. I did not have the ability to do that. I could tell she had multiple problems. Although I have helped many people I seem to know when it is impossible for me to do so. I was honest with her and told her I knew my limits and could only do what I could do. I did not see her again. I only hope that she was able to solve her problems.

Late in the 1990s, when I met Sandra, the woman on the bus whose plant was sticking in my face, she said to me, "You have great powers I can feel them". I asked her what she meant, and she then told me she was a spiritualist. She asked me if I was a healer and I said I was. I told her not to get me wrong because I am not a faith healer. At my church we have five faith healers. When I asked them what they had healed, each one of them told me they had

Chapter Ten

never healed anyone. I asked them why they then all call themselves faith healers when they have never healed anyone. They all told me they believe in healing, that is why they call themselves faith healers. I certainly could not agree with them. I said people think you can heal but as far as I am concerned this is not the case and they should explain to people all the facts of what a faith healer entails so people will understand what exactly they are getting themselves involved in.

The spiritualist asked me if I could heal her shoulder and I said to her I thought you could heal. She then said to me if any one of them tell me they can heal, they are not telling me the truth, because they just listen to dead people. She told me that is what they are good at. I was quite shocked, I always heard spiritualists could heal.

She asked me if she could come for healing and I asked her how long she had had the bad shoulder. She answered for a few years. I told her it would take a few months coming once a week. She was doing very well as the months went by.

She asked me if she could bring her friend who lived in Surrey. She also had a lot of pain. Within a few months they both became pain free and completely better.

One day whilst I was healing, the spiritualist asked me if I had a tray and a small glass. She had brought the alphabet from A to Z in small pieces of paper. She then put these items around the tray with the glass in the middle. Her hand remained on the top of the glass. She kept saying is there anyone up there who wants to leave a message?

The glass kept moving. She would then take up the piece of paper with the alphabet on it. This went on for quite a while till the glass stopped moving.

Once she aligned all the pieces of paper together, she said to me, "Who is Rose Reuben?"

The name rang a bell to me but at that moment in time, I just could not place where I knew it from until it clicked. It was the woman who gave birth to me. She then claimed the woman had told her she was sorry. What a cheek!

After all this time! After all the pain she had caused me! She bound my small legs to a chair when I was a baby so that I was unable to crawl or move and all I received was a pathetic apology through a medium. What sort of a woman is she? Why would a so-called mother subject a child she carried for nine months in her womb to such brutality?

Imagine! Someone coming to me for healing and the session that was meant to be about them, ended up being about me. A dark secret that I have been repressing for years being exposed. Unveiled before me by a stranger who I originally encountered on the bus.

My soul felt uneasy as a God-fearing woman dabbling with the unknown is not something I am comfortable with.

Chapter Eleven

A man I once called my friend helped me discover where the majority of my family were. They were said to be experts in garment making. The woman who gave birth to me, her husband, and my supposed sister migrated to Canada first class (proves they had money). From what I heard, the rest of the family were said to be scattered around the globe, in London, Manchester and America. Hopefully, if they ever get a chance to read my book, my story will trigger off a memory to them about me.

Funnily enough there was a rich Jewish girl that used to go to my school. I was only about eight and this girl's mother used to always bring dinner for her and me as well. I never questioned why she used to feed me I just used to take it. I thought probably she pitied me but as I mentioned before I just accepted it.

One day I overheard the young girl asking her mother, "Why do you feed that girl in my school?" Her mother responded, "She's family". At that age I was unable to understand what it was all about. I was a bit embarrassed to tell you the truth, being that I was the only brown girl in the school, so I kept what I had heard to myself and pushed it to the back of my mind. If I knew then what I know now I would have been bold and brave and asked the woman what she meant by calling me family.

School was a difficult time for me, there was a little ginger-haired boy that would always try to bully me. He would put snowballs down my back in the winter and punch me. This went on for months until I gathered the courage to tell Mother Connie what had been happening. With rage and hurt in her eyes she marched down to the school and reported it to the headmistress.

The little ginger boy attended the boys' school just a few yards away. So, the headmistress alerted the head teacher at his school. She took me to find the boy that had been bullying me. They singled him out and before I knew it, I heard an almighty BANG! The head teacher gave him a good hiding. He never bothered me again after that.

What will always stick in my mind was the head teacher telling the young boy, "This young girl is a princess". I felt so protected. This was not the first time that a male figure had made me feel special.

A friend of Mother Connie used to phone a shopkeeper to watch me as I arrived and returned from his shop. I would always go there for biscuits. He'd give me a very big bag. I will never forget what he said to me: "Be careful, never let any man come near you. If any man on the street ever tries to approach you, just know you are safe around me. Just find me and I will make sure I take you straight back to your mum".

I think he was just ensuring that no harm came to me, as there were some funny men on the roads back then. They were always trying to lure the young girls on the road.

I always stood out from the crowd with my long wavy hair; I was different from the rest.

All the Jews seemed to look after me; it was like they knew I had Jewish blood. Even when I went to the corner shop the owner would always treat me better than the rest of the children and give me extra chocolate peanuts. He would always allow me, and only me, to get six bags with only a penny. No one else though.

I was never mean. I am a giving person and I would always share with those around me. The Jewish women in the cake shop were the same. I would buy cake and she would put the money back in the bag. I was clearly blessed from a young age although I did not have the best start to life, Jesus blessed me all the time.

The person I do miss the most is my foster mother, Connie. She raised me as her own and made such an impact in my life. She was the one who made me the woman I am today.

I wished at that time in my life I knew I was a healer. Mother Connie suffered terribly with asthma. I could have used my gift to heal her. She had done so much for me I just wish I had the chance to give something back to her. If only I had known.

Sometimes things like this do not happen straight away; everything happens in good time, as they say. Once, I was trying to be proactive as I believe that it is wrong to keep your blessing to yourself. I built up the courage to go to my local MP, Diana Abbot's office in Stoke Newington. I wanted her to know what I could do for other people. I thought that she would embrace what I had to say.

I wrote a letter to her, but I got no response, so then I went to see her, and she still was not interested. She did not want to give me the time of day. I was appalled that a pillar of the community would not even acknowledge or listen to me. A lot of Londoners could have had healing but are suffering from cancer out there because of the likes of her.

Without Mother Connie I was absolutely lost. Her father was a priest and a dedicated man. She had three sisters and they were all well brought up and sophisticated women. They were not the type to talk about anyone or gossip. As their father was a priest, he did not allow them to have any relationships with men. It's a shame as I know due to their good morals they would have been excellent mothers and wives. Instead, they helped run an orphanage for teenage girls, but at least they had the opportunity to help disadvantaged young girls and pass on their life skills later on as women. They all dedicated their lives to giving back to others. You rarely meet ladies like them today, constantly putting themselves out to help people.

I was fortunate to be adopted by Mother Connie at four years old. She had me baptised and I was brought up as a Christian. I was always happy to be with her. We were dedicated to each other and she always taught me about Jesus Christ and how to be a decent God-fearing Christian woman.

The love we both have for Jesus Christ is amazing. We attended church three times on a Sunday and on Saturday mornings and I adored every minute of it. Churches back then were different to how they are now. The passion people had for going to church back then was amazing and everyone was so honest and trustworthy. Now there's always constant speculation surrounding the church. This was not the case in my day though.

Mother Connie's house was like nothing I had seen before! It was three houses joined together. It was her childhood home. Her father, being a priest, was able to orchestrate the joining of the houses. I will never forget the enormous backyard. There was enough space for all of us to run around in. Our dog, Crackers, was a character. He protected us all. There were so many of us at that house. I lived with Mother Connie in our own apartment/private rooms in the house. As the orphanage was so huge, we were able to have our own private sanctuary regardless of how many other girls were living there.

As I think back to what the house was like, it was the best children's home, probably, out there. Toys everywhere: rocking horses, bicycles of all sizes, cradles, dolls, you name it, we had it. You would never get anything like that now. It was a safe haven for any young girl. You could sleep where you wanted and when you wanted. Everyone had their own room, and their own bed but there was always an empty cradle big enough for anyone that wanted to have a nap in the nursery.

I will never get tired of speaking about Mother Connie. I would have no problem writing a whole book about her as she was truly an inspiration to me. There was never a day that we did not speak. Anything she told me to do I would follow, except when I was young and would refuse to eat my vegetables and meat. I was just never a fan, but as Mother Connie always said if you do not eat your meat and veg you will never grow up to be big and strong (as all mothers say). Eventually I started to listen and eat up.

To this day I sometimes get tired of eating meat but maybe Mother Connie was right. I am not necessarily strong physically, but mentally I definitely am. I feel that if it was not for her, I would never have received the blessing from Christ to be a healer.

I always complained when I was small that my hands were too big for such a small girl; they did not seem in proportion. Mother Connie would always try and reverse my negative thoughts by saying that God is going to use your hands to do wonderful things. Was she not right! I bet deep down she always knew that I was harbouring this gift, but she never told me; she was just waiting for it to manifest.

Mother Connie was just full of love. She loved animals and was always giving to, not only usual charities, but animal charities as well. She never gave to receive. It was always from her heart. She was just the epitome of what any decent woman should be like: kind, gentle and God-fearing.

A very small child came to me with her mother and father. The little child had cancer. She had a tumour in the brain so I had to put my hand on her head. My hand would get very hot and she did not like the heat. Her mother was so anxious to seek fame through her child being sick. She had seen a man on the television who claimed he could heal, I also had seen him on the television. He came from America. I had actually seen her with her daughter on the television, with this so-called healer. I am afraid after her session with him, one of her family told me she had died. If she had stayed with me, she would have been alive today. I did tell the mother it would take time, but you cannot stop people doing what they want to do, whether it is good or bad. Her family thought she was silly to take her to the American who called himself a healer just to get famous and be on the television. The poor child (of course) would not understand, her life could have been saved if her mother had not been in so much of a hurry. She could have put up with the very 'hot hands' and saved her daughter's life. It seems such a shame.

A few years ago, I met this woman who used to do agency work. She came to the library where I was working as if she was out of breath. She had heard about my healing hands. I was very busy at the time, so I told her I had not got any time to talk to her about my healing hands at work. I did not know her from Adam. She introduced herself right away and asked me if I could heal her back. She told me she was worried about not being able to walk at all. I repeated to her that I was at work in the office, as she could see. I was also healing other people at the same time and so was not available to treat her then. I was very sorry. She was one of those pushy people, determined to get what she wanted at any cost. I could not get rid of her. In the end I gave her a few sessions until her back got completely better. She did not give me a penny, but she told me she would do my feet. She told me she was doing people's feet to make herself quite a bit of money.

I could not believe it when she did my feet, she had the cheek to charge me £40. I just could not believe it.

Some people have the cheek of the living devil. She told me she was buying a beautiful house for herself and daughter. Would you believe that I got a visit from this said woman and daughter asking me if I wanted my feet done again? I told her to get out; she did not seem to have any shame. She was just doing too much. Then she asked me if I could do something for her. I said, "Certainly not!" I had had my fill of this woman, I did not want any more of her. I had had enough. I was tired and just wanted to rest awhile in peace and quiet. You cannot get much of that these days.

I had to keep seeing this woman because she had an agency job in the same building but thank the Lord it was not too near me. This woman was not easily put off. She used to come and see me at my office. I never said a word to her as I was always busy, but she kept coming back all the time and just looking. The girls working for me asked me who she was. I told them her name was Glenda, she came to me to heal her back pain (that I had healed), and that she had treated my feet and charged me £40.

They could not believe I had given her the money and said, "it seems she is looking for another £40 to do your feet again". I told them she should be so lucky. I told them I did not know why she kept coming down. Maybe she does not have enough work. I eventually had to tell her if she did not stop coming down, I would have to report her to her boss.

Chapter Eleven

It seemed as if she was a very fast worker; she told me this and it was verified at her office. I told the girls not to take any notice of her because I did not want to get her in any trouble. It paid off because we were a girl short and had a lot of typing to catch up on. Through my kindness she gave me a hand and was so quick the other girls were very surprised. She helped us out a lot, so it all turned out for the best.

I met a lady who came to see me. She had breast cancer. She brought her small son too. I knew right away I was going to have trouble with the boy. I could see he had no discipline whatsoever. I told the mother not to bring the boy next time she came for healing. Unfortunately, she rang me and asked me if I could come to see her at the hospital as she had to go in urgently. I told her I did not do visits, but she begged me and said her husband would bring me in the car. How could I refuse? She was crying and very upset. Her husband picked me up. I had not decided to go then, but when he came, I went with him.

When we got to the hospital we had to go in the lift. It felt very creepy to me and when we got in the ward, I felt so sorry all those people there had cancer. I just could not believe so many people had cancer all at once. That was when it crossed my mind. If Diane Abbott had been caring, how many people I could have healed. Instead of her shooing me out of her office, I felt so sad how people like her could hold down a good job.

When I got in the ward my friend was delighted to see me. I kept my hand on her all the time where she had the cancer. I stayed there with her until the time was ready to go. She was so thankful. When we started to go, she ran after us and told us the tumour had burst where my hand had been. She was over the moon. But there was a long way to go yet and she told me she would be coming back to visit me. As I told her before, she had to leave her son with her mother when she came.

She phoned me to tell me she was at home and wanted to make an appointment. When she turned up, she had her son with her which I told her not to do. While she was healing on the settee, he was doing a lot of banging around the flat. I was worried to know what he was up to because cancer cases take three hours, such hours I do not want to do again it's not that I am being pusillanimous but it's not necessary to treat a patient non-stop for three hours and that is a very long time for him to be having a good time around the place.

The boy was so undisciplined he had completely broken in pieces my brand-new pine toilet seat. I was so cross I telephoned her and told her, if and when you came again, not to bring her son but to leave him with her mother. He causes too much damage. He was even younger than the boy who lived in the flat above me. He was a menace as well. Sometimes I could not sleep until the early hours of the morning. He bangs and slides furniture all over the flat. I sometimes cannot get anywhere near closing my eyes until the next day.

The boy who came with his mother was about nearing five years old, while the boy who lived in the flat above me you just could not know his age because he didn't seem to grow at all I think he should see a doctor.

The mother who came to me for her healing had to go back in hospital again. She asked me if her husband could pick me up again and bring me to the hospital. I could not say no although I was very tired. Immediately I got there, she asked me to put my hands on her breast, where she had the cancer. I stayed with her for a long time. Eventually, I told her I had to go home to rest. I promised I would come again. That pleased her.

I was just about going down the stairs, when we heard a loud scream. Her husband wondered what was wrong. She said her breast had started leaking again. This was the second time of visiting her in hospital. I said surely that was a good thing. We could not go back in the ward because she could not explain to the doctor who I was and why I was there. The doctor was very surprised that anything had happened. I told her she was very clever not to tell the doctor anything. You see, doctors do not like people like me, so I went home and rested.

I still was not happy, because they sent her home far too quickly. I spoke to her husband and I suggested to him to take his son to his wife's mother. I then went home and got a good rest. The mother rang me again and asked me if she could come and I told her without her son. Would you believe it she brought her son again and this time he started breaking up my beautiful china. I told her she would have to leave. I couldn't take anymore of her son's behaviour. She became rather rude so I told her she would have to hold her son until the three hours were up. I told her I could never take her son again, and that would mean I could not take her anymore with her son. I did feel rather sorry for her, though I knew her mother could not tolerate him either. She was not young; I do not think many people would be able to tolerate him. He was just beyond handling. Just like the boy who lived above me. A person can only take so much. It seems such a shame that you know you can heal a patient, but because of her son's behaviour, hardly anyone can touch him or discipline him and that included myself. My healing takes such a long time that if only someone could take him in hand or look after him, I would be able to work and help his mother.

I feel that the mother and father would like this, but it all takes money that they could not afford, even to give me a donation, because they were buying themselves a house. It is very difficult to heal some people; they just cannot win. It is such a pity some of them go about it all the wrong way. My mother would always say that there is nothing like discipline from a very young age and I agreed with her, every step of the way. I will certainly pray for them.

A young Indian man came to me with a terrible back pain; he told me he had been to see his doctor with no results. He had sent him for an x-ray, but they could not find anything wrong. Someone told him about me so he phoned to ask me if he could make an appointment.

I started to give him two hours a week. As the weeks went by, he asked me how long I had been a healer and how I knew I was one. I told him about the vision I had seen in 1983 of Jesus Christ the Son of God. He said, "God has certainly given you very strong hands, my back is so much better. It is hard to believe I have had this bad

Chapter Eleven

back so long. I know you are going to get it completely better. How can I ever thank you? I wondered if I could ask you a favour". I asked him what the favour was, and he told me he had a lot of friends and family in the Indian community and is it possible he could tell them all about me. He wanted me to just keep my healing hands for them alone and not do anyone else.

I said, "I couldn't do that, I am English through and through. I could not let my own people down and normally I do most people who want my help and am always glad to give it. I know a lot of people are very poorly and need my help. They don't know about me, at least you have got rid of your pain, you are very lucky". He agreed, and I told him he could still tell them and when they are almost better, I could finish the healing on the telephone.

He said he was very happy to have met me. He said he had never met anyone with my power and I told him there must be a lot of people like me, but he just did not know where they lived.

It is a great pity; they should all be well-known so they can help many people. Believe me this world would be a much better place to live in. There would be less pain and fewer people dying unnecessarily.

After a good while the toung Indian was so excited and told me that the pain had completely gone. He told me he had never heard of this type of healing before. He also said to me, "Dorothy the whole world should know about this!" I told him he could tell all the people who need help. He should tell them, but to remember you have to have the hands first, otherwise it would not work. He did not know how to thank me so I told him to remember to always pray and thank the Lord.

In the 1980s I lived in a flat where a woman moved in on the ground floor. What a troublemaker she was. She told me she was a dressmaker. When I came home from the office, all I used to see were quite a few men sitting in the hallway. That was pretty frightening for me. I asked the woman what was going on and why the men were blocking up the passage. If they were customers, why were they not inside her flat instead of hanging around in the passage. She told me she was cleaning. It seemed such a poor excuse. Thank goodness I never saw them again. I did not like the look of any of them.

One day I took a half day off from the office to do some shopping. After a little while my telephone started to ring; it was the woman who moved in downstairs. She asked me if I could do her a favour.

I asked what it was, and she said she was expecting a man to come to her and when you hear him ring my bell, I should tell him she was not in. I said I would. She looked rather frightened. She knew of course I never went down to the door. I always opened my window. She said if he asked me when she would be back; I should tell him I do not know. When he came, I told him that I did not know when she would be back; he looked disappointed. I came in from the window, and would you believe it, he came back in about an hour. I did not answer again.

The said woman stole my cat. She turned out to be a terrible person. Her daughter was no better than her. When she visited, I had quite a lot of trouble with the both of them. When you have people like them living in the same property, it is pretty scary. You always have to be on your guard, because you do not know what is going to happen next.

I got a friend of mine to look for my cat before my neighbour took it. He found it in the cellar. She tied the cat up, so my friend untied it and brought it to me in the kitchen. You would have thought my cat would have been very careful to go near the woman again, but you cannot always tell what the woman enticed it with. By the time my friend looked for him again down in the cellar, she had taken the cat away. One of my neighbours told me they saw her carrying a cat in a big plastic clear box. I was so sorry to lose my cat. If you lose your dog you can call the police, but not for a cat. When I told my neighbour, he said if he had realised it was my cat, he would have spoken to her, but honestly, I don't think he would have because none of the neighbours liked her. They were all very sorry I had lost my cat, but they were all frightened of her. I did not blame them. I did not like her myself; there was something about her that was very sinister and deep. Anyone who can tie up a cat must be evil.

It is such a pity that we sometimes have to live in the same premises as some unsavoury characters. If we could only choose, but you have to have money to be able to buy your own place. Oh well, you can dream sometimes!

A chap came to see me who lived in the same block of flats, he had a terrible pain. I tell everyone who comes to see me for healing that I cannot heal in a minute. It all takes time depending on what is wrong. Some illnesses take longer to heal than others, but it is a shame that some people do not have any patience. I cannot do anything about that. It saddens me that the person is not going to get better, because they do not have any patience. I always think if only they could just try a bit harder to help themselves. I phoned his wife to ask her how he was. She said I told him he should have kept up the appointments. Her reply was, "Dorothy, I thank you for what you did for him, but sadly he died". I was so sorry I hardly knew what to say. I was very anxious to see the gentleman's wife, to talk to her and console her about her husband's death. When I went to see her, I was told she was at the hospital. I wondered if she was visiting someone, so I telephoned her to see if I had missed her, only to be told again that she was admitted to the hospital. When I inquired when she was expected home, I was told she was seriously ill with a tumour in the brain. I was flabbergasted, I have seen so many husbands and wives die after each other; it is quite uncanny, but this thing happens so often. I was sorry I was not able to tell her that I had healed quite a few tumours, but knowing her very well, I knew she would have been delighted to know that I could heal cancer. I somehow knew she would have loved to live a lot longer than she did. What a waste! To think such a lovely person so full of life, just like my friend Joyce who was so full of life also. There is nothing I can do for her now except to say a prayer for her and her husband and ask God to bless them both.

What I have found out is that some people do hide their illnesses; that quite surprised me because you never know who can help you without telling other people. I certainly would not hide my illness.

Since 1983, the time I was blessed by Jesus Christ, I have to tell you many more cases of healing I have done. From 1992, a young woman came to me, with a terrible pain. I used to treat her for two hours every week. It certainly helped. I cannot remember how many months it took, but she certainly got better. She told me she could not thank me enough. She did not realise that a natural healer like me could heal arthritis. She always thought it was an illness that could never be healed. She has always understood that – even doctors tell you that, they do not have a clue that arthritis could be healed. They will always tell you after you have had an x-ray. They always say it is your age. The doctors would be very displeased if they thought a lady like myself could heal that dreadful disease. That would stop them talking about your age when you are ill.

In America they would appreciate you much more than in Britain. I know as I have had a lot of invitations to go there. Personally, I know I would be better off in America, even though I have cured a few Americans who had knee problems but for whatever reason America seems too far away from home.

If there is anyone who can do what I can do, I would certainly like to know them because I do not think anyone can do what I can. Simply the best is how my past patients describe me.

I had a call from a young woman in Tottenham who wanted to know if she could come and see me. She had something wrong with her breast. She knew it was cancer.

I asked her if she had seen her doctor and she said her doctor sent her to get an x-ray, and they verified it was cancer. She asked me if I would treat her and would prefer my hands instead of the radiotherapy. She had heard terrible things about that treatment. I told her that she must not tell her doctor about her healing with me because he would not be very pleased. She told me she would not tell her doctor that she was going to a healer, because she knew full well, he would not like it. She soon started three hours a week; I give three hours for cancer, unless the person wants sessions twice a week. I told her that doctors and some nurses, and ministers in the church do not like me also. I am afraid it is just one of those things. The more you can heal chronic diseases, the more they do not like you. The Macmillan nurses do not like me either.

I healed a young lad who had a cancerous tumour in the brain in 1988. He had six weeks to live and his adopted mother brought him to me for healing. I used to give him lots of hours because he was so near to death and in a wheelchair. He could not talk or walk, after having the hands he gradually started to slowly get better.

One day, when his mother took him home after hours of healing, one of the MacMillan nurses was waiting for the young lad. When he came home, she was very annoyed and said to his mother, "Where have you been with the boy? I have been waiting a very long time". The mother told the MacMillan nurse that they had just come from a healer and that they go quite often. The nurse was furious. She said to the mother you should not be going to a healer.

Chapter Eleven

The mother asked her why not and if she wanted him to die. The Macmillan nurse did not answer. You see, they are there to look after you when you are dying.

I make sure that sick people visit me at all times. If it is impossible for them to visit me, I will explain to them what the MacMillan nurses are there for. I do not want the embarrassment of the whole procedure, so they will understand my not visiting them. That is the best way out.

I am very pleased to see that the young lad was getting on so well. He got married and had a child. The woman he married already had two children. He is now living in Hastings and drives a nice car. He is a very fortunate lad. From 1988 he had six weeks to live, and now he is as right as rain and as happy as a lark.

He printed me a beautiful letter, stating his gratitude to me for saving his life. It read:

> *"Our Father who resides in Heaven,*
> *Whose son died in your name,*
> *Once again you have given us a handle,*
> *To carry your eternal flame.*
> *The Lord has set us a task,*
> *Faith in you we seek,*
> *When doctors send us home to die,*
> *God's gift is Dorothy in Greek.*
> *He who asks nothing except our faith,*
> *Has entrusted one from this Earth,*
> *Placed a power in her hands,*
> *For you have seen her worth.*
> *You in your wisdom who has judged,*

Whose path is always straight and
Placed your gift inside this woman
Whose name is Dorothy Rodgers
I give thanks for your generosity,
For allowing her to save me,
And pray that you bless her forever,
This gentle and caring lady.
AMEN
For Dorothy
2001"

That is why we should all believe in God, through Jesus Christ. He is the only saviour who can bless you with this wonderful gift.

I asked him when he came to see me if he ever prayed and thanked God for his healing. He did not seem so sure. I told him he should do that every day. I asked him if he told other people about the healing, because I told him it is the word of mouth. He told me he had not because he had moved far away since his illness and no one would believe him.

He has come down to see me with his family about three times. He always wanted me to put my hands on him again and he said each time I put my hands on him he could see well. There seemed to be something wrong with his eyes as well. He also told me anytime he came to see me he could see much better each time he left. I reminded him to pray, as I told him without the Lord none of this could have happened. I am hoping he got the message. He did however tell me that he did pray and thank God, and that made me very happy.

Chapter Eleven

I got a call from a lady in Muswell Hill called Delilah. She wanted to see me and said it was very important to her. She seemed very upset and told me she had something wrong with her breast. I asked her if she had seen the doctor and she said he had sent her to the x-ray, and they told her it was cancer. She did not want to have the treatment so she asked me if I could use my hands. She had heard that radiotherapy was not very nice. I told her I did not mind but she must not tell her doctor because they do not like people like me. She had to be very careful. I told her we could start right away, as long as I knew where to put my hands. I also told her we could start at three hours a week. It is not a quick fix; it starts very gradually. In the meantime, I told her to just try and relax.

Delilah told me she had never heard of anyone healing cancer with their hands, as she said it is the best way to heal anything at all. She also said she could imagine doctors would be very upset that they could not do the same as me. She was a very interesting lady to talk to. She asked me how I had so much patience to stay for three hours healing. I told her everybody who came here asks me the same thing. I also told her when Jesus Christ gave me the gift of healing hands. He knew then I had a lot of patience.

I told Delilah that when she got better, she should tell someone else and she said she would be too glad to tell anyone, only if they are nice.

Delilah would sleep for about an hour during the session which I told her was very good because you get very relaxed. Healing is much better when you are relaxed. She was from the West Indies, a very small part, St Lucia. I have met quite a few people from there and they are very nice and educated. She used to tell me about her hometown and that she would love to invite me for a long holiday.

As the time went by Delilah told me she felt a lot better. I asked her if she felt worse at the beginning and she told me that she did. I told her that is exactly how it should be. I was glad to see she had patience. I wondered what she was going to tell her doctor and told her just be very careful and make sure she got all her benefits. I assured her not to worry as she could see herself well on the road to recovery.

I could see the change in her. I assume she very much believed in God and that makes me very happy. None of this wonderful healing could go on without Jesus Christ the Son of God. I knew without asking she will constantly be praying to the Lord, and that is just what I want. Some people forget all about where the healing comes from. You must never stop praying and thanking God for your complete recovery. I pray to God all the time, thanking him for my healing hands and that so many people get the benefits of them, especially the chronic diseases.

I do not know if I have already told you, my adopted mother was a dedicated Christian and her father was a priest. So, you see I was brought up in the Christian world and love every minute of it. In my mind, my mother should have been made a saint. She was always there to help people. When I used to complain about my very big hands,

Chapter Eleven

she used to say to me, "You're going to do wonderful things with your hands my child".

She never told me what it was, I honestly think she knew. She was such a remarkable person. I have never met anyone like her. I do not think I ever will. They do not make people like her today.

I had a telephone call from a lady in Muswell Hill (we shall her call her Zoe). She had a pain in her leg and said the pain was killing her. I asked her if she had been to see her doctor. She said he had sent her for an x-ray, the doctor had told her she had arthritis and that she would have to start to take pills. She asked me if I could treat her. As I tell everyone who comes for healing, I told her it would take a few months with her coming once a week for two hours. She said she would be very happy, as she knew someone else I had healed who had the same complaint.

Zoe was a very interesting person. The things she told me were quite remarkable. I looked forward to seeing her every week. She told me her doctor would not be pleased to find out that a lady could heal arthritis. She also told me that no one could heal such a disease. I told her not to tell her doctor as doctors and nurses don't like me at all, even ministers in the church don't like me either, and she told me if more people knew about me, they would be on top of the world. She told me not to bother about any of them and the people I have healed love me. She also said, "Why bother about them? I love you and will never forget you. You would be getting hundreds of people". I told her I would not be able to manage too many people and I do not let people worry me. I asked the lady how she was feeling with her pain and she told me she could hardly believe it because she could feel the pain slowly disappearing.

She also said, "I know you don't want me to tell the doctor, but I'll have to tell the doctor because I don't want any more pills from him". That did make sense. I certainly miss her, but she is now completely pain free. We said our goodbyes.

I had a call from another woman, Elsa, from Welwyn Garden City. She looked very distressed. I asked her what was wrong, and she told me she had a pain in a not very nice place.

I asked her if she had seen her doctor and she said he sent her to get an x-ray and that, she said worried her. They always like to talk about your age, and she said, "That really annoys me". She said, "I wouldn't mind if they were talking about getting you better, but it is all about that horrible therapy, and honestly I wouldn't like that treatment at all. I wondered Dorothy, if you would mind me asking you if I could have your hands? I have heard they are sound and very powerful". I said, "I suppose you heard the healing takes some time". She said she had and if I do not mind, she was anxious to start. I said I will start her on three hours a week. I told her again that it is rather slow but sound.

I also told her at first, the pain gets a bit worse, then slowly it starts getting better, but it takes a few months. I also cautioned her to keep up her appointments if she wanted to get better, as these things take time. That is

Chapter Eleven

why I work sometimes very late in the night, but it is all worthwhile to see the results, and of course the both of us have to have patience.

We got on very well together. Elsa would tell me lots of things about her upbringing. Her mum and dad were pretty close. Elsa was brought up in Hertfordshire and had sisters and brothers. They were a very close family. She was sorry to hear that I only had my adopted mother until I was 16 years of age and was certain I must have missed my adopted mother terribly when she had to go in a convent, and they wouldn't let me see her. She said it was terrible and told me she had heard about the nuns a long time ago. Their behaviour was disgraceful and pernicious, with me being only 16 years of age I would not know what to do. As I have said before, I was sorry I did not go to the police, but at that age, you would not think about that.

Elsa thought it was a great pity my birth mother treated me so badly. Through that I did not know any of my other relatives. I suppose when they read my book things will click. By that time, it won't bother me at all.

After healing Elsa, she said to me, "I see God will bless you all the way, especially the wonderful gift God has blessed you with. I know a lot of people who say they can heal, but not one of them can heal like you. Your gift is very special Dorothy, anyone who you heal are very blessed. I will be telling all my relatives and friends about you. It seems as if I have had a big burden lifted off my shoulders through you Dorothy, how can I ever thank you enough? I must tell you I feel so much better; I may be going to work abroad when I get better. I have a brother working abroad, and he would love me to come over where he resides the money is very good, and the houses are very big in America". I told her that was why her burden was lifted. I was so pleased for her. It was like she will be starting anew.

I had a call from another man with a heart problem he asked me if I thought he could be a healer. I told him I did not have a clue. Personally, I had never met a healer like myself. It would be difficult for me to know. I said to him I would love to meet a healer like myself. We could both help each other. He said my hands are very strong and he could feel them so much; he said he meant the power in them. He seemed very grateful. I told him that once people get better they never seem to tell anyone else and I am happy to include that once I heal people they never visit a hospital again, but I am often displeased that they never share the information of who healed them, I always wonder why. He told me he could not wait to tell his friends and family about me. He did not know that anyone could heal arthritis and was so glad he did not need to have an operation.

Often the doctors will tell their patients that no one can heal arthritis, but I can, and I do.

When I first went to The Lawns to learn about computing at Computer Age UK, because my computer was new, nobody could help me, until a new voluntary worker came along. He was an expert on all computers and writing letters. His name was Duncan and he said he would be glad to help me with my laptop. The people who were in charge all thought he was all right. I was glad to get the help. He told me it would be better for him to

Chapter Eleven

visit me once a week. I realised he was just after as much money as he could get.

Duncan's behaviour was disgraceful, he was known to the police; he told me that himself. He used to post letters, and take peoples watches to the jewellers. He once took a diamond out of my watch and told the jeweller it was his watch. When he brought my watch back, I asked him what in the world had gone wrong, as there was a hole in the watch. The hole was not there when I gave it to him. He brazenly told me the diamond must have dropped out of the watch, but I knew this was not true. I realised Duncan had a way of stealing and pretending he knew nothing about it. What a sad, sick man. Someone told me to report him to the police, but I did not. I thought it would be a waste of time.

I got a call from a gentleman in Hertfordshire called Edward. He had a pain in his back, I asked him if he had been to the doctor and he said to me he had, a long time ago. I understand that the doctors really have a hard time knowing what is wrong. I suppose if they have pain themselves it would be hard for them to find out what to do about it and what exact medicine to take.

I started healing Edward and I told him it would take a long time. He said he appreciated my honesty and said I got this gift from God. He said Jesus used to heal people quickly, I told him I am not Jesus Christ I am just one of his servants, working on his behalf. Quite a lot of my healing takes time and it depends on what it is or how long the sickness has been there. After he had been with me a few months, he was very happy. His pain was less. He said to me he could not believe it. All that time has been ill and suffering in pain and not knowing where else to seek help; thank goodness to have found you he kept saying. He appreciated my patience and my powerful healing hands. He thanked me with all his heart. I remember him saying, "Dorothy, may God bless you always". I thought that was very nice. Edward did tell other people. That is one gentleman I will never forget.

I had another call from a gentleman in Palmers Green by the name of Joseph who had a pain in his hip. Joseph was a supervisor in an agency and told me it was very awkward for him to play golf. The pain he said, was terrible. I asked him if he had been to the doctor and he told me he had no time for the doctors. Joseph asked me if I could help him and if it would be possible for me to start on him right away. I started giving him two hours a week of healing. He asked me if it would be all right to bring another pair of trousers for the healing so he could change when we had finished. He changed in my bedroom, which I said he could. One day by that time, another patient arrived and I forgot all about Joseph. I have never seen such a vain person. He took one hour to change into his trousers, my patient who came after him asked me if she could use the bathroom. She must have seen Joseph in my bedroom because once she came out, she said to me, "I thought you told me you didn't have a man friend". I told her I did not have one and she asked, "What is that man doing in your bedroom?" That was when I remembered he was changing his pants. I went to the bedroom door and asked him what was wrong. He apologised. He had two hours healing and it took him one hour to put on his pants! Personally, I have never seen anyone like him before. I was very glad when he got better. A man like that will drive anybody up the wall. He was so full of himself.

A young Chinese girl came to me from the West End. Her name was Inez. She had two bad feet going up to her legs. She was a very nice girl. I treated one foot at a time. I gave her three hours a week because she was very worried about both feet. Slowly they started to get better.

Inez was a very charming person. She loved watching snooker. Personally, I do not like it but we would always watch it until she fell asleep. People always used to tell me my hands, not only healed, but also put them to sleep as well. Inez eventually got her feet better.

Unfortunately, the most surprising thing happened. I met the lady who recommended me to Inez and asked her how she was getting on. She said she forgot to tell me Inez died of a heart attack. I was shocked. I said, "Why didn't she tell me about her heart? I could have helped her with my hands". I was very upset; what a waste, such a nice girl. What a shame. Sometimes you feel like giving up but of course you cannot do that. I will just pray that her soul rests in peace.

I then got another telephone call from a lady in Wood Green called Brenda. She told me she had heard about the lady I had healed at St Mary's Church, Stoke Newington in 1984. Brenda then told me she had cancer. I asked her if she had seen her doctor and she said he had sent her for an x-ray. She was very upset and asked me if I would not mind healing her. She would prefer my hands on her for treatment more than what the doctor's treatment would be. I started treating her for three hours a week. That certainly brought a smile to her face and it made me feel much better.

Brenda talked and told me a lot about her family. She had lost both her parents, but they were good parents, much better than mine. I told her she was very lucky she had a sister and a brother. They were both very concerned for her, and very happy to find out how she found someone genuine. She told them about St Mary's Church, and they asked her to give them all the details.

I told Brenda I was very lucky to have been adopted by a marvellous lady who was an angel; kind and dedicated. I also told her how she taught me so many different things. I remember until today, though that was a long time ago and how she was quite remarkable and trustworthy. The lady having the treatment told me her parents were just the same. She was very grateful to me and said she had never heard of anyone else being able to heal cancer.

A woman came to me from the same church as the woman called Janice. She told me she had had three operations and each time the pain kept coming back. She asked me if I could start giving her my hand treatment. I started to give her two hours a week and she was getting on very well.

She asked me if she could bring her dog. I said, "Certainly not as you see I have a cat". She said to me, "My dog is terrified of cats". She kept on about it. I told her that if she brought her dog and my cat is frightened, she would immediately have to go. Janice agreed and promised to do as I said. However, when she brought the dog I was flabbergasted. It was one big poodle. Janice took the dog straight into the dining room and it ate all my cat's food right away then he started to chase my cat up the stairs. Terrified, I told her to take the dog and go right away. After that, she very reluctantly phoned me to make another appointment. I agreed to it but told her to come without her dog. When she came again, she said she wished she had her dog with her. I told her I would never tolerate her dog ever again. After a while, her pain completely went. She told me she had mentioned to her doctor that she was going to a healer. He was very interested and asked her if she could bring me down to see him. She told him she did not really know if she will come because she is her own person.

Janice then asked me if I would go to see her doctor. I said, "What for?" She said the doctor wanted to examine my chest and brain. I asked her what she thought he would find. I then assured her he would not find anything, and I would not go anyway. One thing that must be understood is that my healing hands have nothing to do with brains or chest, but a gift that is only to the chosen few.

Janice then asked me if I could lend her £20. I did. She gave it back to me very quickly and then asked me if I could lend her £600. I asked her where she thought I would get the money from, as she never gave me a penny for all the time, I spent healing her. I must be the poorest healer in England.

Personally, I have never met a woman like her before. Janice would ask me when I did my shopping and believe me she would turn up at the door immediately the shopping arrived. Then she would help herself to cheese and biscuits without even asking me. Then one day she brought two women to see me while I was healing a gentleman and asked me if I could tell her two friends all about my life. I said, "Number one, I am healing and number two, I have no intention of telling her or her friends anything". She then thanked me for getting her better and told me she had got herself a job in Wales. I hoped she would be more settled in her new job. I felt very sorry for all the people she owed money to. I was very pleased she did not owe me a large sum of money as she owed a lot of people money.

The gentleman I was healing at the time that Janice came with her friends, said to me, "Dorothy, you have to be very careful of getting involved with anyone like her again. You should get someone to protect you". I said that would be difficult because everybody needs to be paid and I myself would not have enough money to pay such person. He seemed to be very worried and concerned about me; something would have to be done. I also told him I would be more careful in the future. One has to be these days. I told him I would not take anyone else unless they are recommended by someone. By that time, I was able to concentrate more on the gentleman. He had pain in his leg and right down to his hip. It took me about six months to get rid of all the pain. His doctor told him he would have to live with the pain for the rest of his life. He told me he could not tell his doctor a lady healer had removed the pain with her hands. That would not please him at all. I remember him saying, "I certainly would not give him your name or address. I would be worried; he would not be very nice to you. Be very careful who you give your name to".

After the gentleman got better, I certainly missed him. He was so kind. I said to him, "Surely you will tell your wife?" He told me she was such a miserable woman and he was the only person to put up with her. He said he would not like her to be miserable with me because I was too nice. Now what a lovely compliment he gave me. He would never write but rather telephone me outside to ask if I was still being careful. He said he had a big job on his hands because his wife was very ill. He had to wait on her hand and foot. I told him I would pray for him and his wife. I will never forget him he was such a gentleman.

I had a telephone call from a man in Hertfordshire who had pains in both sides of his hip. I could see it was arthritis. I told him it would take months to get better as I only use my hands and he understood. He told me he had met someone else I had healed. He then said he was very happy to wait; it was much better than going to the doctor and taking pills until the end of his days. I gave him two hours of healing for each week he told me he realised every time he had the hand treatment that he felt different at the beginning; that the pain got worse, then as the time went by the pain reduced. He told me he thought he was very fortunate to meet me and get himself better. Doctors tell everybody that arthritis cannot be cured but they are wrong. He was quite a nice person; easy to talk to and had been to very interesting places and met different people. He certainly knew a lot about travelling, he seemed to have been all over the world. He said to me, "I am sorry I wouldn't tell anyone. I know about you solely because I wouldn't trust any one of them". He said some of them are not even worth it, he had been practically all over the world, and had never met or heard of anyone like me. I couldn't help but smile, this was all due to the wonderful gift God gave me and he quite agreed with me that I had been blessed.

It took quite a long time to heal this man as he had arthritis on both sides. I can't remember how long it took, but I am sure it took a very long time. I really miss him because he told me things I have never heard of and he made me very wise to lots of things. I was very happy for him; he was getting so much better and having less pain. I asked him if he was going abroad again, and he said he was going to settle down, buy a flat and going to study the ministry. I think that is just what will suit him fine. He is that kind of man, very caring and always aware of other people. I will always pray for him for he is such a kind man.

I had a telephone call from a woman who already knew she had cancer. I asked her if she had been having treatment and what sort. She said she had been having radiotherapy and chemotherapy but wanted me to treat her very quickly. I told her I am only a servant of Jesus Christ and my healing takes a long time. I also told her I would only be able to treat her for three hours a week because I heal other people as well. She asked me how I knew I could heal cancer. My reply to her was, "I have more or less told you it is a gift from God".

I knew I had a very difficult woman here. She said she wanted to start as soon as possible. I started healing her for three hours a week. She could take it or leave it, but she took it.

Her cancer was very painful. It was on her breast and it had spread. She said to me how she had never heard of anyone else who can heal cancer and asked why I did not put an advertisement in the paper. I told her I would prefer patients telling each other. Besides, I do not think it would be safe for me putting it in an advertisement since I live on my own. I would never do it anyway. She then asked me if I ever got tired of healing. She said she very much admired me putting up with all the people who come to me for healing. I remember her saying, "I would never do it, some of them must be really miserable. You don't even make much money". I replied, "You seem to have got it in a nutshell. I suppose it is just one of those things. We all have to put up with awkward people".

I must admit it was not very nice healing this lady; she never stopped complaining. You certainly have to have patience with someone like that. I felt very sorry for her and could not wait for her to get better.

With the gift I have, I have to tolerate such a lot of questions all the time and keep telling people the same thing over and over again.

I was very happy when the lady started to get better because she would soon be finished with her healing treatment. I do not think she ever told anyone else about the healing, but as long as she was all right. She would not think of anyone else but herself. Unfortunately, I have met a lot of people like her. She thanked me after her complete healing. I told her I would pray for her. She told me not to bother.

I then got another call from a woman in Cambridge. She also had cancer. Her name was Ruth. I asked her if she had seen her doctor. She said she had and that she had no intention of taking their treatment. She said she thought it was dangerous. She had also met someone I had healed.

Ruth told me she got very excited and wanted to know how I discovered I could heal such a disease like that. I had to go over it all again and tell her about the vision I had seen in 1983 of Jesus Christ. I told her I know a lot of people would not believe me, but I do not mind, I really would not tell or make up a story like that. I would not have so much power if I did not tell the truth. She said to me I should not bother what other people thought as she knew I was telling the truth. She said anyone who has the pleasure of meeting you would know you are telling the truth also.

She asked me if it would be possible for me to start healing on her. I told her she will get three hours a week of healing, but it would take a long time to get her better. Ruth did not mind. She was only too glad to get some help.

Ruth said it is because of the fact that I am very kind, and God knows I am not greedy either; that is why I was chosen. I said to her we will never know. I will just continue as usual.

Ruth took a long time to get better, though it was very tiring for me. Three hours is a very long time though she was quite satisfied.

Ruth was a most unusual person. All the time I had to be answering questions like, "What do I feel in my hands? Why are your hands so big?" I said God must have given me these big hands on purpose. Ruth then asked why the doctors, nurses, and ministers in the church do not like me. I told her I did not know why. Maybe they wanted the gift as well. I could not explain it to her. She said it was strange as she would have thought they would like me in case they got ill themselves. It would be somewhere they could go to seek help and treatment, but I guess the doctors themselves are too proud. I told her none of them would come to me – they would be too proud to do that.

Ruth once asked me what I did for enjoyment as my husband had died (which I told her). That was a very difficult question to answer. I suppose my healing was some satisfaction. I always felt saving lives and getting rid of people's pain made me quite contented.

When I told her we all have gifts, Ruth told me she had not got any. I told her she had but she did not realise what it was. She told me none of her family had any gifts she knew about and she wished she had a gift of healing. I said to her many are called but few are chosen. She then told me she was getting very much better.

When Ruth finally got better, she asked me what she could do for me to show me how grateful she was. I told her I was only too glad she was well enough. I might tell you I was very satisfied. She told me she thought she was going to die. I told her she must always pray and thank God for the healing because if it was not through God none of it would have happened. She said she had not prayed in a very long time, but she certainly would now she was healed. Though people like her never tell anyone else.

I then started to heal a man from the church whose name was Fiz. He had ulcers in his stomach. It took a little time to get him better. I gave him two hours of healing each week. He was a church man and it was nice to talk about God with him. Fiz was the caretaker of the church he attended. He was certainly studied in flowers. He used to grow beautiful flowers all around the church. This was quite some time ago.

Fiz told me long ago about his illness, but it was his wife who reminded me of it. She said she got very worried when he had it because he was very sick. She was very grateful to me when I started healing him; though it took quite a little time to heal. I was very happy to heal him. I do not think for one minute the doctor could have healed him. It is a shame that doctors, nurses, and ministers in the church could not get together and work together so as to provide solutions rather than have things remain in permafrost. That would solve a lot of problems.

I was very glad that Fiz got completely better. He was helpful in the church. He practically runs the whole church. What they would do without him I will never know. Fiz is the backbone of everything, but what I noticed was that he never told anyone else about the healing.

I had a call from a man who lived in Essex by the name of Frank. He had a pain in his back. I asked him if he had been to see his doctor and he said his doctor did not know what it was. He sent him to the hospital to get an x-ray and they still did not know what it was. The doctor gave him pills which did not seem to work. Someone told him about me, so he called to ask me if it was possible for him to come to me for treatment. I told him I would give him two hours a week. He was very happy about that.

Frank said to me, none of the medical staff could help him, only me. What he said was incredible. He also said to me he did not know what to say.

After each healing session, Frank always put a donation on the table. As soon as my hands got on his back, he would go fast asleep. He told me he could not think of anything nicer. He used to sleep at almost every session and told me my hands made him sleep. He told me many of his friends who had come to me had told him they also slept. They said it was my hands. I told him it would take a little time. He did not mind at all how long it took as he knew he was getting better. He said to me, "What more could a person ask for?" He just kept thanking me all the time and asking me what he could do for me. I continuously told him that as long as he got better, I was happy.

Frank said I must get very tired when healing. I told him I did get tired. He then said, "Words can't say how grateful I am to you for your patience and kindness".

Frank told me he had a big job lined up abroad and he could take it with ease now that he was better. He assured me that should he ever get ill again he would come to me for treatments, but I assured him that that wouldn't be necessary as he is healed; but to also make sure that his food be his medicine and to exercise even for once each week. I certainly will miss him. He was very happy when the pain started to go.

He was absolutely flabbergasted. He said he liked listening to the prayers I always say at the beginning of every session. He would say, "May God bless you always, Dorothy, and may I thank you with all my heart. I will never forget you". I told him I was very happy to see him completely healed and told him I would pray for him all the time.

I then got a telephone call from a woman in Palmers Green. Her name was Jean. She had cancer and I asked her if she have seen her doctor. She told me her doctor had sent her to the hospital. They confirmed it was cancer. Jean definitely did not want the treatment they gave her which was radiotherapy.

Jean told me she would much prefer my hands. She told me my treatment was safer, permanent, and much less painful. I said to her you do get some pain with the hands but not as bad as the radiotherapy. It is when the hands get to the root of the cancer that it can cause pain. Of course, you have to put up with that. She told me she was so thankful that someone told her about me. She certainly loved the prayers. At the beginning of the healing she certainly did not believe very much in God. She certainly believes in God now. She asked me when I knew I could heal such a serious disease. I told her I had seen a vision in 1983 of Jesus Christ. I also told her when I tell people I have healing hands, some people do not believe me, but I do not let that worry me. I know what I saw, and I am very proud that I was chosen.

Jean said to me, "Dorothy you have made me very happy. I thought my life was over. I realise it is just starting again, thanks to you. I know when you have finished, there will be no more pain". I have not had so many hugs and kisses for a long time.

I might tell you that knowing you have just saved someone's life and stopped the pain is so fulfilling and peaceful. Of course, all of this comes from God. What a wonderful gift. I myself thank God every morning and every night. I feel God has really and truly blessed me. I will never stop praising the Lord. God is the whole of my world. Without God I could do nothing.

Jean and I talked and talked. She said she could barely believe it herself that she was healed. How fortunate she had met the person who told her about me. She had to admit she didn't believe at first, as she said, "You don't meet many genuine healers, plenty of them say they can heal but when you go to them they can't heal at all!" I was so happy that Jean got completely better.

I then had another call from a lady in Streatham, Beryl by name. She had a lot of pain all over her body. I asked her if she had seen her doctor, she said she had, and he had sent her to the hospital, and they said it was arthritis. She said, "All they want to do is operate on you. Some of my friends have had the operation and they are still in pain, so they give you pills. The doctor will tell you there is no cure for arthritis. I did not know it could be healed, till someone gave me your name and told me I did not need to have an operation. She herself could hardly believe it. I was thrilled, but then worried I wouldn't get the appointment with you".

I started to give Beryl two hours a week of treatment. I told her the healing takes quite a long time. She did not mind. She thought herself very lucky and she asked me if I could tell her how I found out I could heal these types of diseases. I told her about the vision I saw of Jesus Christ. She asked, like others, "Dorothy do you know why you were chosen?" My reply to her was, "I honestly don't know".

Beryl asked me if I feel any different to other people. I told her I was brought up by a Christian lady and her father was a priest. I also told her I used to go to church once on Saturday and three times on Sunday, so I had God in me all the time and I liked it. I suppose it is the way you are brought up. Some people tell me it is because of my childhood before my Christian mother adopted me. I think there is something to say about that.

Beryl was a very nice lady and she told me the different experiences she had had. Some of them were very interesting. Beryl had been to quite a few places. Trinidad, Jamaica, America, Malta and many more places. She told me she thought her travelling days were over because of the arthritis she had. She was glad she would be able to travel once more.

Chapter Eleven

Beryl said, "Only through you, Dorothy. I am so grateful. It is so distressing when you have to stumble around and have to use sticks and frames. I know arthritis does not get better with pills. It gets worse and it travels all over the body.

The older you get the worse it becomes. It is not very nice. I am so grateful to you I just do not know what to say only thank you with all my heart and may God bless you always".

Some people really appreciate what you can do for them. They are just lost for words.

When I was working in the Civil Service one of the supervisors took his hand and spanked me on my bottom. I was so furious. I said to him, "How dare you do that!" I told him he was out of order and he said to me, "Who do you think you are? Gold?" I said to him, "Yes and silver. Don't you dare lift you hand to me ever again". That was the first time anybody has ever done that to me, and I hope it will be the last. I told one of my colleagues, Molly, and she said to me, "Some of the men are rude and cheeky. I have had the same thing happen to me. I tell them off. Some of them think they are God's gift to women". Molly told me that when she reported the man; he got a promotion!

I then had a telephone call from a couple. A husband and wife who needed help; the wife mainly. It was a pain in her hip and back in a very awkward place for me to put my hands. I asked them what the doctor had told them, they said he had sent them both to the hospital for an x-ray. They said the x-ray did not show anything, so they had to go again and have another one.

They told me they heard about me and preferred to come to me, saying, "That is if you wouldn't mind healing us". I said I would do what I could. I started giving them two hours of healings a week.

I really felt very awkward healing her. I had to bend a funny way in the chair. I would never take on a case like that ever again. I did not know if I would finish this one as it is the worst one, I have ever done. I have done many such cases where I did not know what I was doing and still got the patient better, but this one I was twisting my back far too much and feeling very uncomfortable. I was afraid to tell them I had tried my hardest, but I could not continue. I was so sorry I had to tell them it was my first case that I had done that way. I hoped it would be my last.

I had a phone call from a lady called Anne. She was from North London. A friend had told her about the policeman I had healed. I asked her if she had seen her doctor. She said her doctor had sent her to the hospital and they confirmed she had cancer. Anne told me the doctor told her she would have to have the treatment of radiotherapy. She was terrified of the treatment and did not want it at all. She said to me, "I am hoping you will not let me down. I would be so grateful if it would be possible to have treatment with you". I told her when she makes an appointment, we can discuss it.

When Anne came, I gave her three hours a week for treatment. I told her it would take quite a few months. Anne was very happy with that.

Anne was quite interesting and very inquisitive. She wanted to know how I found out I could heal such a disease. I told her about the vision of Jesus Christ on 3 January 1983.

I will never forget something so precious for the rest of my life. Jesus blessed me with healing hands; that is why my hands are so big and powerful.

The people I haven't healed are the people who are racist and don't like brown skin, as well as people who have had only one session and left on their own. In a way I feel sorry for them.

When people did not like me for my skin colour, I personally cannot see anything wrong with being a brown-skinned woman. People would go on holiday to get like me and would be proud of their tanned skin. I think my skin is just as nice as anyone's, and besides, when I was younger a lot of men were so attracted to me due to my hue.

The patients are very happy when they feel my healing hands on them because they are very firm. What I cannot understand is how people come to me for healing and they do not believe in God. But they can come to a person who can heal a dreadful disease like cancer, arthritis and other diseases. This gift comes from God.

The next person who came to me was a man and his wife – Mr and Mrs Smith. Mrs Smith had cancer. Mr Smith had heard of the policeman (Christian Luke Barker) I had healed who had a cancerous tumour in his brain. Mr Smith asked me if I could heal his wife. I asked him if he had been to see her doctor. He said he had and added, "But my wife I'm sure would not like the treatment they give in the hospital. Your hands would be ideal. Not so much pain".

Christian Luke Barker told him he got better in 1993. Mr Smith said, "Now when your hands heal it is for good. When they give you treatment it is only temporary. So which one is better? I am asking you please could you start on my wife?"

I told him I would give her three hours a week of hand healing. He just did not know how to thank me, and they asked me why I did not put my healing gift in the paper. I said I could not do that because I live on my own. The people I heal should tell other people. That would be much safer for me. He then said, "When you tell some people they don't believe because it is such a dreadful disease. It is a shame because in London alone loads of people are suffering from cancer, even little children, and big people. They would be over the moon to hear about you. I feel, Dorothy, you need some protection". I said, "That is quite right. If I had protection I could heal so many more people".

Mr and Mrs Smith were both very kind and used to bring me all sorts of things such as baked cakes, as well as other things. They could not do enough for me and would buy me all sorts of other things. Mrs Smith said to me, "Dorothy, it seems as if the pain gets worse at the beginning". I told her she was quite right. It will slowly start getting less and less. It just takes a long time to heal but as they say, when it is finished it is permanent. She said, "You could get so many people better. That would be marvellous". Mr Smith then said, "We will tell as many people as we can, but then again we would be worried about you because in today's world you can't trust many people".

I certainly missed them when they got better. I had so many hugs and kisses. They were both lovely people. As they said, there are a lot of phoney healers and that is why people do not believe in healers. They both said it is such a shame, as doctors, nurses, and ministers in the church do not like me. They both saw it as jealousy because they could not heal other people themselves. They also both said the whole world needs people like me.

Mrs Smith said to me, "Don't you get fed up with having to explain the same thing over and over again, and the long hours you stay with people. You must get very tired". I told her I get used to it and I do not mind it at all. She then told me that it is because I have a lot of patience. She admired me tremendously, and was so happy that we met, and the fact she got better made it so completely awesome. Some people stay in my memory because of their gratitude and for showing their appreciation.

I had a telephone call from a man in East London called Robert. He told me he had seen his doctor and had started the treatment at the hospital. Robert was horrified to find out what the treatment did to him. Eventually he started an investigation himself and heard of someone who had cancer and was now better. Robert said he was then desperate to find out who had healed the person and then got a telephone number.

He said, "I still thought it was phoney because really and truly I just couldn't believe it. I had never heard of anyone who could heal cancer. When I eventually rang the number, I heard a voice so sweet to my ears. It said, 'Hello, can I help you?' I asked if it would be possible to come and see you. We made an appointment and I was worried that you would say you could not take on anybody else, but you told me you could only take me once a week for three hours. I might tell you I was over the moon when I asked you how much money that would cost me per session, I thought it would be thousands of pounds and you said to me I can just put a donation on the table. I thought I was dreaming".

I found him to be different from other patients I have treated, but extremely pleasant and very well-mannered. I found he was very kind asking me if I needed anything and if he could help me with anything I needed doing. I thought that was very considerate. I told him it was very nice of him, but he must not worry, and if I wanted any help, I would ask him. I thanked him for suggesting such a kind thought. He was a very unique man and very interesting to talk to. Robert used to tell me things I knew nothing about. I realised then that you are never too old to learn. We are learning all the time.

As the healing went on, Robert told me how he felt when my hands were on him for three hours. He said after a few weeks he felt terrible pain. He knew that was my hands attacking the roots of the cancer. I told him he would have to put up with the pain for quite some time because that is how the hands work and he would try and have patience.

After a while, Robert said, "My symptoms initially seemed to increase but are now beginning to subside and I know that by continuing with the healing sessions I shall soon be fully healthy again".

Chapter Eleven

As the months went by, he said he felt quite excited. He said the strange thing was when he told a few of his friends they did not believe him. Robert clearly stated, "I thought well, if they didn't believe me why bother about them. I'm sorry I just didn't have time for any of them". I told him it was because I was not well known. If I had been well known it would be a different matter. If people had seen me in public, that it would be very different. As the saying goes, 'everything comes to those who wait'. Not that I would like too many patients for now because I am growing older and by having too many patients, the strain would be too much.

As I said, Robert taught me a lot about my own healing by giving me all the facts about the different pains he had while healing. I said to him, "Sometimes I get a strange feeling when I am healing and I get nothing, but the healing still goes on". He said to me, "Till the day I die I will never forget you". He was a very charming man. I was so happy I could get him well again some people stay in your mind for a very long time.

I then had another call from a man who lived up in Balham, South London. His name was Sunny. Sunny told me he had pains nearly all over his body. I asked him if he had been to see his doctor and he said he had. Sunny said to me there is not much the doctor can do really; only give you tablets. He said they help a little bit, but then the pain comes back and when you keep taking those tablets, they give you it does nothing at all. Even the doctor does not know what is wrong and even the x-ray did not show anything either. Sunny then asked me if I could help him. I said it would be rather difficult for me not knowing what I am healing or what is causing the pain. I told him I would try and give him two hours a week of healing sessions. Sunny said he would be very grateful and that would suit him fine. I told him I did not know how long it would take as I did not know what was wrong with him. He would just have to have patience.

He told me where the pain was and to tell you the truth, I did not look forward to the stress and strain, but what could I do? I could not leave him in pain. He had faith in me. It would not be the first time I had healed someone when I did not know what was wrong with them.

I was pleased to hear he believed in God. The person who told him about me said I always say prayers at the beginning of every healing session. Sunny said he knew then I was a very powerful healer. He had met some of the people I had healed, and they spoke very highly of me to him. Especially about how my hands are very strong and that it was a pity that more powerful healers are not recognised so they can help more people. I very much agreed with him. I told him that on the news a lot of people have lost their lives with cancer, especially in London. All over the world in fact, but I explained to him I just do not like travelling, as I worried about my birth certificate issues. I think that has been a limitation of my gift as I believe that if I had taken all the invitations I have had to travel globally, I believe that I would have been able to heal more people and save many more lives. I just have to trust in God that he knows where I should be and who I should help.

Chapter Eleven

I have had so many opportunities to travel to America, but on my birth certificate as registered by my birth mother, who herself was white, registered me as a white girl rather than as a child of mixed parentage because she didn't want her family members to find out that her baby was of mixed race. So as to avoid people finding out about me being the only brown-skinned girl in the community, my birth mother tied up my legs to prevent me ever crawling out.

I told Sunny to just relax and pray and he will find everything will be all right. It just takes time.

Sunny told me he had never heard of anyone being able to heal arthritis. I told him it will take time though. Doctors do not like people like me.

Sunny told me he would be frightened to tell anyone else, especially If they do not know a person very well. He said I should have someone for protection. I told him I do not intend to do any more healing without protection. I think in this day and age; it would be very risky, and we are all getting older. It is so hard to trust anyone today, even friends today are very unreliable. Things you hear about what friends do are just too much to comprehend.

I had a phone call from a man in Stamford Hill called Frank. Frank said he had a lot of pain. I asked him if he had been to see his doctor, he said he had. His doctor had sent him for an x-ray and told him he had arthritis. He said all they wanted to do was to operate or give him pills, which do not get rid of the pain. Frank asked me if he could make an appointment. He told me he was very frightened. I said to him I could only give him two hours a week and I didn't know how long it would take because these things take time.

Frank said he would be very grateful if we could start the healing session right away. I was very happy to help him. I certainly do not like to see someone who is very sad after being healed and could not believe how lucky he was. He told me he had met someone I had healed which is why he felt such a relief. I told him not to worry. The pain gets a bit worse at the beginning and then it starts to subside very slowly.

When I first moved to Clissold Crescent in the late 1970s and early 1980s, most of the people I met warned me about the Stoke Newington police and to be very careful of them. I thanked each one of them for the warning. Believe me the police in Stoke Newington haven't changed. They did nothing about the woman running the laundry with dangerous chemicals that lived above me in my flat. When she had finished washing she wickedly made sure that underneath my windows was where she dumped all the dangerous chemicals from the laundry, right outside my window so I could breathe in the toxic fumes.

She did this for 18 years and paid the Stoke Newington police for the privilege. The police knew what was going on and how dangerous it was for me to breathe in all the fumes from the laundry but they couldn't care less; and as soon as she went to America the woman who took over her flat just carried on with the laundry business and spreading the same dangerous chemicals around my window. If it hadn't been for my very strong belief in standing your ground and fighting for your rights, I wouldn't be in this world and she would have got away with my death; but fortunately I am still here hoping I can do a lot more healing in the near future. I hope I can get rid of that terrible laundry with those dangerous chemicals which are still going on right now above my flat. I cannot say they have not made me feel very ill all the time. It was no use telling the doctors; they could not do anything about it. Anyway, one has to put up with this when you have policemen who are making money out of it. I think the whole thing is disgraceful. I know it was only through the Lord that I am here today and with the gift God gave me.

There was no one to help me at all, and even when I wrote to Diane Abbott, she still found some excuse, getting someone from the council to type a letter saying that I asked them to cut down a tree. Have you ever heard of someone who feeds birds everyday telling anyone to cut down a tree? I do not think so. I know the trees are for the birds and as I said I was brought up with birds. Dianne Abbott made that excuse because of the way she shooed me out of her office when I asked her to tell other people about my healing so I could save lives. I have been feeding birds all my life and I will never stop. The birds did wonderful things in the war, so I heard. They must have saved a lot of lives. We should all treat the birds with respect. I shall for as long as I live.

When I first moved into this particular flat, the British Gas kept harassing me to get a new boiler. I told them there was nothing wrong with the boiler I had. It was giving me very good service; in fact it lasted me for years. I moved here in 1989 and my boiler lasted until 2014.

The British Gas, in 2009, told me when you get a new boiler you pay less money to British Gas. I thought there was something wrong with my boiler, but it was a mistake. The gas man who came to see what was wrong was very quick with his hands. I had been washing and cleaning my utensils as he rang the bell. I was putting my utensils on the side (I wish now I had put them in the drawer). When he left, I looked to put them away in the drawer and found they had vanished. My lovely utensils. I will say I had never seen a gas man steal anything like that before. I wrote to the British Gas about the incident, but they never answered. Unless it is about money, they could not care less. When my boiler went, I applied to British Gas for a new boiler. They sent an engineer to put one in. Would you believe it? The boiler had a leak in it! They charged me £3746.58. The boiler itself was on sale for £1000. It was put in in July and did not work properly until August 2014.

When the boiler broke down, they sent a very young man. He said the new boiler had a water leak. He was right. The second gas man stayed in the bathroom for quite a long time. I wondered what he was doing so I went to have a look. He was sitting in my bathroom cleaning his filthy greasy tools in my bath and using my face towel to wipe them with. When I asked him what he was doing, he said nothing. He had covered over the face towels so I could not see the filthy grease stains. If he had asked me, I would have given him a piece of material. Instead of that,

Chapter Eleven

I had to throw away my face towel. The other one was brand new. I had to put it twice in the washing machine to get the grease stain out.

The new boiler had been installed so high I couldn't reach it. I think they do these things deliberately. The British Gas had even put the passage heater so high that I have to strain myself to reach it. They seem to find pleasure in doing these things to upset people.

The man who put the boiler in said he had to do something in the bedroom. He made such a mess of the bedroom, even pulling out the aerial out of my television. I asked him if he could put the aerial back in and he told me he did not know how to do it. The cheek of the man! I had to hire a television engineer who charged me £40 to put one in which took two minutes. The British Gas should have paid that. I honestly think British Gas should be monitored every month for their behaviour. I think a lot of people would agree with me.

Arthritis is so painful. There are thousands of people that have arthritis and many other diseases. I well remember healing a lady who had cancer in her breast. Her name was Lucy. She stayed quite a few months having treatment. Lucy certainly did tell other people who had cancer in their breasts, but I find a lot of people do not tell anybody else of who healed them. I find that very strange. If it was me, I would be only too happy to tell other people of where to get help from a proper healer because there are so many phonies saying they are healers.

I had a woman named Velma come to visit me for healing. She said she had a tumour in the brain, then as

I was putting my hand on her head, she told me that she was a healer also. I asked why she did not try and heal herself. Velma said she would do that, but she just wanted to know what I did. I thought that was very strange. She said she felt my hand on her head. I asked her what in the world she meant. She told me she had never met a genuine healer before. Anyway, she never came back so I think there was nothing wrong with her.

I did not get anything from Velma's head. She told me she wanted to know just what I did when I healed people, so I said to her, "Are you really a healer or are you trying to become one?" She said she would love to be able to heal all sorts of diseases like I can. I think she was up to hocus pocus. I told Velma it would not be possible for me to teach her as I got this gift from Jesus Christ and it is not something you can pass on to anyone else. She said she was sorry for wasting my time and then asked me if I had prayed to be a healer. I told her I had never even thought of it. I was very proud that Jesus Christ had blessed me with such a wonderful gift. I told her she was not the first person who had asked me that question, but as I say God gives us all gifts.

Velma wanted to know how, if I did not pray to be a healer, why it was that God had given me the gift and why I was chosen. My reply to her was that it would be impossible for me to answer and I have not got any idea. I said to her to keep praying because God listens to all our prayers, and I prayed for her. She was very disappointed. I told her she was a very young girl and she simply does not know what is in store for her.

I remember a woman I met, Joan by name, from Buckinghamshire. She was a very wealthy woman with a holiday home in London. She told me she was a healer and she gave me a terrible pinch on my leg which hurt very much. I asked her "What in the world did you do that for?" She said to me she does it to all her patients. I told her to stop doing it because it hurt very much and that would harm people instead of healing them. I also told her never to do that to me again, otherwise I would not ever come back to her. I did not think it was good at all and if she claimed she could heal, what in the world would I be coming back to see her for? She said she was sorry, but of all the healers that she knew, including herself, she thought I was the most powerful of them all. I honestly do not think she was a healer at all.

I met a minister who was connected to a church in America. He told me someone had told him about me and asked if he could talk to me. I agreed but was flabbergasted by what he said to me. He told me what they did in America is that they all got together in a group and tried to heal until their hands burnt like real fire. The minister said they would love you over there.

I made it very clear to him that I would not be associated with anything like that. He then told me that the devil creeps in. I was disgusted. I would never be into anything like that, especially when he asked me if I would come over. I said certainly not, under any circumstances would I even think of going to see something dreadful like that. It shocked me even more when he said he understood that I am a Christian. I said to him, "How right you are. I respect the gift God gave me and it is only for healing, saving lives and helping people with their pain. All that dreadful behaviour about the devil, I have nothing to do with that sort of behaviour. I cannot even imagine things like that going on; how crazy this man was just to imagine ministers in the church doing things like that. It quite amazes me. I have never heard of such things like that before.

I remember a chap who came to see me once and asked me if he could join with me in my healing. I asked him what sort of a healer he was, and he told me he was a spiritualist. I then told him I knew nothing about that sort of healing and that I heal through Jesus Christ. I am one of his servants that heals directly through the Lord Jesus Christ. I told him I was very sorry, but he could not join me at all. I told him, "I wish very much that I could meet a healer like myself. We certainly would have a lot to talk about and what a lot of people we could heal between the two of us".

It would be so wonderful, but I have never heard of so many things about so-called healers. I wonder if I could trust any one of them. A certain friend of mine told me she thought it would be very unlikely, but I told her in this big world you never know what is around the corner. She certainly agreed. Then I told her it is a shame that some people you heal never tell anyone else and I think that is very sad.

I knew before I had been chosen as a healer, that if I discovered anything or anyone who could help me,

I would tell as many people as I could. But everybody is not the same. As long as they are all right nothing seems to bother them. It is like that lovely young girl I healed at St Mary's Church. Even her own husband never told anyone I had healed his wife of cancer. Somebody told me it did not take him long to move to Birmingham, and according to what they told me, he got married again. It is unbelievable he never told anyone about the healer who healed his first wife so that other people could get healed as well. There are so many people who need help. Why are people so selfish and only think of themselves?

I once asked a friend of mine if she would believe me if I told her I could heal cancer. She told me certainly not. You see, she did not know until after I had the accident. I had to smile because I know it is hard to believe that anyone can heal cancer, especially because it is such a dreadful disease. When God gives you a gift such as given unto me, you have to try to treat as many people as you can, and you just wish people would try even to tell their friends.

Now of course it would not matter, as I am writing this book about my life. More people will know what I can do. Even people abroad. However, everybody would have to be monitored as you just cannot take people into your home in this day and age. One has to be very careful.

I remember once a young woman phoned me and asked if I could meet her at Liverpool Station. I asked her, "Why in the world would I want to meet you there just out of the blue?" She told me that one of her family was ill in hospital with tubes all over them. I told her I was very sorry, but firstly, I never meet people at stations and if anyone wants me to go to the hospital, they automatically pick me up and bring me back in a car. Secondly, I would not dream of going anywhere to see people I do not know. Thirdly, I asked her if she thought for one minute that a hospital was going to like me interfering, when they have tubes all over a patient. I then apologised again and explained to her that I do not do those sorts of things anymore since the time when a woman came to me for treatment with cancer in her stomach.

I made sure to get all the cancer out of her stomach and then her eldest son encouraged her to have an experimental operation after I had healed her; I was quite appalled. All they wanted to do was experiment on her because they could not understand why the cancer had gone. I warned her not to allow the doctors to touch her because I knew fully well what they were playing at. After they had finished their experiment, they camouflaged and covered her with tubes. I did mention this before; I felt very sorry for her children.

That poor lady had to die, leaving her family so depressed and sad. The doctors that were investigating her went on as if nothing had happened. Their disgraceful behaviour made me feel very sick and I cried. After all, I had spent hours with my hands on her and she knew she should have never allowed the doctor to touch her at all.

I promised myself I will not mind how long it takes me, but I am going to write about it even though it took place in 1992. I have never forgotten about it. Things like this grieve me very much. I hope that someone at least will talk to the doctor about it and to the nurses who were there, and to make sure it does not happen again.

I have healed quite a lot of people with cancer in all different places. This lady I am talking about actually worked at St Thomas's Hospital. She thought she was going to get special treatment. Instead, just look at what they did to her. What she suffered must have been awful. The doctors did not blink an eyelid. Everything to them was normal. Things like that are bound to stick in your mind forever I only hope those particular doctors will be told never to do that again.

It is most distressing. Doctors are supposed to make people better, not make them suffer through their disgraceful behaviour. The doctor should not have done anything to her at all.

The doctors asked me when I had my accident and went to the hospital, if I wanted an operation. I told them certainly not. I had met a woman in the ambulance going to the foot clinic the day before that. She told me she allowed them at Homerton Hospital to operate on her knee and she said she was very sorry she let them do that. She said her knee was worse now than it was before. That is a chance we have to take sometimes, but a doctor told me once a while ago that it depends on who the doctor is. If the operation comes out all right, he told me really it depends on how much experience that that doctor has.

I have met a lot of people who have had their knees done and they have all complained of terrible pains. It is a pity that the doctors cannot do something instead of operating. That is where the trouble starts. I do not like to see people in pain, especially as I have healing hands. Of course, I cannot heal everybody. I wish I could but that would be impossible. That is why I wish I could find someone who could heal like myself. I used to hear a lot about healers a few years ago. Where have they all gone? You never hear about any healers today. Maybe it is because so many people are against them.

I remember a doctor called John. He was not afraid of anything. If you were having trouble with anyone, he would try very hard to sort it out, especially if it was affecting your health. John would get down to business and see what he could do. He was also very dedicated and genuine, but unfortunately, he is not in this world now. John is dead. It was a pleasure to go and see him. He never complained about anything and was always very anxious to find out how you were.

John told me if he knew I had healing hands when I knew him, he would not have been against anything like that. He said he would have been very interested and want to know everything. I know I would have told him as much as I could, as he always said we all have gifts. John was a doctor you could tell anything to. You could always ask his advice on anything, even if you thought it did not make sense. He would always put you at ease. Many people who knew him always spoke well of him and always mentioned how clever he was. What a pleasure it was to see him.

John had so much patience and always understood everyone. I will never forget him and nor will many other people I know. It is very sad how doctors of today dismiss you and you always have a feeling they have not got the time of day for you. They can make you feel embarrassed and glad to get you out. I always wonder now if they ever knew what I could do, and how they would feel. I know they would not like me at all.

When I am in a hospital, I make sure I never mention to anyone of them what I am capable of and the gift God gave me. I do not think any one of them would like it. I know full well to keep my mouth shut.

I did once hear a nurse say to her colleague that I am always using my hands. I wonder why the nurse had said that. I suppose it is just one of those things. Lots of people use their hands. The nurse said, sometimes our own hands are a comfort, and I thought to myself how right she was. My hands are quite a comfort to me, and they have been a comfort to quite a lot of people. How many? I cannot count.

I remember two very young ladies coming to me. They asked me how much I charged for my healing and I told them just to put down a donation. They said to me, "Dorothy, I think you must be the poorest healer in the world, and we know you can heal serious diseases! So why not charge a fee?" They also both said I am too kind and too patient. One of them pointed out that everyone is just grabbing money today, left, right and centre, and you could be making a small fortune with your healing session, but hey, that was then, and these days things have changed. I certainly wouldn't want to be left behind or out of pocket, even though time is money. I still have a lot of sympathy for my patients hence I would let it be known to them to let their conscience be their guide. I told them about when I went to Malta to heal people. I could not take any money from the people at all, not even donations because Malta was in a bad way and the people were suffering. The then Prime Minister of Malta was mismanaging all their tax money and so many of them had very bad nerves.

In Malta so many people lined up for me to heal them. They all wanted my hands on their heads, even for an hour. So many elderly, children, mothers; they were all in a very bad state. The people who came to see me were all from different homes in Malta. They all said my hands made their heads stronger and reduced their nerves. They said my healing made them calmer and relaxed. Some even asked if it was possible that my healing should continue every night, but I told them I had lots of other people to heal. I did however try to fit some of them in, but not all the time as I was certainly very busy in Malta.

I also told the ladies about one of the businesswomen in Malta who asked me if I would consider taking an offer of staying in Malta. She said they would build me a beautiful house and there would be people to do my cooking, cleaning, and washing; all I would have to do is use my hands to heal people. I thanked her for such an offer, but I could not take it. I explained to the woman that I could not take up the offer especially with the thought of me missing England. I was born in England and I am so attached to the easiness or availability of most things. I could never live in Malta anyway; it is not my sort of country.

I met a few English girls in Malta who agreed with me that I would never get used to living over there. They had their husbands over there and to tell you the truth, I was glad to get back home to England. I really do not think I would ever go back to Malta again. I did not like the ways they treated their animals in Malta.

When we were landing in Malta, the plane was wobbling all over the place. We all thought it was going to crash land. It was pretty frightening. The return journey was all right.

The two young girls who came to me for healing told me that coming to me was very interesting and they were happy with my healing hands. They said, "We know you will get a lot of people come to you for healing because the majority want everything for nothing". They both advised me to get much bigger donations, especially with the fact that I have my heating and everything else to pay for. Of course, they were right.

Given the economic situations that we all face at the moment it does make sense to charge a fee per session. Also, I have even considered hiring an assistant to help me out as this is necessary, and besides, the assistant could also be there for the sake of protection. Things would have to be very much different.

The two ladies both told me not to let so many people get away without giving a larger donation, otherwise I should not help them at all. They both kept on repeating that you do not meet or hear about people like me very often. Especially someone who can heal cancer and arthritis. They also both said if it had been them healing, that they would be millionaires by now. They said people like me, the whole world is in search of. I really do not know if that is true, but I do know a lot of people want help.

More people should get together and find out who the genuine healers are. Doctors should accept real healers and be glad for their help. That is why God gives certain people healing powers, so they can heal people.

The two young girls were very grateful to me for healing them and as they got better, they both went overseas for a vacation, but prior to me healing them they wouldn't go on holiday because they were scared of their illnesses worsening. They said when they tell people about what I can do they do not believe It. That is the trouble with people today; they try to find the people that I have healed so that they can verify it or give a testimony of being healed.

Actually, I have volumes of names of people that have been healed by me, and only with their permission would I reveal their names. It is so easy for the majority of people to have petulant thoughts because they don't knows what a person is capable of doing.

Anyone can go to those who have given me permission for their names to be published in my book for testimonies. They will find out the truth there.

One of the ladies on her last visit to me said they both wished me all God's blessings and said they hoped I would get someone strong and good to protect me and see no harm comes to me because they say in this day and age you have to be very careful who you are dealing with.

People sometimes appear to be all right, then you find out they are not.

They asked me to pray for them all the time and they promised me they would pray for me. I think that is very nice. I think prayers go a long way. Without prayers there is nothing. I think as long as Jesus is there in my life then I feel very safe. I also have a guardian angel all the time.

I then had a middle-aged man called Sager. He asked me on the phone if he could come for healing. I asked him what was wrong and he told me he had a pain in his back. When he came, he told me he had the pain for a long time. I asked him, "Why haven't you been to your doctor to see what it is?" He told me he had seen his doctor a long time ago, and he just gave him pills. He told me the pills were no good. The doctor told him if they did not work, he would try another pill. He tried another pill and that did not work either. Then out of the blue, a friend told him about a healer. His friend told him I was first class. Sager said to me that his friend was not lying about me being first class. I had to smile. I told him it is because all these healings came from Jesus Christ the Son of God. I asked him what he thought about my statements. To my astonishment, he thought that was the most wonderful thing he had ever heard.

Sager said to me, "Now I know I am going to get better. I know the pain will never come back once you have healed it". I told him how right he is. The fact that he had faith in Jesus Christ made me feel very happy because his faith alone is so sound. I have never had anyone say that before and yet I have healed so many people with all different diseases. At first, they are not too sure until after they start feeling a lot better. Sometimes at first, they feel a little bit worse. Then it starts getting better very slowly, so you see I quite admired this man.

Sager's wife was over the moon when he told her to believe that he had been completely healed. He said to me that he could not thank me enough and that he told his doctor about me getting him completely better; though his doctor did not like it at all.

Sager told me his doctor said I must have a lot of money through my healing. But he told him it was a very small donation that he gave the lady. His doctor said I must be a very unusual person because today everybody is after money. Sager told the doctor that he did not think there is another healer like me. He also told him I am a very special lady. He told me he was sure the doctor wanted to ask for my name, but he would not have given it to the doctor anyway. Sager said the doctor was so desperate to find out how I was to be able to heal a disease that he himself could not heal, but he told the doctor that he was made aware that she has a healing hand, a gift from the Almighty One who gave me the gift, and that is why I am so special. Sager told the doctor I had healed all different diseases and he asked him if I can heal cancer. Sager answered him yes, and that he had the proof as well.

The doctor told Sager that he did not think he would see him again. I told him it would be very unlikely. The doctor asked him if he should strike his name off his list. Sager told him it was the best thing to do because he would not be coming back there again. Sager said the doctor was very nice and that he would not strike him off. Sager knew it was in my interest not to supply any information about me to the doctor. The doctor did not know how to ask him because at first when he told him about me, he was not pleased at all. What a pity doctors cannot get together with genuine healers like myself. It would be better for the doctors and very much better for other people. It makes you wonder what they are made of. After all they know that God gives everybody gifts, but strangely doctors do not believe in God, but in themselves.

Sager said to me, "Dorothy, I'm so glad I met you; if I hadn't, I would still have the pain now. My wife is very happy as she said she knows where to go if ever she is in any pain. She said having healing hands that comes from Jesus Christ is the most wonderful thing I have ever heard of and I agreed with her. She said you are so special that the Lord chose you to do such a dedicated and precious work". I said to him I am a servant of Jesus Christ. I am very proud to have been chosen as I told her we all have our special gifts. I told him how people always ask me if I prayed to be a healer and I did not. I was very surprised when I saw the vision of Jesus Christ telling me that I had healing hands. I always remember my Mother Connie saying to me when I asked her why God gave me such big hands. She always used to say to me, "You are going to do wonderful things with your hands my child". She never told me what it was.

I always wonder if she knew but never told me. I could have healed her and kept her longer with me instead of her going to the convent and then the nuns not wanting to see me, slamming the door in my face.

Sager's wife said to me, "God knew he had chosen a kind and dedicated lady". I told her that was very nice of her to say. She said it was true. I wished her and her husband all the best wishes. I told her I would pray for the both of them. They said they would both pray for me. I thanked them very much. I knew he was completely without pain.

I had a call from a woman who asked me if she could come for healing. Her name was Carmen. I asked her what was wrong, and she told me she had arthritis in her knee and hip. I told her it would take a few months, and she said she did not mind because her doctor told her that nobody could heal arthritis and it would be better that she had an operation. Carmen told him she did not want an operation. A friend of hers had an operation on her hip and it had hurt her even more than before. Someone fortunately told her about me. She told me she was so relieved. She thought to herself, fancy going through the rest of her life with such pain. Carmen was surprised why the doctor would tell her that nobody could heal arthritis, yet I could. I told her that the doctors do not like the idea of any healer being able to heal cancer or arthritis, bear in mind that being sick or being in pain keeps the doctors employed.

The doctors do not recognise women like me being able to heal through Jesus Christ. I think really it is just jealousy because they cannot do it themselves.

Carmen asked if I ever felt embarrassed. I said not at all. I do not take a blind bit of notice of the doctors.

They do not have my healing hands. I bet they wish they had. Perhaps a few of the doctors can treat patients to get better, but at a cost. I have the Lord on my side and always a guardian angel with me. I feel very secure and safe.

Carmen said to me, "I have never met anyone like you before in all my life. I do not know how to thank the man who told me about you. It seems to me like a dream but I realise I am wide awake. I have been talking to a few friends of mine and they all say I wish I had met her before. I would never have had my operation which they say hurts them even more now than it did before. They are asking me to ask you if you can help them after they have had an operation". I told her (as I could not recall at the time) that I have never really healed anyone who has had an operation because the damage has been done, you can't undo an operation. They themselves seem to think once they have had an operation, that is it. I told her I honestly do not know.

I only try to heal people who have not had an operation, but I do feel very sorry for them being left with so much pain. Even myself when I went into hospital, they kept asking me if I wanted an operation (due to getting a bad hip that had been caused by my accident when I was laying on my bedroom floor for two days). I said certainly not and that was it. I am very glad I did not ever have an operation. As the time went on, the woman's pain, as I told you before, would get worse and then slowly started to get better. And she told me this was exactly how it felt. Carmen asked me how I know and I told her it happens to everybody I heal. She was quite astonished and very happy that her pain was going away. I told her not to forget to thank God for her healing; she promised she would pray all the time. Carmen also said that she would pray for me also. She said, "You have a lot of patience and you are very kind. That is why the Lord has chosen you". I replied that that it was very nice of her to say. It seemed a lot of people often say this to me.

I then had a telephone call from a very young man who asked me if he could come for healing. His name was Nicholas and he was from Cyprus. When I asked him what was wrong, he told me he was feeling very depressed and he could not sleep at night. I told him I did not do that type of complaint, but I asked if he had seen his doctor. Nicholas said he had. He said to me, "You know what they are like". He was very sad I said I would do what I could for him. I told him I would hold his head for two hours each week as he knew I had other people on the queue. I said to him it may be something that needs healing in the brain. That might just be what the brain needs.

Though I told Nicholas that, now I remember I have done awkward things like that before. Like when I healed a woman from Spain who had not slept for about 20 years, and believe me, she slept like a log after that.

As the months went by Nicholas said to me, "You know Dorothy, just as you said, I have started to feel better slowly. I bet in a few months I will be as right as rain. I just cannot believe it. You see the doctors do not have your healing hands".

Nicholas was a very interesting young man. He had all sorts of plans for himself. When he got completely better, he went abroad. He did not take my address, so I never heard from him again, except before he went abroad Nicholas did phone me and thanked me for giving him his life back. I told him to pray and thank Jesus Christ because without Jesus it would not have happened; also, he promised to pray for me as well. I thanked him and I know he would make something really worthwhile for himself one day.

I do not just pray for people I have healed. I pray for everyone and of course my friends. I do hope to be able to heal a lot more people than I healed before, and believe me, I healed quite a lot. It is such a shame that some of the people that are healed by me do not tell other people.

One man who was very nice to me told me he was frightened to tell other people of who I was in case they harmed me. This time I will make it a duty to always have someone with me when I am doing healing sessions. I'm sure after the book on my life is finished, which is the book you are reading at present, I will be able to get a lot of help. People will then understand what I am capable of.

Cancer, arthritis, and heart problems are the main ones that I heal more easily than other diseases. At this point in time, I am just typing what I remember in the journey of my life, but come to think of it, what is life? Most people have no understanding of what life is all about. The whole experience of life is to enjoy it by manufacturing happiness into your life. As time goes by, sometimes I may have to repeat myself because I had so many patients and they all want to know everything from the beginning.

I met a young man and his girlfriend once. They both asked me if I could help them. I asked them what the matter was and they both told me they have been on drugs for a long time and would like to quit. I asked them why they did not go to rehab and they said they had but it did not work. I then asked them what they wanted me to do, and they both said they wanted me to put my healing hands on their heads for a couple of hours every day. I told them I could not do that. I could only put my healing hands on them both once a week or twice a week as I had other patients before them in desperate situations that are in need of urgent healing. They said they could not even give me a donation, but I told them not to worry. They gave me a guitar. The only thing is, I didn't know what to do with it as I cannot play guitar. I thought I'd wait for some lad or a young girl who was interested in guitars and give it to them.

The two of them lived next door to me for quite a time. They both told me as soon as they felt a lot better, they would be off to America. I did feel very sorry for them, especially when they told me they had never felt so good in years, as the healing took its effect. I told them they would both have to be very careful not to get on drugs again. They said they would be. They were both writers of songs and playwrights. I told them I would pray for them both and wished them every success. I felt very happy when they told me they were getting ready to start travelling to America. They asked me if I would ever go there and I said that I would like to go there one day. They both said I would make lots of money in America, much more than in England because I have very strong healing hands and can heal all sorts of diseases. I told them I would not feel very safe because of my birth certificate. If I should travel to America as a white person the Americans would be suspicious or curious to which part of me is white European. Besides, I was going to get married, but my friend had a stroke.

At the time I had just seen the vision of Jesus Christ telling me I had healing hands To begin with, I experimented on Baboni who was a dear friend of mine in hospital. I didn't know where to put my healing hands on him so I just placed my hands on his stomach. I was placing my hands on Baboni's stomach instead of putting my hands on his head; that was one mistake I made throughout my experiences in healing people, but I had only just got the gift of healing. All the same, I visited Baboni everyday while he was in hospital.

I realised it was incorrect, when I started to put my hands on Baboni's head whilst he was in the hospital. The doctor was giving me dirty looks. He asked me what I was doing. I felt very embarrassed and I was worried I would not be able to save him. The doctor had put a fan right on his bed. I thought that was very strange because I felt his body and his head were quite normal. The doctor was looking at me as if to say 'please leave'. The next day I went to visit him – he was dead. I then asked the doctor why he had put a fan on his bed when he was not hot at all. He said to me, "You don't know anything at all". Little did he know he was talking to a powerful healer but there was nothing I could do. I was very sad. I certainly did not like that doctor but since then I have become so wise, I will certainly speak up much more now if I see a need to. Especially if it is someone I know.

I have seen such a lot of things happening in hospitals. It makes me very annoyed that I did not speak up before especially with Barbara, the lady I healed with cancer in her stomach. The doctor decided to experiment on her. I was furious to know what they had done to her. It was a few years ago, but when her sons asked me if they could pick me up, I said yes. When I got to the hospital, her daughter told me she had not opened her eyes all the time she had sat beside her bed. She told me as soon as she heard my footsteps coming, she opened her eyes. I looked on her and she was pleading to me to help her; talking with her eyes, telling me she was sorry she had not followed my advice. I will never forget for the rest of my days. I could see she was in a terrible lot of pain.

I am very sorry I did not give the doctor a good talking to and ask him how would he feel if he was in Barbara's shoes. How terrible it is to have no feelings, no compassions for another human begin who trusted you and your profession as a doctor. This is a betrayal of trust. I will never forget her pleading eyes until the day I die, asking me to help her.

After the hospital staff admitted they had punctured her lung, the children of Barbara asked the doctor to turn her on her side, so that I could put my healing hands on her or to allow me to examine her, but the doctor refused to comply because the he knew what damage he had done.

The medical people did not want me to put my hands on her. They were afraid I would feel far too much damage. I do hope they will read this book on my life; it is bound to jog a few memories. I do hope one day they will say they are sorry to her family and pay compensation.

After that terrible experience of Barbara, I remembered a lot things from my youth days. I had some terrible times before I got married; all on my own, wondering where the next meal was coming from, having no relatives, no mother or father, no cousins, aunties or uncles, sisters or brothers; no one at all to call family. It is a very bad feeling. You feel quite lost with men coming on to you that you do not even like. It made me wish I had a father to protect me and advise me.

I was very good at putting off men I did not like. But at the same time I was sometimes very frightened and wished I could still have my wonderful mother whom the nuns wouldn't allow me to see; due to the thoughts of nuns not wanting me to inherit anything of my mother, but wanting my inheritance to go to them instead. I guess that is why I didn't inherit anything from her will when she went to sleep. Little did my mother know that when I came to visit her the nuns would slam the doors in my face and refuse me visits to my her.

When I was 17, I desperately wanted to see my adopted mother again and talk to her for a very long time. I wanted to listen to her talking to me, giving me a lot of advice about always remembering to say my prayers and asking Jesus to help me with any difficult situations. She would always say that God would be with me all the time but when I realised I would never see her any more I was so sad. It doesn't worry me to be alone now because I am much older and I am used to being by myself; but I have friends both young old, especially a young man called Ali. He is of African race and he is always kind and helpful. I like Ali; he's always on hand.

But of course, I did not know I had healing hands until many years after. I knew at that time my Mother Connie wouldn't be alive, but I hope she knows now that I am a healer and that I saw the vision of Jesus Christ in 1983, telling me I had healing hands. That, I will never forget until the day I die. What a wonderful feeling to know you have been chosen with such a wonderful gift and to know you can save people's lives and help them with their pain. The joy, the smile on people's faces when I hear them gives me a wonderful feeling.

I notice when I have many people to heal, I am so relieved when the last one leaves. I always thank God for being there with me, then I try to relax.

I always think when good things happen to you, it always comes from Jesus Christ. Who else could it possibly come from? I do not know why but I always feel sorry for people who do not believe in God.

I always have that kind of feeling when I have met people who are ill or in pain. That was before I knew I had healing hands and they always ask God to help them. I used to think how in the world they could not believe in God, yet when they are in pain, they call on God. I used to think that was very strange. They must believe in God if they call on God, so why do they deny it?

Chapter Eleven

When I became a healer through Jesus Christ, I always used to ask people if they believed in God. They always used to say they did. One day, a man asked me if I would treat anyone who did not believe in God. I said, yes of course. I would expect them to believe in God after the healing. Why wouldn't they? I think some people do not realise what they are saying. They of course never have any experience.

I certainly remember the hard times I had when I was young all on my own. I used to remember so many different people I have met, especially when I lived in Cheshire. I met some nice young people who used to treat me very nicely and try to bring me into their group. We used to talk a lot about life and I always wondered what I would be doing for a living. I remember when I was younger, I used to tell people I wouldn't like to live until I'm very old and they all used to say as long as your healthy you should like to live to any age. I thought about that a lot.

I used to like the people in Cheshire; they were a good crowd and they were always ready to give you a helping hand. Not like the people of today, they are all for themselves, and you have to be very careful.

I remember when I was in Jamaica and we had a terrible hurricane. We all thought we were going to die. It battered the house we were in and we all had to shelter under half a roof. It was terrible. Everything we had was soaking wet. I wondered how we were all going to manage. We were like that for days on end. I had forgotten about it because I blocked it out of my mind. I had never experienced anything like that before. That is why I was glad to be back home in England rather than continuing to live in Jamaica.

I was so glad that hurricanes did not occur in England. Though I have seen on the television where a lot of people have to go upstairs or the rooftop because everything they have gets wet. I do feel sorry for people who live in those places near to the seas and oceans. I honestly hope I never have to go through that sort of experience again, but life is very funny. One never knows what you have to go through in life, you just have to pray nothing like that happens again.

People in the West Indies I hear, often have to put up with that sort of thing. They are brave to put up with living with hurricanes. Some of the things I had to put up with I wonder now how I managed to survive them all; as far as I am concerned, it is the Lord God that always has been there for me and always to my rescue.

My friend, Paula, who lives in the same block I live in used to say to me, "Dorothy, how in the world do you live on your own?" I would say to her that you get used to it. She used to tell me she would be frightened to live on her own. I said to her I very much like living on my own. I like the peace and quiet. Mind you, it has not always been quiet. I told her I would never get a man like Baboni again; the one who just had a stroke. I did not know where to put my hands on him because I had just seen the vision of Christ as I explained it before. Now of course, I would know what to do.

When Paula had a stroke 14 years ago, she asked me if I could help her. She said her doctor asked her who her next of kin was, which scared her. Paula also told me her doctor told her she had a lot of blood clots and asked me if I could get rid of them for her. I asked her if she knew where they were and she said she did, so I worked on those blood clots every week until they all disappeared.

I gave Paula three hours of healing a week and she thanked me very much. We became good friends and always kept in touch with each other. We also sent each other birthday and Christmas cards. We always talked when she came down to shop and she would say to me, "Dorothy, I wish I was dead". This was 14 years after I had healed her. I said to her, "You shouldn't say things like that. Can I help you in anyway?" Paula replied, "I am getting on in age now and I am in too much pain. I'm not happy at all". I felt very sorry for her. She lives upstairs in a block of flats and I wished I could have gotten her a downstairs apartment so she could get out more often, as it was difficult for her to come down the stairs.

Then, someone told me Paula had died. I could not believe it. Her partner did not tell me at all. I rang him and asked him where Paula had died, and he told me in the bathroom. I could not understand why he did not tell me himself, knowing we were friends. Then after that someone told me that Paula's partner had taken to drinking since Paula died and he must have had far too much because he died as well. Paula wanted to leave her flat in her will to her cousin in Belgium. I was worried because she never gave me her cousin's address in Belgium. I will have to try to hurry with this book because that is the only way I can get help to her family.

I have been a healer a long time now and I hope never to stop healing people. I seem to know automatically where to put my hands when a person comes to me for healing and tells me what is wrong.

Sometimes when a patient comes to me with a new type of disease I have not heard of, I look it up in the medical book and that gives me all the answers as to where to put my healing hands. There are quite a lot of diseases I have not even heard of, nor treated, but I have treated most common diseases including cancer. I know there are a lot of diseases, but I suppose I will never know them all. There are far too many.

When a woman came to me with psoriasis, I had never heard of it before. I could not find it in the medical book, so I asked a doctor what caused the disease. He told me it was something to do with the brain, so I concentrated on the brain. I gave the girl three hours of healing a week and it certainly worked; she was completely healed. It took me about six to seven months, and it all cleared up much to the satisfaction of the girl because the doctor told me there was no cure for it. I have since heard quite a few people have it. it must be very irritable to have.

A man called Colin asked me if he could come for healing and when I asked him what was wrong, he told me that he had something like a paralysis down his left side. I asked if he had been to see his doctor. He answered yes. Colin said all his doctor said was, "You don't feel it now". He replied, "No I don't".

Colin asked his doctor if he could do something so that the feeling would not come back again, and the doctor told him to keep on waiting until the pain goes away. How ridiculous a statement. A friend of Colin, whom I have healed, told Colin to make an appointment with me. He told Colin I had greater powers than the doctor. His friend also told him that I would place my healing hands on his head because his type of illnesses come from the brain.

I told Colin his friend is right about his illness being brain related. I explained to him that I would hold his head for three hours every week until he does not have the paralysis feeling again. Colin said he was quite happy with that.

Colin knew I had a lot of patients at the time. He asked me if I could keep attending to him for quite a few months and I said I would try, and if that made him happy, I would be glad to treat him for as long as he wanted.

Colin told me since I had been holding his head, he had no more of the paralysis feeling. I said I was very glad for him because I know it is very frightening to think you are going to have a stroke or anything of that nature. Colin said to me, "Your hands are very strong, and anyone could see that the gift you have comes from God".

I told him, "You are quite right. I am glad to know you believe in God. Without God I would never have been given such a gift". He was very interested in me telling him about seeing Jesus Christ's face in a vision in 1983. I asked him who told him about me. He said the person had met me quite a few times. He came from Hertfordshire for healing. Colin told me he was over the moon because he said I allowed the person that told him of me to come over for healing sessions for a long time – his name is Christian

Luke Barker. He told me he feels better because before he came to you, he was having these paralysis feelings often and now, since he has been coming to me for healing, all the paralysis has gone. However, he asked again if I did not mind if he came over for a longer healing session just to be sure. I told him that would be all right as I had not healed anyone with paralysis before, but I told him the experience was very good and I fancy the challenge if anyone else should come to me with the same problem. I am more than prepared to heal even more diseases than I can spell or pronounce.

I was glad to be able to heal Colin and that he was happy with my healing hands. He was a very interesting man and he certainly told me a lot of things I myself had never heard of.

Colin knew a lot about the world and its politics and told me about all the places he had been to. I told him I would be eventually writing a book about my life and he said he would love to read it. He said to me, "If I travel the globe, people would not want to lose me because my healing hands are very powerful and strong". He could see I was dedicated to God. I told him about my adopted mother who was a dedicated Christian. Her father was a priest and I told him she was an angel. My childhood with her was unique and she was a wonderful mother. She taught me so many things.

I was very pleased with Colin's progress. He never had any more paralysis. I took him in for healing sessions for about six months. That was quite a few years ago and I know he was cured. He rang me and told me he was going away to a job and I wished him the best of health. I told him not to forget to pray. He said he certainly would and that he would pray for me. That sort of thing makes you feel so happy to know that God has given you such a powerful gift. What more could anyone wish for?

Someone told me about a meeting that was taking place at Homerton Hospital which also has a church. There seemed to be a special department there and lots of people were there. Pastors, ministers, as well as doctors and sick people. The person who informed me about the meeting told me I would be the best person to go to the meeting, but I was not so sure. When I approached the sister of the hospital there, she was not so sure either because these people do not like healers and I could see right away. The minister who came from America certainly did not like me at all. He said to me we do not want people like you here. I was quite shocked and I thought what a rude man! He said to me, he did not want evangelism here. He was practically telling me to get out. I told the sister and she said, "if I was you, I wouldn't hang around". I left and that taught me a lesson. I realised ministers in the church were very spiteful including the pastors, priests, doctors and nurses.

I could have healed one of the patients that was there. She had cancer in her arm. There was also another lady who had it in her breasts. I tried to make eye contact with the lady with the cancer in her arm, but she did not look at me at all. Neither did the one who had it in her breasts.

I thought to myself that God made sure I was a very strong person and could hold myself quite high. I always knew I had Jesus Christ on my side and that gave me a lot of strength. Even up to now I feel strong and I always feel that someone is with me who is much stronger than myself.

What I had to put up with around the ministers in the church was simply awful. They were so against me. I think if it had been someone not as broad-shouldered as myself, they certainly would have given up. Sometimes I was insulted so badly that I used to wonder myself whether I was ever going to give up saving lives and helping people with their pain with all the harassment I was getting.

A friend of mine told me if she had known that I was going to the meeting at the church, she would have told me not to even talk to the minister of the hospital church because people who know him say that he is full of himself. She said, "Seeing you and knowing you have a powerful gift, I know he would insult you because that is how he is. He is so wrapped up in himself and he does not see anyone else. I know quite a lot of people he has been rude to. I'm so sorry I didn't see you before; I could have warned you".

One wonders why he ever became a minister but as she said, a lot of the ministers are not into God. You hear about them every day; they are just doing a job. She said to me, "I know you have had quite a lot of experience with quite a few ministers and pastors since you have had your gift". I said, "How right you are. I have certainly met quite a few of them and the experience I have had with them I wouldn't like anyone else to experience".

I know God protects me all the time. I wonder what they will think if they ever read my life book. What a shock they will get when they learn I can heal cancer and arthritis and lots of other diseases. I wonder what their thoughts will be of me.

I always think to myself perhaps it's about time I stop healing people, but it was when I met Christian Luke Barker's mother and father and they brought their son for healing that I started to have a lot of courage to heal quite a lot of people in Tottenham, Barnet, Muswell Hill, Palmers Green, London, Peterborough, Hertfordshire, Ireland and lots of other places. Both Christian Luke Barker and his parents used to tell people about my healing.

I still go to the clinic every six weeks. I will admit they are very good. I am so glad to be home and getting stronger all the time. Getting the treadmill was the best thing I could have done. You see, I was not getting enough exercise before. I now walk every day on my treadmill and hope to get my book finished very soon. I am working very hard on it and I have to thank Rebecca for checking it for me as I write. It gave me more courage to get on with it quicker. I feel at last I am getting down to brass tacks. You see I have never written a book before and it is not easy. I think it is quite a big job, especially if you have not written one before.

This is the only way I can tell people what I can do and have the proof, especially about the church where I healed Brenda who was dying of cancer. The people in Italy would be very surprised when they hear the truth and then I will be able to start healing again. It can be checked by Brenda's husband, Adrian King, who now lives in Birmingham.

I am getting much stronger despite all the insults I had been getting over the years. Some people would have just given up, but not me. I knew I always had Jesus Christ on my side and that is what made me continue. I can also not forget the help of:

Hackney Volunteer Befriending Service
Unit 2, 15 Ramsgate Street, London E8 2FD.

They are no longer at this address as the landlord had put up the rent and forced them out. Instead of allowing them to pay their rent as normal each year, they were told that from now on their rent was double and as such forcing them to vacate the property and move elsewhere; but they are not happy at their new address. I would never have anything to do with Hackney Council if given a choice. These folks at the council are just in it for their salaries than providing a good quality of services. The sort of people at Hackney Council are so terrible at closing most places where people socialise, even as I write this book. I will be annoyed if this centre is closed down, and so will a lot of other people.

The centre is based in Shoreditch now, but things are different from before. I would not want to have anything to do with these types of people that own Ramsgate Street. I met Rebecca through the Befriending Service and as I have mentioned, what a wonderful help she has been. What a wonderful set of people the Hackney Volunteer Befriending Service are. Had it not been for them, I would not be as far as I am now in completing this book.

I did not know if I told you that a doctor told me it wasn't fair for me to have such a powerful gift because he had to study for a few years, and I didn't study at all. I told him I have a lot of people against me all the time, whereas he being a doctor, people just sing his praises while he heals people by reading from a text book and people think that doctors are the best things since sliced bread when in fact you are but chemical people that just feed the mind up with what you call medicines, many of which are full of cocaine. Besides, doctors use jargon languages to describe the details that the medicines contain, but if they were confident then it would be written in plain English what these medicines contain. Mind you, I am not saying that people do not like me, just the opposite. They do like me sometimes more than the doctors, especially if the doctors have made a blunder.

Doctors only heal by drugs and I heal with my hands. Though one doctor wanted to examine my chest part and my head. I asked him what he expected to find, and I told him straight that he would not find anything. I know that for certain so that was the end of that.

I would not let any doctor experiment on me, especially after what I saw them do to another lady. I was shocked. I am sure they cannot force me, and I would never have an operation with just any doctor. I would be very cautious with which doctor I have an operation with.

I remember a few years ago I met one of the women who I saw in Mother Connie's home where I lived with her. Her name was Ruby. She was so nice to me and said, "You have certainly grown up from the last time I saw you". I asked her in which occupation she was in, but I did not get a proper answer from her, so I let it go. One day while she was around, I wanted to go to the shops. She asked me where I was going, and I told her I was going to buy something at the shop. She then asked if she could come with me and I thought that was rather strange. Why in the world would she want to come to the shop with me to buy something? I replied by asking her if she had not got anything to do and she said she had not.

I did not know what to think of Ruby when she told me she was hungry. That pretty much shocked me, so I asked her if she would like to stay for dinner. She said she would be very thankful as she did not know the last time, she had had a proper meal. I just could not understand. I asked her who she lived with and she said she lived by herself. I felt very sorry for her, but I just could not make her out. I got a bit worried and I wondered what in the world she was up to. I then told her she would have to go after I had made her some dinner because the place did not belong to me and she agreed. After she had eaten, I had to go to the bathroom and told her I would not be long. When I got back, she had stolen a couple of my dresses, money and had run off. I just could not believe my eyes. How could she do something like that? She was just waiting for the opportunity to steal. I contacted the police. The police asked me what she looked like. When I described her, the police said she is one of the worst women thieves that we have in this district, and said to me, "If you see her again, don't have anything to do with her". I told him I certainly would not. The policeman then said, "She was just

Chapter Eleven

waiting for the opportunity and as soon as you went to the bathroom that was it for her". He also told me that she had been to prison quite often and they do not think she will ever stop stealing. That was just her way of living and it seemed she does not like any other way.

I said to the policeman, "How in the world will she end up?" He said, "That really is her own problem. Nobody can help her. She does not want any help". I thought that was very sad, but as the policeman said that was her problem. He told me they had even tried to help her, but she was not interested. The policeman said, "I think she must like going to prison. She certainly does not like to work and that is the whole story".

I remember bumping into a girl who once lived in the same home as I was living in with my adopted mother. Her name was Pearl. She said to me she was glad to see me and that I looked very well. I asked her how she was. She told me she lived with her boyfriend and they both worked. She was very happy, and I told her I was very glad she was all right. I mentioned Ruby to her, and she remembered at once. Pearl said she was not surprised about her behaviour as she never seemed to fit in anywhere. Pearl also said that was the life Ruby liked and nobody could help her.

Pearl then said she thought I was much stronger now in my leg department than from what she remembered. I told her it was very nice of her to remember. then she asked me about Mother Connie. At that time, I did not live with her, so I told her that she suffered from asthma and that she had to go in a convent. I explained to Pearl that she had it very bad and she told me to go and see her every day.

When I told Pearl about the first time, I went to see Mother Connie and how the nuns slammed the door in my face and told me never to come back, she was horrified. She said to me, "Of course you didn't know what to do at 16. I would not. I hope one day you can bring them to justice". I said to her, "I hope I can bring them to justice as well". Pearl then said, "I haven't heard very good things about these nuns". I agreed with her. She said to me, "I suppose they wanted your name out of the will Mother Connie made for you. The lot". I told her that was what it is all about. It was pure greed.

I then told Pearl that when Mother Connie goes to rest, I suppose she will learn everything. I told Pearl that I miss her very much because I love her very much, and she said she would miss me very much too because she loved me. We all knew that and she was very sorry the nuns treated me this way. Pearl said they should be ashamed of themselves, especially with the fact that they call themselves Christians. She also said that she wondered what they told Mother Connie. I wondered too. I told her that I thought they must have made up some story to tell her, and that is what saddens me, because none of their story would be true. They gave me such a fright when one of them said, "Don't you ever come back here!" I was flabbergasted. I really did not think people like them could be so nasty. Pearl told me to try and not worry too much and she knew I would pray. Pearl also said she felt like going down there and giving them a good telling off. However, I really did not think it would help because they are too hard faced anyway.

I thanked Pearl very much for her support. It made me feel so much better. We parted and she told me to be very careful of Ruby if I ever met her again and to just ignore her. I said I would.

I remember a gentleman who telephoned me and asked me if he could see me. His name was Michael. I asked him what it was about and he said he thought he had a tumour in his head. I did not understand because he told me he had not been to the doctors, so how could he know he had a tumour. I said, "Why worry about something that you don't know to be true? I then suggested he went to the doctors first so they could send him for an x-ray. After the x-ray, he would be able see what is wrong. I also explained to him that it is after that that I may be able to help him.

Michael said he was worried to go to the doctor. I explained to him again that without going, I would not know what to do. Michael then said he would go to a private doctor. I said to him, "Why waste your money going to a private doctor when an NHS doctor could tell you what is wrong if you go and get an x-ray?" He seemed to be very nervous.

In the end I was able to persuade Michael to go. He asked if he could see me after. I agreed. He then gave me the name of the person who had recommended him to me. When he eventually came, he was very nervous. He told me they had found a lump in his head, but it was not dangerous. I asked him if they gave him a scan and he said they did. I explained to him that lots of people have lumps in their heads, but it is not dangerous. Michael then asked if he could keep in touch with me and I agreed. I said to him, "You know my address and my phone number. Keep in touch whenever you want". He used to phone me every week. This was a long time ago. When he realised he would be all right, he told me he was going abroad to get a very good job. I told him not to worry and to pray to God all the time. I also told him I was sure he would be all right and that I would pray for him as well.

Michael said after talking to me he felt a lot better. I just knew he would be all right. I wished him good health and I told him I did not think he would have any trouble at all with the lump. I also told him that if he did, he knew where to come. After that, I could hear by his voice he was not nervous anymore.

From time to time I meet different women. I met this lady at the home where I lived with Mother Connie. She was very nice, and she was so pleased to see me. She took me to a restaurant and asked me if I ever saw the lady who used to run the premises, Ms Ilsie. I said to her I was pretty shocked when I saw her on the bus. She used to be a tall, beautiful woman and I saw a bent woman – I could not believe it was her. She looked quite distressed. She never liked me, and you know I felt quite sorry for her. She certainly had changed. I could not understand why. If you remembered, she had a boyfriend with a very posh car. I said something must have happened to her and the lady said, "I suppose it was something she did to herself".

This lady asked me if I had met any of the other girls and I told her about Ruby who stole two of my dresses and some money. She said, "I don't think anyone trusted her and you should have remembered her". I told her we

Chapter Eleven

called the police and told her about what they said. She then told me to be very careful as you cannot trust many people today.

As this was a long time ago, it seems as if times never seem to change. It was so lovely seeing her then. I told her about Pearl and how she was very annoyed when I told her Mother Connie had to go into a convent because she was poorly. I also told her how Mother Connie told me to visit her every day and how the nuns slammed the door in my face on the first day I went to visit and told me never to come back here again.

The lady was furious also and she said that it is because Mother Connie was leaving you a will. She said, "I suppose they wanted it all. I wonder what they told your mother. That was a nasty thing to do. I am not surprised. I have heard of some terrible things some of those nuns used to do. Some of them were quite devious. Few people liked them of course, quite a lot of them would have to change their ways now because people wouldn't put up with them".

The lady also told me how she heard how the nuns used to beat children a lot. She said, "I suppose you yourself was frightened to try and see your mother because you must have heard how they treated some children. I am very sorry you could not see her before she passed away but now, she is in Heaven. She will know everything. Those nuns will be punished for what they did to you". I told her that I did not think they would admit to anything they had done but instead pretend that nothing happened. I had heard about them being very good at pretending, as I told

Pearl. She said to me, "Be very careful because you can't trust many people today. I know God will look after you and I hope I will see you often so we can talk". I thanked her very much. I told her I would be extra careful in future and she said again that she was so glad to have seen me.

When I got home, I got a call from a woman who asked me if she could come and see me. Her name was Rosa. I asked her as I always do, who gave her my number and when I recognised the name of the person that gave it to her, I asked her what was wrong and if she had been to see her doctor. She told me she had.

Rosa told me she had cancer in her breast and asked me if it would be possible for her to come up and see me. I told her we would have to make an appointment. I then asked her how far she had to come from and she said Cardiff.

When I told Rosa, I could only treat her once a week she said she would appreciate any time I could be of help to her. We arranged a day that would be convenient to her which was the weekend, so I started giving her three hours of treatment a week. When she came, I said to her that Cardiff was rather a long way to come from. I then asked her if she could not find a healer nearer to her home? Rosa said, "Believe me I have heard of healers but not none like you. Anyway, I have never heard of anyone who can heal cancer, only you, so I am very happy for you to give me three hours of treatment a week. At least I know I am going to get better. Dorothy, I do not mind how long it takes and I am looking forward to seeing you every week. I will be happy to know you better and I will tell you everything about myself".

As I do with others, we always start our sessions with prayer. I continuously told Rosa that without Jesus Christ there would be nothing. When I told her about seeing a vision of the face of Jesus telling me I had healing hands in 1983 she was very interested. She said to me, "That is why you can heal cancer. You got it directly from Jesus Christ".

Rosa was so overjoyed. She said she was speechless. She was so excited. Rosa then said to me, "When any person had something as deadly as cancer, one gets so frightened. You think your life is going to end. Then someone out of the blue tells you about a lady who can heal cancer. It is very hard to believe and then when the person told me you already healed someone who was dying of cancer, I was worried in case you could not treat me. Then I got your phone number and heard your voice. My heart gave quite a jump. When you asked me if I had seen my doctor and when I told you I had breast cancer, it did not seem to alarm you. We started soon after that. I could always feel your hands on me, and I thought what strong hands you have".

I said to her, "The pain will get a little bit worse at the beginning but don't let that worry you. It happens to everyone". Rosa then said, "Your hands are very big. I think God gave you them to heal. What a wonderful thing".

I told her how Mother Connie used to tell me that God gave me big hands because I was going to do wonderful things with them. I also told her how I would always complain to her about my big hands and how she always had to get men's gloves for me, even as a young child.

I explained to Rosa that now I know why I have such big hands. I know it is a wonderful gift and few people can heal cancer, but I told her people do not like me for what I can do. People such as doctors, some nurses, ministers of churches and pastors.

I also told Rosa about the time I had my accident. I made sure not to tell anybody in the hospital what I am capable of doing. I told her how they asked me if I wanted an operation on my hip and I told them certainly not. She said to me, "Those people who don't like you are just spiteful because they can't do what you can. You just have to ignore people like that. They are not worthy of even thinking about".

I did tell Rosa about the lady who had cancer in her stomach whose name was Barbara and what the doctors and nurses did to her. She said to me, "I will not let the doctors touch me after you finish healing me. I wouldn't be so stupid".

Rosa told me about herself. She had a daughter, and she and her husband were not together. She told me she had been on her own for quite a long time and I told her I had been on my own for a very long time too. I explained to her that one gets used to it. Rosa said she could not see herself with anyone else. I told her I felt the same way and when one is getting older you just cannot be bothered. You enjoy being on your own. I told her I would like to write a book about my life one of these days and she told me she would love to read it. I told her at that time I would not know where to start. I have been thinking about writing a book for years.

Chapter Eleven

Rosa said, "I felt that God has really blessed you, because you might know it yourself, there are a lot of healers today who claim they can heal and a lot of them are not really sure of what they can heal. I have visited a lot of them before I heard about you, and I was very disappointed. I wondered whether I was going to meet anyone genuine. I was quite amazed wondering if we did have anyone in England who could really heal until I heard about you. I still was not sure until I heard about you healing the two policemen. It was one of their friends who gave me your telephone number. Can you imagine how I felt right away? I thought I have got my life back and now I am here with you having the treatment of my life. I couldn't be more grateful and why do you just charge just a donation while all the other healers I have met, who don't really know what they can heal, charge a lot of money?"

I told Rosa how I have always thought it is not good to charge a lot of money because people haven't got a lot. I think if you only take a donation people will feel much better, and all of them can afford a donation. They can donate what they can afford and what they want to donate, and they do not have to feel a strain or worry, but it is best to let their conscience be their guide. Rosa then said to me, "No wonder God gave you such a powerful gift, a real healing hand and you are very kind and considerate. If you write a book people all over the world will read it". I then told her how I wondered if I could cope with a lot of people coming to me for healing. I also told her that I believe when God knows you haven't got much time, especially if you are travelling through a foreign country or a district or a long distance, it seems the force that is the healing, even though I heal people with my hands, the force that makes it possible comes from the Almighty.

When I was in Malta, I knew I had not got much time to spend there and I was able to heal people much quicker. I think Jesus Christ does all this because he is the powerful one, not me. I am just the servant and very proud it. I would hope to heal as many people as I can in the future, but I know when that happens, I would need assistance.

I said to Rosa, "I am very happy that everything is going all right for you because you have come such a long way. I think things will go more quickly for you because you have a lot of faith in me due to what I have been blessed with". Then, I asked her, "Will you tell people who have the same complaint as you?" She replied, "I will tell people only when I know they are all right. I wouldn't like to tell anyone of a devious character because today you can't trust many people". I said to her, "How right you are. You have to be very careful these days. That would make more sense". Rosa certainly agreed with me. She herself was coming on very well.

Rosa said to me, "You are right when you said the healing gets a little bit worse at the beginning, then it slowly gets better". She then asked if I had any time when she is better to come and stay with her in Cardiff. She said it would be like a holiday. I said to her, "I had a friend who lived in Cardiff, but she died. I would think about it, but I do not think I would get very much time and I am not too keen on travelling, especially right now. As long as you are completely better, that is all that matters". She said to me, "Dorothy, I will certainly pray for you". I replied, "I will pray for you as well".

Rosa said she would certainly value my prayers. I thought it was nice of her to say that. What she said next quite astonished me. She said, "The world needs someone like you". I said to her, "Why did you say that?" She said, "I just seem to know. Things come to you sometimes and that just came to me. I feel that is true feeling". I did not much agree with that, but I told her we would keep in touch. I told her that I hoped whatever she decides to do, she will be able to do it.

She then said, "If it wasn't for your healing hands, the doctor told me I would have to have therapy and I certainly did not want to have that. My friend a long time ago had therapy and it was not very nice, so I am delighted I would not have to go through what she did. It was awful and a couple of years after that she died".

Rosa then asked me what I thought about what she said. "I suppose that was the only treatment they had at that time and it is rather difficult to know what to say. It is just one of those things. You are not in that position, so we just have to thank God. You are practically better now so I am sure you will be able to go back to work", I said. She replied, "I am grateful to you".

On one of Rosa's last visits, I said to her, "I'm sure you will be glad to tell one of your friends about the healing you received from me". Rosa said she certainly will as long as they are the right persons to tell". On her last visit she said to me, "I will be very careful who I tell about you because I don't want you to come to any harm". I replied, "I do appreciate you being very careful, especially on my behalf". We said cheerio and she asked me if she could come and see me if she ever came to London. I told her I would be glad to see her.

I then had a phone call from a gentleman called Allan. I asked him who gave him my name and my phone number and what was the matter, he said he had heart trouble. I then asked him if he had seen his doctor and what the doctor had said. Allan told me he had seen the doctor and he had sent him for an x-ray. After the x-ray, the doctor confirmed he had heart problems.

Allan told me he was very frightened and when someone told him about me, he felt much better. He then asked me if it was possible for him to make an appointment with me. I agreed and said that I would give him two hours of healing a week. I then explained to him that I would give him one hour of healing on his heart and then another hour on his head.

Allan said that sounded marvellous. He then said to me, "You seem to know what you are doing". I said, "You will see for yourself". We made the appointment for two hours of healing every week. He came from Surrey and he asked me if we could start right away. I told him it would be OK and he seemed very relieved.

I explained to him that I start sessions with a prayer while I lay my hands on the patient. I told Allan I only use my hands at all times, and I do not use anything else. He seemed so content. That made me feel that this patient would be no trouble to heal because he was so relaxed. I told him this and he said to me, "I know you are going to heal me. That is why I feel so relaxed. Just looking at you I felt very secure and the thing is you are not greedy at all though I would be happy to give you much more, but money doesn't seem to bother you". I said to him, "If and when I write my book, as I intend to do so one of these days, surely once the book becomes a bestseller I would need an assistant. He said that made sense. The point remains that the assistant would have to be paid, hence I would be very grateful for a much bigger financial donation. I have to keep repeating this all the time to everyone I heal, even though I don't wish for money, but I have to meet up with my bills.

Allan then asked me when I was going to write a book and what it would be about. I told him it would be about my life, but I did not know when that would be. I told him I was hoping to start soon but I do not know how soon yet. Allan told me he would love to read it. He was very kind, patient and very interesting. It was a pleasure to heal him. He often brought me flowers and presents. He was so thrilled, but disappointed he could not do enough for me.

Allan told me once that my healing was like a dream come true. He said to me, "Your hands are so strong and big. I'm sorry I fell asleep when you laid your hands my head". I told him that a lot of my patients fall asleep and that is the best thing to do. Also, when you fall asleep you are very relaxed and that is the best time to feel at peace. You do not feel a thing and when you wake up you feel so much better. If you could fall asleep during each healing session that would be absolutely wonderful for you. You would not feel a thing and each time you went home you would feel so much better.

Allan then said, "As you said to me that doctors don't like you and some nurses of course, as well do not like you, I realised why. When they check your heart or treat your heart, they do not do it like you. They operate, but you just use your hands. That is why they don't like you". I then asked him what he would tell his doctor when healed. Allan said, "I will just let them look at me. When they cannot fathom out what is going on, I will not tell them anything of you because they are bound to say that the heart is looking a lot better". He also said, "I will never go back so that they will not embarrass you or me, because as you say, they don't like healers. What a pity. They may need your help one day".

I asked Allan if he believed in God and he said he certainly did. I said to him, "If it wasn't for Jesus Christ, I would never have this gift". Allan then asked me if I would tell him what happened when I saw the vision. I told him about seeing the face of Jesus Christ. He then said, "That is why your hands are so powerful and strong. I think I am very fortunate to have met you. I will certainly pray more now to what I have done in the past". I said to him, "I am very glad to hear you say that. I can see you appreciate the healing very much and I know once you get better your heart will stay like that forever". He said to me, "I certainly trust in you and I know it will. I don't know how to thank you".

I assured Allan that as the months go by, he will be back to his normal self again. I then asked him if he would like me to tell him about a lady called Brenda whom I healed at the church in 1984. I told Allan how she asked me if she could come for healing. I asked her what was wrong, and she told me she had cancer all over her body. She told me she could hardly eat and was full of pain. She couldn't sleep at all so I decided to take her in for healing every day until she got over the worst, then I took her in for healing twice each week.

I told Allan how I healed Brenda and how she decided to go on holiday, which I disagreed on, and how she died on the vacation. I told him how upset I was when I found out. I also told him she was an assistant headmistress and how she had so much to live for. Brenda was such a lovely girl and I had treated her for quite some time on her cancer. I did not mind that so much, but if she had just listened to me, she would still be alive. She told me she was going on holiday for five weeks. I told her that was too long after just having treatment for cancer. I advised her to halve her holiday.

Allan said he was very sad for me and he was sure she was sorry she had not listened to me, but that is life. You are sorry when it is too late and you just have to try your best and forget about it, because there is nothing you can do now. I told him he was quite right, but it would take me quite a while to forget her. Still today I remember her.

Allan himself was coming on very well. He asked me if I did not get tired of telling people the same story over and over again, trying to help them when they do not help themselves. I said to him, "You can say that again. Some people are very tiresome. To be a healer you have to have a lot of patience". Allan said, "I can see you have quite a lot of that. I know I am very fortunate to have ever met you. I have to take my friend who told me about you for a slap-up meal and a drink". His heart was very sound by now. I asked him if he was going to see his doctor, but he told me he could not be bothered. I certainly wished him all the best and he could not thank me enough. Alan told me he would never forget me, and I told him not to forget to pray either.

I then got a phone call from a chap who lived quite near me. He told me he had bad feet. His name was Lennie. I asked him what was wrong with them and he told me it was really his ankle. I told him to make sure he washed his feet thoroughly before he came to me. When Lennie arrived, I asked him if he had washed his feet and he said he had, but I did not believe him for one minute. I said to him, "Don't you ever come back if you haven't washed your feet. I won't touch them again if you don't wash your feet and I mean it". Lennie said he was sorry, and he promised he would wash them next time. I told him I would not let him into my clinic if he did not wash his feet and that it was up to him. He eventually came back when he had washed his feet – after all he did not live far from me. Sometimes it is just being too lazy.

I had Lennie for quite a time. Of course, I had other people as well who had all different diseases and it was a good job because this one with the ankle was giving me the creeps. Sometimes people can be very awkward and do not take advice. I was very glad when he got better, but it took quite a long time.

Lennie was not a person you could talk to and I could never understand what he was talking about. His English was very bad. I was so relieved when he got better and was hoping I would never get another patient like him again. Who in the world told him about me I will never know.

I then got another call from a woman called Julia who had a bad knee. At that time, I was healing other people, but I did not mind healing just a knee. Julia told me that she was going to have an operation on it but was very uncertain about it because she had met people who had operations on their knees. They told her the pain was worse than before.

Julia asked me if I could help her with my healing hands, as she would appreciate it very much. I told her I would give her two hours of healing a week and she told me she would be very happy with it because she knows people who have experienced my healing hands on them and were very happy and haven't had any pain after I had healed them. I told her it is not a quick fix. Julia told me one of her friends told her that my healings would only take two hours once a week per session as they were so many patients for me to heal; it took me about five to six months to heal Julia. Her friend told her that my healing is better than having any operation, especially when you have more pains after the operation than you did before.

Julia told me it did not matter if it took one year. She said my healing is the best. I told her to be careful because the doctors do not like me at all, nor some of the nurses and the ministers in the church. Some people are very unhappy about what I can do. Julia then said, "I don't suppose you let that bother you". I said, "Of course I don't. I am very careful who I take in for healing. I always ask my patients who told them about me". She then said, "I don't blame you".

There was one woman I was treating for sickle cell disease. She told me that the pastor at the church she attends asked her why she was coming to the church so regularly, and she told him she was going to a healer. The pastor told her he was very interested and would love to come and see this healer, she told him she would ask the healer's permission before allowing the visit. I told her I did not want any pastor in my clinic. When she told him, he was not satisfied. He wanted to see me because he had not met a healer before. I told her again that I did not want to see a pastor. I said to her, "What in the world would I want to see a pastor for? I am not from a church of God. I am an Anglican". She told me the pastor still insisted that he wanted to meet me, and she had given the pastor my telephone number and address. I told her she shouldn't have given him my address or my telephone number.

Julia's pastor kept telephoning me. I told him I was very busy. He eventually turned up at my home. I was very annoyed. I asked him what he wanted. He said he would just like to talk. I asked him what he would like to talk about, and he said healing. I said to him, "I cannot teach you anything about healing. I think you already know it is a gift from Jesus Christ. Being a pastor, you should

Chapter Eleven

know all about gifts". He then said he wished God had given him a gift of healing. I then asked him, "What do you think I can do about it?" He said, "I know you can't do anything about it, but I have told my bishop about you. I suggested you invite us for dinner". I then said, "Are you forgetting I don't belong to your church? I have no intention of asking you to come to dinner. What in the world do you take me for? I heal. I don't go 'round asking people to come to dinner. That I have never done, and I have no intentions of ever doing it. Now would you like to tell me what you have come here for?"

I nearly died when the pastor suggested he would like to stay with me for the weekend. I got so furious. I said to him, "Would you mind leaving right now?!" I ran to the door and ordered him out. I told him never to come back. Talk about manners! He went and I slammed the door shut. Would you believe it, a few weeks after that he telephoned me and asked me if he could come and see me? I just put down the receiver very quickly. I thought to myself, some people never learn. I asked my friend what she thought of that and she told me, "You did the right thing. It seems to me he had other things on his mind". I said, "I think you're right. I did not trust him in the first place. First he wanted me to cook and then he had the cheek to say he wanted to spend the weekend with me".

Can you understand some of these people who are supposed to be pastors? It makes you wonder why some of the churches are so empty. Of course, some churches would be empty especially with people like him around. I have heard lots of stories about certain pastors and what they get up to with the female congregations. You don't know who to trust in today's world.

I give to charities and some of them drive me up the wall with their behaviour. They are always harassing you for money. They never seem satisfied. It really gets on my nerves. It gets so bad that you wonder why you gave them anything in the first place. You even wonder if it is worth it.

I saw an advertisement on the television for children who needed treatment for their eyes. They were asking people for £2. I answered the advert and as soon as I spoke to the person at the other end of the telephone, I could not believe it. The girl asked me for £5. I said to her, "Why don't you ask for £5 instead of £2 when you advertised? Rather than you immediately jumping on people to ask them for an extra £3". I told the girl that some people may not have the extra bit of money and that they should not do things like that. This can put some people in a very awkward position, but the girl did not seem bothered at all. I then said to her, "Some people will put the phone down right away and I wouldn't blame them. Your behaviour is disgraceful".

Then I got a phone call from a lady called Jo who wanted to bring her two sons that had asthma. They were called Harry and Ben. I gave each one of them two hours of healing a week; they were nice lads. The boys were easy to heal because they were well behaved. You can always see when a child has been well disciplined. It makes such a difference. It was a pleasure to heal them both.

One of the boys asked me if I wanted anything done. I was quite amazed at such manners because most children do not have any. They came every week until they got better, and believe me, children take a much shorter time than adults do. They asked so many questions such as why I was able to heal and not their mother, then I would have to explain that we all have gifts and Jesus Christ gave them to us. They could not understand why we did not all have healing hands and even asked why doctors did not have such gifts as well. I would say, their gifts are different. They deal in medicine. One of the boys then asked, "Isn't it much better to get hands instead of medicine?" I told them that doctors have to study to pass their exams before they become a doctor.

One of the boys asked me if I had to pass any exams and I said only with the Lord. Then he asked me if I prayed to be a healer. I said I did not, and I thought for a small boy, he was very clever. Then he asked me if I made a lot of money. I told him I did not, but some of the healers make a lot of money. The mother then told the boy. "You see, Dorothy only takes donations". They then asked me why. They said to me, "You mean you could be very rich, but you refuse the money?" I said to them, "When you get a bit older you will understand".

Sometimes I will admit, you cannot always answer children's questions. I asked Harry and Ben if they ever said their prayers at night and they both said they did. That really pleased me. I said to them, "Money is very important, but it is not everything". I told them, "Some people don't have very much money to give; that is why I only take donations". Sometimes they said they understood, and they thought that was very nice.

The boys asked me if I was a Christian. That quite amazed me also. I thought to myself, these two boys are going to be very caring and grow up to be fine lads. The sessions for the two lads took quite a lot of time, but you could see they were both getting a lot better. They certainly mentioned it. They would say such things as they thought it was rather strange that a lady could heal men and women with her hands. They said they thought it was a wonderful gift and that God had really blessed me.

When they asked me if I pray to God and thank him for the wonderful gift, he gave me, I told them I never stop praying to God and I do it more than once a day. I asked them if they will pray to God and thank him for their healing and they both said they certainly would. They also said they would tell other children at school and I thought for two small lads, that was very nice. I asked them what they would like to study when they grow up and one of them said to me he would like to play football and the other one said he hadn't thought about anything yet but he did like to play tennis. He was not sure what he would like to do. They certainly know what they want.

The two lovely boys were a credit to their mother. You could see they certainly had a lot of discipline by their behaviour and that they had manners. They were so like some of the boys of today that are so rude and out of control; like the young boy that lives above me. His mother hopes that she will run me out of my own flat so that she can take it over. This woman never seems to stop at anything, all because her father is a millionaire. She is the one who runs a laundry with dangerous chemicals that drain down from upstairs into my small garden. It kills all my plants and flowers to such an extent that all the grass in the garden has died. Nothing can grow on this land. I have complained to Hackney Council and they just fob me off; it is disgraceful. I wrote to the Mayor of Hackney and he wrote and told me it was none of his business because I am not a council tenant. Would you believe such a statement?! Ken Livingston was Mayor at that time (so you can see how long this laundry issue has been going on); he told me to write to Diane Abbott the MP. He said she should stop that right away, but she did nothing! What in the world is this woman doing as an MP, I will never know. She is just full of herself.

I am hoping Prime Minister Theresa May will be in power for years, only if she can offer me help by having an investigation into the corruption that takes place at the Stoke Newington police station. It is a shame that the Prime Minister does not know about the corruption that goes on; after all, this is a Labour-controlled area. So many people know about the Stoke Newington police. I have been told this over the years and that the Labour Party have been corrupt for over 100 years. I am not surprised about some of the things I have heard; they are disgraceful, and from what I have been told they don't get any better, just worse. I do hope they never get in power again; then we can all be a lot happier. With regards to American politics, I do like President Barack Obama and his family, as well as Hilary Clinton and her family.

I hope to be carrying on with my healing as I always do, but I will keep an open eye due to the area in which I live in.

Sometimes it is a nightmare and when you have to deal with the likes of Hackney Council who keep fobbing me off. They're supposed to be in charge but their action is petulant. I do not think too much of the Mayor of Hackney or the MP Diane Abbott. Look at how many people I could have healed when she first got in power. It was a long time ago when I wrote her a letter and also went to see her telling her how I could save a lot of people's lives and help them with their pain. All she says is that she's not interested, FIVE TIMES now. I ask you, what sort of a woman is she? No doubt in my mind that Diane Abbott is not for the ordinary or for black people, but for the bourgeoisies of society. She should be ashamed of herself but that does not seem to bother her. She thinks she can get away with being petulant. She wants to be an MP forever, yet has done nothing worthwhile to remember her by after all these years, then has the nerve to ask me if I would vote for her. Even the Mayor of Hackney had the nerve to ask me if I would vote for him. I would not vote for any one of them, I voted for Amy Gray, a Conservative MP.

I had a call from a lady who told me her brother's wife was very ill and would like to come for healing once a week. I asked her what was wrong and whether she had been to see the doctor. She said the doctors cannot do anything for her; they seem to not bother in treating her. They couldn't do any more for her, her illness had gone too far. I told her it would be impossible for me to treat her once a week, especially with how serious her illnesses had worsened. You have to come every day to get better

Chapter Eleven

and once a week is not enough. That is why I had to tell Brenda, who attends the same church as me to come every day, because I could see she was in a terrible state.

I made sure that this lady came for healing every day because that was the only way I could save her. I have had one or two people come to me in the past who have had serious illnesses and they only wanted to come for healing once a week. When they told me more about the illness, they had, I would be able to tell them whether having two hours a week would be all right or if three hours a week would be better. For a serious illness, daily treatments are needed. I seem to know if they will be all right as sometimes their illness has not spread and is not too serious. It all depends on what illness and how serious it is. Sometimes it does not take long at all; it may be just a little arthritis which has not progressed very far. The hands will get it all better, but if you have had it a long time it will take a lot longer.

Cancer treatment of course takes three hours a week, but if it is aggressive or progressed throughout the body, I am very sorry to tell you she is not going to make it. They begged me to help this lady. I tried to help her, but her illness was too advanced when she came to see me. If she had the sort of cancer Brenda had, I would have been able to heal her just as I did Brenda. Eventually I did my uttermost best to have her healed, but this took me two years to have her completely cancer free.

I then met another lady whose mother-in-law was a friend of mine. I asked her (the daughter-in-law) how her mother-in-law was and she told me she was getting on fine; that she was all right, but when she told me that 12 people had come to her flat (all suffering the same disease as she had), and she told me she never told anyone of them about me it made me think whether she was telling me the truth. So, I telephoned her and I spoke to the father-in-law and I told him his daughter-in-law was telling me that his wife was getting on very well. He was flabbergasted. He told me his wife was seriously ill; so ill she can hardly move. I just could not believe that I had taken so much time to heal her (the daughter-in-law) and all she was doing was making things up to suit herself. I thought to myself, I just can't tolerate people like her. She chain smoked and I wondered who was going to help her because she was fully recovered from what she suffered from, but I certainly would not want to see her again because of her selfishness. Her father-in-law had told me his wife was dying. I think that this woman has no shame, she is selfish, she thinks about herself all the time and no one else; but there is a saying that 'what goes around comes around'. I just have a feeling she will get what is coming to her in the very near future.

I got a letter from the Post Office of someone who was desperately trying to get hold of me. I told the Post Office I had already paid the money to redirect my posts to me, so whoever he or she is, they should write and they should redirect all my letters to me simply by forwarding it to my new address, that is all. I told them whoever it is couldn't be that important otherwise they would know where I had moved to, as I had given all my friends my new address; but I hadn't given that particular woman my new address.

Chapter Eleven

I asked my friend's husband (John) if I should come and visit his wife and he told me she was so very ill and does not want to see anyone. If it had been when his daughter-in-law had been coming that would have been all right, but he told me right now he didn't think she was well enough to see anybody, though he said he would tell her. He told me he hadn't told her about me being told she was getting on very well. He thought that would have upset her even more. I was so sorry for him and his wife. I just did not know what to say. John told me later on when his wife had passed away that the daughter-in-law had the cheek to ask him if he would like to work for her. He just could not believe it. I told him he should just ignore her, and he said his own daughter had asked him to go and live with her and her family. He did just so. I said to John that surely he didn't tell her where his daughter lived and he said certainly not. He said that was the end of ever hearing from her or seeing her, and somehow that made me feel so much better.

I then had a call from a lady who was getting on in age. She asked me if I would help her with her breast and I said to her of course I could. She told me, she had been to her doctor and he had sent her for an x-ray and they had confirmed she had cancer in her breast. One of her dear friends gave her my phone number. I started giving her three hours of treatment a week. What an interesting lady she was, telling me things I did not know anything about. I looked forward to her coming every week. She so appreciated my healing method and said to me she did not want the treatments the doctors give to their patients. She said she had a friend who had the same cancer as she did and she wished she had heard about me and my method of healing, because the treatment she got from the doctors, she said was horrible. Unfortunately, she is not alive now but her friend never forgot what she had been told about the treatment she had. She told me that she had been such a good friend, so when the doctor told her she had cancer, and she heard about someone getting better through my method of healing, she was determined to come to me rather than have the horrible treatments of the hospitals She just could not imagine going through radiotherapy. She told me she was frightened to have all that therapy and when her friend gave her my phone number she was over the moon. She used to bring me little presents which I thought was so nice, but I had to tell her not to waste her money and she would say to me, "Dorothy, I am not wasting my money". She would say, "I don't give you any money, so buying a small present is nothing to what you are doing for me". She used to say to me, "I have never met anyone so kind like you" and then she said, "That is why Jesus Christ chose you. Jesus Christ chose you from the day you were born to your natural mother, but it was good your adopted mother was an angel. She gave you such a nice life till she had to go into the convent with terrible asthma. What a pity you didn't know then that you could heal asthma". She said, "You were only 16 and it wasn't till years after that you saw the vision of Jesus Christ's face telling you of the wonderful gift he had given you; healing hands, what powerful hands, you have been able to heal cancer, arthritis and lots of other diseases".

I told her one doctor told me that it wasn't fair because he had to study for years to qualify as a doctor and I got my healing gift from a force that is the Almighty God, and I had told him we all have gifts.

I said to him he had a gift being a doctor, and he said he would like very much to have healing hands. As It is just one of those things when your gift comes the one that is greater than you. My friend said she knew exactly what I meant and fully agreed with me. She said some things are very awkward to explain, but as she said and I say as well, that all good things come from God and bad things come from the devil. My friend told me she had met a lot of people where she lived who told her that they could heal, but she never found out what they had healed. She then told them she had cancer in her breast, none of them could help her. She told me, "I suppose it just depends on how powerful a healing hands are, it maybe they just heal simple little things". I told her there were quite a few women and men I knew who told me that they were faith healers. When I asked them who they had healed they told me they hadn't healed anyone, but they believe in healing. I said to them you should tell people that you cannot heal rather than call yourselves faith healers. I said to my friend that maybe the people where you live were faith healers, that is why they could not help you. I think it is a rather strange way of telling people you are a faith healer rather than tell people the truth – that you cannot heal, but only believe in healing by faith. To believe is not to know; it means not being certain, because when you are certain you do not believe.

My friend said maybe these faith healers will explain to people better next time.

Anyway, by this time my friend was getting on fine. She told me she could feel the effects of my healing hands; the healing process both during and after each session. My symptoms initially seemed to increase but are now beginning to subside and I know by continuing I shall soon be fully healthy again. And she said, "If it wasn't for you Dorothy, I don't know what I would have done". She used to tell me lots of things about when she went abroad. She said she wondered why I never went to America; they would have appreciated me much more over there. I told her I'd had a lot of invitations to go to America, but it was my birth certificate that stopped me. The Post Office told me if I had shown my birth certificate to the American authorities at the port of entry, they would arrest me because they would say that English people are all white, but the reality is that my mother is white and English and in her ignorance she had me registered as white English, but I am biracial and so I was put off going to America as I didn't want to be locked up in an American jail. I may have had quite a different life if the woman who had given birth to me had not been so irresponsible. She ruined my life in every possible way, but as I told my friend there is nothing, I can do about that and it was a long time ago. My friend said to me, "But you are very light brown". I said, "Yes but I am still brown, and people can see".

I told my friend of an incident on the bus once. I had gone upstairs because there was no room downstairs. As I was getting off the bus a chap said to me, "Are you getting off the bus or what?" I told him I was, and he said to me, "You foreigners". I said to him, "Do you mind? You have a foreign accent and my accent is northern and I happen to be English". I said to him, "Don't kid yourself". It seems like everyone on the bus was listening and they all roared out laughing and said to me, "You tell him girl!" I had to laugh myself – I did not know so many people were listening. I thought that was very funny. My friend asked me if this man was Greek. I said I did not know, but I knew he was not English. She said to me, "I will never know how to thank you, Dorothy, because this thing is so big you will never know". She told me she had gone to tell some of her friends who were supposed to be healers and they were all shocked they said we haven't met anyone who could heal cancer, especially someone who can heal cancer all over the body. They knew I had cancer in my breast, but I told them about the lady you healed who went on holiday to Italy and they asked why you haven't told a lot of people. She told them I had approached Diane Abbott five times, and that she wasn't interested. As my friend and I discussed the problem of Diane Abbott and how in the world she became an MP, we thought it is good to let the public know about her and to let them know just how useless she is to the public, and that nobody wants her as an MP. If you do not tell people they will never know. We wants people like Amy Gray, a Conservative MP. I'm sure if I had told Amy Gray what I told Diane Abbott about me being able to heal people of cancer and other diseases, she would have been glad to tell anyone who is in need of my help, if thought it could save a life or heal their pain.

You can see what kind of person Amy Gray is. She is always helping children and people. What a pity I have never met her, but I hope to meet her in the future. I voted for her because it is someone like her we need, especially in the Stoke Newington area. My friend agreed with me although she does not come from this area. Sometimes it is very good to be alert and watch and see who is the most caring in every possible way. By this time, my friend was completely better; all her cancer had gone, and she was quite happy.

She said to me, "Dorothy you have saved me from all that horrible treatment". She said she will never be able to thank me enough. She said to me that all she had to suffer at the beginning was just a little pain, then it slowly subsided and as she said she thought that was wonderful and that God had blessed her to meet me.

When I first discovered I had healing hands, I would visit elderly homes and treat them. Once I got very close to an elderly lady, Elsie, who lived with her daughter. I used to tell Elsie to be very careful how she opened the door when I came to visit her, and make sure it was me because there were a lot of bad characters where she lived. I told her to always look through her window before she opened her door.

Actually, when I first realised I had healing hands I would go to church and after church I would visit elderly people in old people's homes to offer them my services freely; besides I needed people to know about me and my healing hands because when I tell people that I have healing hands, they don't believe me. I let it be and narrowed my focus on healing the elderly at the old people's home.

One day when I went to visit Elsie and her daughter at their flat, before I got to them a man had already pressed their doorbell and she thought it was me. She told me she thought it was me; I recently told her to be very careful and to look through her window. She said a man came in, looked through her drawers and found nothing. He heard me coming up the stairs and he quickly rushed out. I told her never to do that again and to always look out through her window. I think that taught her a lesson. You see, some people you have to visit because they cannot travel themselves. I used to treat her daughter who wasn't keen on my healing hand on her head for up to three hours because she said my hand got far too hot on her, so really it was useless going there although her mother was a very nice lady. She was always trying to coax her daughter to continue with the treatment. I stayed there for a couple of hours, but it wasn't much good. I kept up my visit with them for a long time and her mother did her very best to make sure her daughter would accept my healing, but to no avail. Then she agreed to take up my healing only for an hour session and not for three hours; besides, her daughter had mental issues. We tried very hard but she wouldn't allow me to keep my healing hands on her head for even two hours before losing concentration. I tried as hard as I could but there was nothing more I could. I would still try because, as her mother said to me, I have a lot patience. I said to be a healer you have to have a lot of patience; it all goes with the healing.

I said to her some people are very awkward. I told her about a woman I used to go and see and when I got to her flat, she used to say to me, "I will be with you in a minute". Every time I went to her it was just the same. I went to the kitchen and all she was doing was looking up at the ceiling. I said to her, "I am leaving now", and as soon as I said that she would come rushing in the sitting room. I said to her if she did not stop wasting my time, I would stop coming to her altogether. I told her I had other patients to visit as well. She used to tell me she would not keep me waiting again, but the following week she would do the same thing.

You see, I used to visit the elderly because it was awkward for them to visit me. When I started to put my hands on the woman who looks up to the ceiling on her stomach, she would say to me, "Could you keep it there for much longer because it feels so nice?" I told her I thought two hours was long enough. She was very much more different than the other lady I had just been to. The other lady did not like my hand on her head because it was too hot. Anyway, this woman's husband used to ask me to put my hands on his hands because he said his hands hurt him, so after two hours on his wife's stomach I had to spend two hours on his hands. After visiting them for quite a few months I could not believe it when her husband told me he could hold his cigarette much better now. I said to him he should not be smoking because it is not good for him. I said I did not get his hand better for him to smoke. I said he must try and give up smoking and he said he could never give it up. Well after hearing that, there was

Chapter Eleven

nothing much I could do, so the wife said to me you can stay longer on my stomach when you come again. I said to her two hours are quite enough. I said you waste far too much time looking up to the ceiling; you seem to forget I have other people to see as well as you two. I told her if I have to wait any longer for her I am going to stop coming. I said she would drive anybody's patience to distraction. She said she was very sorry, and she would never do it again, but be sure when I got there the next week, the very same thing happened!

I do not really know who the kind gentleman was, but somebody seems to have come to my aid on the lawn which surrounds my flat. The women who live on the other side have always invited their friend's children to come and play football right outside my window, even knocking the ball on my window and cracking it. I was tired of telling them to stop it, all you got was rudeness from their friend's children. They invite their friends to play on their bicycles and kids break up sticks and throw them at my window. I was tired of telling them to stop. The lease on the property instructs that nobody should use the lawn as a playground; that space belongs to the person who lives in flat No. 1 and that is me.

I believe some kind person told them to stop playing football on my lawn and to stop hitting the ball against my wall. This woman lives in flat No. 10 and never works but looks after other people's children, as well her own children. Whoever told them to stop hitting the ball against my wall and window I am very grateful to for giving me back at least my peace of mind. The amount of times I told them to stop made no difference. They still kept on with quite a lot of verbal abuse and it was embarrassing when I sometimes went shopping and came back home. I could see about 20 children on the lawn each day all playing games outside my window. It really disgusted me how these people can rent a flat and then take over the whole block with their petulant ways of life. It never used to be like that when I first moved into my flat. I had English neighbours then and they were nice neighbours, but when they moved out, along came Orthodox Jewish neighbours and their children, and the start of my nightmare – they had unruly children, totally out of order.

Ever since these Orthodox Jews and their wives moved into my block of flats, they just took over the whole block, never going to work, but producing children every year and these children invite other children over to my block of flats. These children are growing up to be a menace, but I was hoping that had all stopped, but it hasn't stopped as they have actually broken my bedroom window.

I had to call the police, and would you believe it they are still playing football against my wall and window. When I tell them to stop they come right up to my window and tell me to shut up and get out. I have never seen such rude children in all my life. I have no intention of moving from here. I aim to continue doing my healing right where I am based.

I am by this time still visiting some of the elderly because as I stated before, it is awkward for them to visit me. I was treating a couple of them with knees problems as it is difficult for me to do their hips. I certainly would not take on anyone with bad hips, only knees because some of them are very heavy and I would not take on such a task, but doing their knees was all right. Those women healed by me all appreciated what I did, especially when their knees started to get better. I could have healed their hips, but it was difficult for those with hip problems to turn on their side. I used to tell them it was not a quick fix and they used to tell me they had never had anyone to heal them with their knees until I came along. They did not know how to thank me. Two of them once asked me who pays me for this and I said that nobody does. They asked how I manage, and I told them I go to work and only do this after church every Sunday. Two of them said to me they had never heard of anyone doing such a thing like this for nothing. As a matter of fact, they told me that they did not know anyone could help them with such an illness. Then they started to question how it is they had never known anyone who could heal arthritis at all. they had heard the doctor say often that nobody could heal arthritis, but I can. I would say to them don't mention me to your doctor because they certainly don't like people like me, but being elderly they didn't understand where I am coming from; two of them used to say to me, "But couldn't you help the doctors as well?" I used to say to them that I would not even try because they would not believe what I could do, so it is better to leave them alone. They asked me how I got to have such strong healing hands and I would tell them that I saw a vision of Jesus Christ's face in 1983. I told them few people would believe me. I told them also that I healed a lady who had cancer all over her body and it could be proven by St Mary's Church in Stoke Newington. They were so glad of what I told them and said a lot of people would be jealous including the doctors. I told them that some of the nurses do not like me either, would you believe it quite a lot of the ministers in the church do not like me too. They could not believe how ridiculous these people are. I said to them they should always pray and thank God for the healing. They used to tell me each time I visit them next that they had started praying to Jesus Christ, that they would continue to pray all the time; and that made me feel so happy. They used to ask me if God heard their prayers. I told them that God heard their prayers and that God was answering their prayers. They knew in their hearts that what I was telling them was the truth.

The women asked me if I would be visiting people all the time at their houses. I said I did not think I would be able to continue visiting people at their houses, but people would have to come to me instead. I told them that as times goes by I would be in need of an assistant to help when people come for healing, and they agreed. I had to tell each one of them that when I visit them they should always look through the window before opening the door. I told them you have to be very careful these days, always make sure you know the person at the other side of the door, never open the door unless you know the person. I used to tell them I cannot understand how elderly people, both men and women open the door so easily to people they don't know. I made it clear to them I personally would never open my door to people uninvited or unwanted because such types are just looking to steal whatever money or valuables you have. I told them to be very careful and sometimes these strangers want to hurt you, so don't take any chances and always pray to God who hears us all if we call. They each told me they looked forward to seeing me every Sunday after church service. I looked forward to seeing them. It is a nice feeling when God gives you a gift. It is nice to use it to the best of your ability, especially to the elderly. I remember when I first realised I had been blessed with a wonderful gift given to me by Jesus Christ, one of my friends said to me if I was you I wouldn't bother with people who are over 65 years of age. I said to him, "Are you serious? I would heal people who are very old". It does not matter to me how old they are, the people I used to go to were nearly all in their eighties, some of them in their seventies. I think when they are older, they need help more than anyone else. Some of them used to tell me it is a good job you are here to help us because the doctors could not do what you are doing for us. Most of the time they just give us pills; that is all the help we receive from the doctors. I somehow used to feel sorry for them.

I know when you're getting older, people can get very awkward; that is why you have to have a lot of patience and believe me, God gave me a lot of patience. I sometimes wonder why I have so much patience because holding people's heads for three hours in a healing session is quite a long time, but I only do that time if people have cancer. If they have arthritis I hold them for two hours, but it really depends how bad the arthritis is. Sometimes it does not take so long – it really depends how long they have had the illness for. Of course, with some of the elderly they have had it a very long time so it takes a long time to heal. I know I used to think that they would get very irritable if the healing session exceeded two hours, but I was quite surprised as soon as my hands got right on the spot of their illnesses or pain, I would tell them to relax and they would sit there as soon as the hands were on the exact spot of their pain, and then they would fall fast asleep. I would have to wake them up and tell them the two hours were up. They would say to me, "You mean the two hours have gone so soon?" I would tell them they went fast asleep and they would say to me, "That is your hands, Dorothy, they make you fall asleep". They were not the only ones to have experienced this. I used to say to them that is the best thing to do because that means you are completely relaxed, and I told them that the healing would be much quicker if they are relaxed.

I used to have one lady who was so grateful to me, she used to say to me, "Please Dorothy, stay for dinner". I used to say I couldn't because I had someone else to visit and she would beg and I would tell her to stop worrying herself because I already had a very big breakfast.

I could hardly eat anything now anyway. I just did not want to give any of the elderly any trouble, especially when they did everything for themselves such as cooking for themselves, not to mention cooking for two. I was so happy when they would say to me, "Oh Dorothy, I feel so much better, much less pain". I would say be very careful what you tell the doctors as I have already told you that the doctors do not like me at all, so please do not tell them my name or anything about me. I think that would be much better. I never told my patients where I lived. Even when I went in hospital nobody knew me and I never told anyone that I was a healer because as I have mentioned before, doctors don't like me at all. If they had found out, who would know what the consequences would have been? It is better to be safe more than sorry, so I was very proud of myself that I had kept it very quiet. I made sure not to invite anyone to the hospital just in case anyone happened to let it slip that I had healed them. So, you see, I got no visitors whatsoever, only a couple of women from the church I had recently joined. They did not know about my healing abilities and they only came twice. I was glad when I left both hospitals – the Middlesex and Homerton. I started to live a normal life again.

Before I went into hospital I had not started writing. It was years after that I started writing again about the people I have healed. I had a call from a man who had a dodgy heart. He asked me if I could help him. I knew he had been to see his doctor and I told him what I did when someone came to me with a bad heart. I would take them in for three hours of healing sessions once a week. I would put my hands on their heart and spleen for an hour and a half, then put my hands on their head for another hour and a half. Would you believe a female friend of mine who knew more about the body than I do told me where to put my hands when I had someone with heart troubles, and it worked? The man I was healing was quite a big man, very tall. I could see how delighted he was with the treatment. When I told him I hadn't got a clue where to put my hands, it was my friend who told me where to put them. He said to me it is a good job you have at least one good friend because some people would be so jealous that you had such strong healing hands; they would be reluctant to tell you anything. How right he was. My female friend, who I am very sorry to say, went into hospital for a slight stomach trouble without telling me at all. Then I heard from one of her relatives she had died. I could not believe it. So I certainly had no friend to ask for further advice on medical issues. The man I was healing said he was so sorry. I told him I had medical books that I looked in to find out where to put my hands he said I was full of ideas. I told him that was through Jesus Christ, who blessed me with this gift. He told me he could never stop thanking his friend who told him about me and believe me, I did not know the person at all. He said to me, "I have to thank you for my life". He was a very kind and interesting person. He said he had never heard of any healers who can do what I do, such as heal cancer, arthritis and do hearts and other things. He said to me, "Dorothy no wonder the doctors don't like you". He said to me, "I'm sure, Dorothy, you are a very strong person. I can see that you will not let these people bother you at all". I said to him how right you are and I told him one day I am going to write a book about my life and he said, "When you do write this book, that lots of people will love you and trust you and they will all see just how strong and kind you are".

The man then went on to say that he is going to pay his doctor a visit, and on his next appointment with me he will tell me all that took place. He said, "I bet my doctor will get a shock when he notices how improved I am". He was smiling all over his face. When I saw him on his next appointment with me, he said to me the doctor said to him that it seems as if the heart is getting better all by itself. My friend nearly laughed out loud at this, but he tried to control himself because he knew if he told the doctor he had been to one of the greatest healers in history, he would not have liked it at all. I said to him, "I don't think for one minute I am one of the greatest healers in history. Where in the world you got that from I don't really know, but I think I have heard of great healers in the world". He said, "Yes, in Jesus Christ's time when he was on the earth but I'm not referring to that time. Remember you got this gift from Jesus Christ in a vision". I said that yes, I knew this. He said to me, "It is only when you write your book about your life, that is when people will know". He went on to say to me, "Dorothy, I think I am one of the lucky men to have ever met you, and as I promised you, I will always pray and thank God for my healing just as you want me to do", and he said he will always pray for me as well and pray that God will always protect me. I thought that was very nice.

The man told me, he knew his heart was getting stronger through my strong hands. I told him that when I was a child I used to complain about my hands being so big and how my mother used to tell me I am going to do wonderful things with them. I always wondered if she knew what I could do or would be able to do with my hands. I still wonder why she never told me. She made me realise that perhaps she too had a vision about me, and what my hands would do in my journey of life; and here I am healing people. It has always had me thinking if she knew I could heal why didn't she tell me? I wonder that because she suffered from asthma and I could have healed her and looked after her. My patient said maybe she was not supposed to tell you, but you will never know. She may not have known. I said to him, "It is no use me worrying about that now". He said to me, "You are right. Everything happens for a purpose", and he said, "Thank the Lord that you were chosen", and he told me he would only tell people about me when he found out what kind persons they are and what their occupation is. I would not like to introduce the wrong persons to me at all, because as I know myself, there are not many people that you can trust today. I told him how right he was and it seems to get worse these days as people seem to have lost the sense of humanity and compassion.

I told him about going on holiday to Liverpool, when I had my beautiful case stolen which was packed with all new clothes and photos of Mother Connie and myself. I was so upset I just did not know what to do. I went straight back home. That was a real disappointment.

That is the world today, full of unreliable, opportunistic people just looking to find what does not belong to them. Then he told me about his own experience of what happened to him. He was going on holiday abroad, and he was robbed also, while he was sitting down waiting for the plane to arrive and then he fell asleep. Once asleep, an opportunistic individual robbed him. He told me he was going to make sure that never happened to him again; certainly, a lesson well learnt. He said it was better that when you travel with your luggage that you keep the handle round your wrist, then if you do go to sleep you can feel someone taking the handle off your wrist. He said to me it was a pity I did not have a handle on my case. I could have put it on my knee. I told him I would make sure that never happened again. He said to me, these days you have to be very careful.

I told the man about when I was travelling once when I had to stop at a station. It was a very hot day too, so I bought myself a large ice cream and as I was enjoying it, a woman came next to me with a big dog. All of a sudden the dog grabbed the ice cream out of my hand. I was quite shocked and the woman told me she was sorry, but a man who was standing next to me told me she trains the dog to steal ice cream from women and kids. She is quite a character; she does it deliberately. This way she does not have to buy the dog any ice cream. I said to the man I had never heard of anything like that before and he said the woman should be reported to the police; she has been doing this for a long time. I asked my patient what he thought about that, and he said the man was right, she should be reported to the police. He said people pay a lot of money for a large ice cream. I said to him that the man who told me that was looking out to see if he could see a policeman, but could not see one. The woman was quite quick to move on once the dog got hold of the ice cream and the man told me that is what she does all the time. I was certainly very shocked to find out that the woman trained the dog to do such a thing. The man told me he didn't know how many ice creams that dog has every day, and my patient said to me how we learn new things about what people get up to in this world. He told me not to go there anymore and I said I wouldn't. He said if I did he would come with me.

I told my patient that after the incident with the dog it was within a couple of years I saw the vision of Jesus Christ and I was able to heal myself and he said that was a good thing. He said to me I would gladly take you anywhere you want to go. I told him I was all right but if I wanted to go anywhere and I was a bit nervous I would ask him to come with me. He was such a nice man. I told him it was a very nice offer and I would not forget it, but at the moment I am quite all right. He always asked me if I wanted anything and I told him I did not, but I thanked him for asking. He was such a kind man. He often brought fish and chips with him; enough for two, and he would ask if we should have them before we start the healing session or after, and I would ask him if he was hungry and he would ask me if I was hungry. I said I can always warm up the fish and chips in the microwave when we finished, given that his healing session with me was for three hours; one hour and a half on his heart and spleen and the other one and half hours on his head. We both really enjoyed the fish and chips and he would say he would see me next week, and believe me, I always enjoyed seeing him.

Chapter Eleven

I told this man about the lovely girl I healed in 1984. She had cancer all over her body. I could see she was very ill, so I said to her, "Brenda, please come every day till you start eating properly and feeling stronger", and she said to me, "Are you sure, Dorothy?" I said of course I was. She was worried because she told me she would not be able to even put down a small donation and I said to her, "Don't worry about donation, your health comes first; your health is your wealth". I took her in for healing every day for a few months and she said to me she felt on top of the world and I said to her that made me feel very happy. While I was healing her, Adrian her husband watched the television and one day she said to him, "I see Dorothy has a big tin of paint. Don't you think it would be nice if you could do some painting for her?" and he certainly got to work. So, as I told my friend, sometimes it pays not to worry about money, especially when people can do other things.

Brenda's husband told me that when Brenda feels so much better they will both be going on holidays. I said to her that is nice I asked her where she was going, and she said Italy. I said that was nice and I asked her how long she was going for and she said to me for five weeks. I was quite surprised I said to her Brenda halve your holiday. I said to her when you have had cancer all over your body the way you have had it weakens the system. I kept saying to her please Brenda halve your holiday, I was not happy. Anyway, the day came when she went on her holiday, she wrote me a beautiful card saying how she was eating well and feeling no pain. She said, "All through you Dorothy.

How can I ever thank you for your strong hands and your patience". I can only hope that she is all right and to continue in strengthening herself and her wellbeing. When the five weeks holidays had finished, I saw her husband by himself. I asked him where is Brenda? He told me as they were just driving through Italy she said to him, "Adrian, I'm so sorry I didn't do what Dorothy told me to do", and he asked what she was worried about because they were going home now and she said that is what she was worried about. She just fell over in the car, and he could not believe it, she was dead. He said, "I had to take her body to the Italian police station. I told the police that my wife was dying of cancer". He told me her body was taken to one of the top hospitals where all the top doctors practiced. He was so upset and just didn't know what to do. As soon as Adrian heard from the hospital in Italy he went to collect his wife's body. The doctors (about seven of them – men and women) in white coats said to him, "What sort of doctors do you have in England? Your wife did not have a trace of cancer in her body. She died of a heart attack". Now what do you think about that? If she had listened to me, she would still be here with us, alive and happy. I was so upset. Until today I have never forgotten her she was such a lovely girl, an assistant headmistress who had all her life before her. I was rather cross with her because she did not take heed to my advice. She was sorry when it was too late, and my friend said to me it was such a pity. I asked my friend why is it that people don't listen to a healer, and he said to me if I had warned him about anything he would certainly have listened, especially to someone like me with such strong hands and so kind. I was very glad when he got completely better. I asked him if he would get himself examined by his doctor and he said certainly not. He said to me, "Dorothy, I trust I will never have another heart attack", and I said to him, "I am happy to hear you say that". I would certainly miss him coming once a week but I was very happy to see him get completely well. Some people ask me why I give people so many hours of healing for the different diseases they have. I tell them it is my way of healing but I think things will be different now, as we all know things change.

I think to get a cleaner today is very difficult. I feel very sorry for the cleaning companies. They get people applying for cleaning jobs and they do not know anything about the individual – and anyone can get a fake reference. I had one thief; she was a very crafty person who stole six spoons. I could not keep any hand cream in the kitchen or bathroom either. She stole so many other things; it was impossible to keep watch on her. I had to phone and ask the company to get someone else; they were very good that way.

It is such a shame you cannot trust many people today. I feel very pleased that cleaner has gone. I hope everything is back to normal now. Before I had this woman cleaner, there was another man cleaner called Don that used to come around. You had to watch him as well, as he would be giving you a hard luck story and would then want to borrow money. I am hoping I will be all right now as I have gotten rid of the two of them, but I still do not know what is ahead. If it is not one thing it is another. I once lent £50 to one of my cleaners and was surprised that he paid it back. He cleaned my windows and then cleaned my cooker. When he called me to look at the cooker, he turned it on unattended without lighting it. I quickly turned the cooker off and asked him what he was playing at. I honestly think there was something wrong with him. I made sure then to get myself another cleaner. I had nothing more to do with him. A lot of my things went missing, surely stolen by these so-called cleaners. The message is simple, and the message is that a lot of people like the simple way out and mostly these sort of people want what you've got, but I if I take them to the river or sea I hope they know how to cross that river or sea because if not, then they shouldn't be jealous or envious of what a person has achieved or what a person has. This is why people mostly steal; because they like the easy way out and the easy way is to steal from other people. Sometimes you have to be very careful as recently one of the men who live in the flats reported to the gas company, telling them that the gas was coming from my flat. The gas company sent someone to investigate further. A gas leak was detected and I asked the gas man to tell my neighbours of this. The gas leak was fixed and there had never been an issue since.

The man who had been asked to clean the gas cooker for the £50 loan had called me and switched the gas appliances on. I then quickly switched off the gas appliances and told him to advise those living above me that he had switched the cooker and heater on himself, for whatever reason I will never know, but it still baffles me as to his behaviour; probably he might not be right in the head. How dare anyone come to my house and switch my gas cooker on without my permission, having gas escape from the cooker. This could've had a very dangerous consequences. In the end, the gas man told me as long as I am all right there is nothing more to worry about. He just smiled and told me to take care of myself. I said I would.

I must tell whoever reads my book that I do not know anything about the body or anatomy. I only know that Jesus Christ blessed me with very strong healing hands, but if anyone comes to me with a disease that I have not heard of I just look in the medical book and read up on it and identify what exactly the medical condition is and the cause of it. With the help of the medical book, it enables me to place my healing hands at the exact spot of the pain or diseases. I haven't heard of a lot of illnesses; I haven't even got a clue on how to spell the words of these diseases, so it is rather difficult for me, but I have a very dear friend who has just passed her medical exams. She is an English rose and so reliable. I feel I can always ask her for help. She has also helped me in every way with my laptop. Without this lovely lady I would never have been able to complete this book.

Some diseases I can't heal because if the patients only come once a week for healing it is not enough. There are illnesses that are far too serious, and you need more healing contact time than once a week. People do not seem to understand at all that illnesses are different, and it depends how severe they are. I mean I am fully booked up but willing to accommodate people with severe illnesses as long as they attend the healing sessions as prescribed by me. When people get to know that I can heal cancer, they become very interested. There are a lot of people all over Britain, in fact all over the world, who need my help. I will give it to as many people as I can, because that is why Jesus Christ gave me the gift in the first place; to help people all over the world. However, from now on, I will always have to have someone with me for assistance. When I meet people who are very ill and then they come to me for healing and I see the progress of them getting well again, it is the most satisfying feeling of my life. It is a most wonderful feeling. I do hope that people who do not believe in God will start believing in God because I work through God as a channel.

I had a phone call from a lady called Sally who asked me if it was possible to visit me because she was very worried. She would not tell me anything on the phone because some people are like that. I arranged for her to come and see me, and she told me that she knew something was very wrong and I asked her what was wrong. She looked at me as if she was embarrassed so I said to her, "If you don't tell me, how in the world will I be able to help you?" She then told me that she was going off her food and her stomach was hurting her. I asked her if she had seen the doctor and she said she had. He had sent her to have an x-ray, and her doctor told her she had cancer. I asked her why she was so frightened and who had told her about me. I said, "Didn't anyone tell you I had healed quite a few people who had cancer?" She said she had heard but was wondering whether I would help her or not. She told me she had heard about the lady I had healed

Chapter Eleven

with cancer all over her body. I said that was right and, "I will certainly heal you as well, but for goodness sake don't ask the doctor to do anything to you after I have healed you. It will take a little time". I told her about the lady I had healed who had cancer in her stomach like hers and what she did after, and she said she wouldn't do anything like that. . I told the lady if I ever get to write a book about my life, I will certainly write it all down. She told me, "I would do the same, but I am lucky to have you to make me better. I would never let anyone else touch me". I told her when this lady first came to me, she told me she went to the doctor at the hospital where she worked. She told them her stomach hurt her and that she could not eat, and they told her to come back when she could eat. Now I tried to tell her they didn't mean that literally, because they know when you have cancer you wouldn't be able to eat again, but they didn't realise she was going to meet someone who could heal cancer. So when she went back to them and told them she could eat and that her stomach didn't hurt her again, they couldn't understand why. Her doctors decided to investigate, rather than leave her alone to live the rest of her life. They had no right to do what they did. My friend said to me, "Just like you Dorothy, I would have felt very sorry for her that someone could do such a dreadful thing and walk off as if nothing had happened". I said to her to make sure she will always remember this story, and she said to me she will never forget it for the rest of her life.

Sally was getting on very well with her healing. She told me she hardly had any pain now. I asked her if she would inform other people of her being healed and she said, "Only if I know them well enough to be of a good character because I want you to be safe". "I'm afraid a lot of my patients say the same thing. They are mostly worried about me, but some are just selfish and don't want anyone to get better but only themselves. These type of people I do not much bother with, after all it is nice to see other people helping others. That is what I aim to do all the time, only I have to be very cautious these days because you can't trust many people". I told her I will always have to have someone with me now when I am healing because from what I am hearing in today's news shows me what a sad world we are living in.

I think I have told you a bit about the Stoke Newington police station. They should be ashamed of themselves. We all pay a lot of money in taxes every month, but they never seem to be satisfied. Where I lived once in Clissold Crescent, Stoke Newington, the landlord moved gypsies on the ground floor. When I told the landlord they were doing a lot of stealing, he told me he was sorry. He had been given good references from them and he said he did not know they were false. He told me they had lived there for six months and paid one month's rent. He told me he was trying to get them out through the courts. When two men off the streets spoke to me about gypsies, I was very upset because they told me they were pretending to be healers. Now this was in the late 1970s and I myself had not seen the vision of Jesus Christ telling me I had healing hands by then. I didn't see the vision until 1983. I told this gypsy she should stop taking money from people and stealing.

Chapter Eleven

She told me they pay the Stoke Newington police who are on their book. I could hardly believe such a thing. The people on the street asked me to get a petition and a lot of local people signed it. The gypsies were going into people's houses and stealing things and the Stoke Newington police station were getting all the benefits; money and likewise. The whole thing was quite disgraceful. This in addition to the 'laundry' using dangerous chemicals upstairs for their laundry business, and now also a factory.

I just couldn't believe when I saw all the stuff coming in every day into the people's flat above me; pure factory stuff, and if you were coming into the main entrance door you couldn't get in until they moved all of their factory equipment. I certainly could not get to my flat, the passage was obstructed due to the prams, bicycles, cases and (when it arrives) factory equipment; it was awful. One cannot move and the fireman said the passage should be left empty otherwise it could be a very serious illegality, being an obstruction in an emergency. These people think that they can do anything and get away with it; nobody bothers. The fire brigade should be helped by the police, but it seems the police are too busy doing other things for themselves. I hear it is only the sergeants and senior officers who do these sort of things that the Stoke Newington police station are up to. If the junior ranking police officers acted the way that their superiors do the people would not complain about Stoke Newington police station and their behaviour would have been appreciated by the public, and the public would have trust with the police. But when some officers put on their uniform at

Stoke Newington police station the public just wonder what hocus pocus they are getting at. It is quite worrying to have a police force like them, with no public confidence in them.

I was robbed by one of the actual workers from the hospital who came to fix my bed after my accident. When I found out, I called the Metropolitan Police on the 101 number because I trusted them much more than the Stoke Newington police. Then when one of the police officers at Stoke Newington police station saw my name at the police station, he said he knew who I was and that he has known me to be a hardworking and respectable lady. He asked what my name was doing in a police station. The Metropolitan Police told the Stoke Newington police station that I had been robbed by one of the workers in the hospital. They (Stoke Newington police) asked the 101 Metropolitan Police if they could take over the case because they claimed to know me. Then they had the nerve to phone me and tell me they had taken the case over, and to date have done nothing. As a matter of fact, they do come to my building for a reason – to collect money from the people who live above my flat (a backhander), so as to allow them to continue operating their illegal laundry business with the dangerous chemicals. They did not want me to tell the 101 Metropolitan Police about the dangerous laundry they were being paid for; that is how they knew me! The police are employed to stop this kind of awful behaviour. Oh, but not the Stoke Newington police; people are afraid to report anything to them because all they do is say sorry, and that's the matter closed.

Chapter Eleven

Although some people would be afraid to write about this dreadful police station, someone has got to do it so as to reassure the community once again and to make people feel safer. I am a very God-fearing person who has decided to help people the best way I can, not just saving people's lives and helping them with their pain, but helping them to educate themselves on all matters relating to Stoke Newington police. I am sure lots of people would be very grateful to me for doing this. I have heard so many stories about the Stoke Newington police and I myself have had my share of experiences with them. I think it is about time they were brought to justice. I telephoned them not too long ago and asked them to tell the people above me that they are directly burying these dangerous chemicals underneath and around my window, and it's about time someone put to a stop to these sort of behaviour.

All that happened with the police was a visit by about four of them who looked at what those people had done. It can be easily seen that there was no grass at all underneath my window and the surrounding area, all damaged by the chemicals thrown down from the occupants above me. The police who were sent down to investigate the matter didn't see me peeping out of my window. All they did was to have a laugh and joke of the situation. I wondered what they were thinking. I expect we all know; that is just the kind of people they are. They have no shame and not one word did they say to me, I was not surprised.

Some of these Orthodox Jews living in my block of flats are the strangest people I have ever known. They have a way to pull their chairs around the floor with no carpet and it makes the strangest of sounds. They do it all the time. It seems they let their children do all the pulling and it seems to please them to make such a noise. This usually goes on nearly all night. I remember when I first moved into my flat, there were two English people who lived above me who I got on well with. They lived a couple of floors above me and they complained to me how these children pull the chairs and make a lot of noise and that it went on all night too. I felt very sorry for them because it is not very nice when you can't get a good night's sleep. Sleep is important because that's when your body heals itself and rejuvenates itself; so I can understand the frustration of a person not getting a good sleep. I was very lucky that an elderly lady lived above me. We got on very well together. I had no trouble sleeping until unfortunately, the lady passed away. It was then my headache started in 1996. Ever since I have been suffering from sleep deprivation due to the noises that these Orthodox Jews and their children make. It is most distressing. The two English people living a couple of floors above me eventually moved out. They could not put up with the noise. I think I will prosecute these noise polluters. It would make a difference, especially if they have to pay money in compensation. I'm sure that would solve the problem and would help a lot of people, including myself, who lived with these types of people. When it comes to slamming doors, it never stops. I have never lived in such a place where so many people slam the main door from the morning hours throughout the night. It goes on in my

Chapter Eleven

block of flats, but these days you cannot move in and out of flats as they are hard to come by. There is a shortage of flats in London, and if you haven't got much money, then it's best to stand your ground and fight for your right. I certainly would not like to give that woman above me my flat. I can hear her now bringing in a lot of her factory equipment very late in the night. That woman has become quite a menace with her laundry and her factory businesses in a block of flats – never seen this before in my life. It certainly would be a waste of time telling the Hackney Council about this. They would fob me off like they have been doing all the time, and the Mayor of Hackney and Diane Abbott are very good at making excuses. Now I hear that Diane Abbott has got a promotion. Well that is the Labour Party for you. I am very glad I am not a member of the Labour Party. Their members ring my bell all the time; I do not answer it when it rings as I know it is not for me.

One day about 3 o'clock in the morning my bell rang. I did not answer because no one has ever rung my doorbell at such hours, but it kept ringing, so I had to get up at that hour. When I answered the doorbell and asked who it was and what they wanted, a man shouted it was a pizza delivery. I thought to myself, what a nightmare. I said to the man, "I don't eat pizza. Please get your flat number right and stop disturbing people at this hour of the morning". I did wonder who in the world could be eating pizza at that hour of the morning. I gave the man a good telling off and told him never to ring my bell ever again. In all my life I have never seen people coming and going so late in the night. If and when any of these Jews move flats it is always late in the night and the door entrance never stops opening and banging late in the night and continues in the morning.

I usually give a lot of my clothes to charity when I have finished with them and they are still very good to wear, but some of these charities go too far. They keep bothering you all the time; they never stop. One gets fed up with them – some of them can become rather rude and demanding and I think this can put people off.

A man telephoned me and asked me if he could make an appointment. I asked him what was wrong and he told me he would prefer to discuss it with me in person. I told him he could come as soon as possible. I could hear by his voice he was very worried. When he came over, he told me that he had Parkinson's disease. I told him with a serious disease like that he would have to visit me three times a week. He said to me that would worry him because he would not have the money to pay me. I told him not to worry about the money, people only give me donations. With your disease you would not have to give me anything. I told him to let me get him better first, then let your conscience be your guide. He told me that would be taking liberties. I said it would not. I told him your health comes first, your health is your wealth. When he started coming for healing, I could see his illness had degenerated too far, so I warned him not to stop coming for healing. When I started healing him, he told me that when my hands were on him the shaking stopped, and as time went by, he got better. He stopped coming and ran away without even a donation of thank you, and yet I prayed for him and telephoned him and told him if he didn't keep coming for treatment it wouldn't be good. He was such a nice man in behaviour and as such, I was so sad for him, but there was nothing I could do. I suppose he was too proud; but at least his shaking has stopped. Listen, healing is priceless, and some people take it for granted.

I just remembered a lady named Myrtle whom I healed from arthritis. She had it very bad in both of her knees. I told her she would need healing sessions which she attended, and made progress. Within five months she got better. She was so appreciative of being healed that she gave me a monetary donation. Some people are like that; they are not full of themselves and are willing to tell other people of who healed them, whereas some people will come and not even put down a penny on the table. Everybody is so different. Some people have no conscious way of reasoning; it is always about them and no one else.

I remember a man who came to me and had not even made an appointment. When I asked him who he was, he told me some cock and bull story about a friend of mine who had given him my address. He claimed he had a tumour in his brain. I took him for three hours a day for healing and when he left, I checked up with my friend and he told me he had not given the man my address at all. He had the nerve to give me his telephone number to make another appointment. I rang him and told him never to come again. I didn't want to argue with him. This is why I have to have someone with me at all times as my assistant, because I heard that this particular man was a bit of a character, and as I am not the only one who heals tumours, he could easily go to someone else. I would not want him back anyway; it was rather strange when I was healing him. I did not feel good at all and he had the cheek to inform me he did not want any prayers. I must add that not all the people who come to me believe in Jesus Christ, but I still heal them, hoping when they get better, they will believe; but I never impose my religion on anyone. My job is to heal both the believer and non-believer. Somehow, I could not with these sorts of patients that do not want prayers at all. It did not feel right, and I was not surprised when I checked with my friend and he told me he had not given him my address. He told me to be very careful who I take into my home. I made sure that never happened again.

I had quite an expensive video recorder and the man who used to fix videos and televisions asked me if I would sell it to him for his son. At first, I told him I would sell it, then I changed my mind. He paid me but I gave him the money back because I decided I did not want to sell it after all. When he returned the video recorder I put it straight on top of my wardrobe. Long after the time had passed (like a few years) I decided to use it. Much to my horror, the gentleman who was putting back the video recorder near to the television asked me if anyone had interfered with it. I said only the man I was going to sell it to, then I changed my mind. He said to me, "He did not want you to use it again". I asked him what he meant. He said he put a lot of dirt in it so I could never play it again and I said, "What a terrible thing to do. He got angry with me just because I changed my mind about selling it to him". He said to me that he had never seen anything so disgusting and that man should be ashamed of himself. I quite agreed with him.

When I called up the man I sold the video to and asked him why he damaged it, he denied it and told me he had done no such thing it. I told him the video recorder is full of dirt and he replied that he never saw any dirt inside the video, so I said to him the dirt must have got inside the video recorder itself, but when someone is guilty, they will try to twist things around. I was really upset because it was the best video player I had owned. I knew it would have lasted me a very long time but there was nothing I could do about it. I would have loved to have got some DVDs of Nat King Cole and Frank Sinatra and a lot of the old singers. But I do not have the video or DVDs of these great singers, but I do have their records. The videos and DVD players are easier to play than the big records. I think so. When you have not got a good video but lots of tapes there is nothing you can do about it. I would love to get one of Dr Charles Stanley's beautiful sermons on the television. He was a fantastic preacher and when he does preach it seems as if he is directly having a conversation with you; very captivating indeed. His programme was called 'Day Star'. How shameful that this programme is off the air; I would love it to come back again. If I could do anything to help bring back that programme I would. I also like to listen to the Betty and James Robison television programme. I once sent them both a very small sum of money. It was just a one-off. I suppose they will still remember it. I would like to send them both and Dr Charles Stanley some more money when I can afford it. I certainly do miss his preaching service. I think he is a wonderful preacher; he always preaches something different and he is such a dedicated church minister. He is so different to the other preachers. I certainly like his preaching very much. I also like Joel Osteen Joyce Myers as well as a lot of other church ministers on Day Star. I still give money to a lot of other charities, but some of them do drive you up the wall. My favourite is IFAW; they do not pester you like some of these other charities do.

I hope after I have finished writing my book and I continue healing people again; I would like to get a makeover from the Scottish man who introduced himself as John. John sells special chairs that would suit my patients and not only that, but these chairs will also enable me to do my work as a healer more effectively. Makeovers are quite stunning, and I would certainly love to get one. I think if I did get one my healing would be much more relaxing and comfortable for all. I do hope I am not just dreaming. Oh well, time will tell. I hope you know that I write this book as I remember things that have occurred in my life; but my interest is to write this book and inform the whole world of my capabilities.

When I was growing up, I always had very thick hair. Sometimes I would wear it high on the top of my head or curl it all over. Lots of people used to think I had been to the hairdressers but I used to tell them I did it myself. Some women even used to pull out a strand. I suppose they used to think it was a wig. I would get very cross and ask them why they had pulled my hair. They used to look surprised and tell me that they were sorry, but they thought it was a wig. I would say to them even if it was a wig they had no right to pull it at all. They would say they could not believe that it was real hair. I would say to them that is a load of rubbish, lots of people have thick hair like me. It became quite a worry of who was going to pull my hair next, even when I went on a shopping trip with a lot of the Dial a Ride passengers' bus and one of the women on the bus pulled my hair so hard that it hurt me. She honestly thought that my hair would come off, thinking it was a wig on my head. I asked her what in the world had she pulled my hair for, and she said she really thought it was a wig. I told her I could have her charged for assaulting me in that rude manner and she said she was sorry. I gave her such a good telling off. I made sure she did not do that to anyone else again. Just because she had on a wig herself, she thought I had on a wig as well.

I think there is a lot wrong with people wearing wigs, because the wearing of wigs only proves how a person has no confidence in themselves, or how they are trying to imitate who they are not. Some of the wigs look very nice, if I must say, but these wigs are dangerous and full of chemicals. Besides, putting on a wig is not really safe because a person wearing a wig can accidently set themselves on fire. I myself would never dream of pulling off anybody's wig. I think that would be very rude. I could understand the wearing of wigs, especially if you the lazy type of person, all those who wear wigs only have to put on a wig and take it off as it suits them but all that hotness and smells coming from the head, how terrible it must be; all in the name of beauty. I have to go to the hairdressers very soon because my birthday is coming up and my friends are coming to take me out. Believe me, it will cost me quite a lot of money, but I am always proud of my hair because it is so thick. I will always be proud of my hair. I suppose you get it from your parents.

I had a call from a gentleman who asked me if he could book an appointment with me. We arranged one and he told me he had this dreadful disease called motor neurone disease. I said to him I was very sorry I could not treat him for that disease once a week. I would have to treat him every day because his disease is too serious to be treated once a week. It has to be done very often otherwise it will never get better. He told me that he could not come every day; he did not seem to think it was serious enough. I was quite astonished. I asked him if he had been to the doctor and he said he had. I asked him, "Didn't the doctor tell you this disease you had was very serious?" He said that the doctor did tell him that. I just wondered what he really expected me to do. He then said to me, "Do you mean you will not treat me?" I said to him, "Of course I will, but it won't be much good healing only for once a week". I told him it would be hopeless, but he did not seem to understand.

I felt very sorry for him but really there was nothing I could do. He certainly needs me treating him daily. He still would not take my advice seriously and he insisted on coming for healing once a week, but as time went on he stopped coming for his healing sessions because he became too ill to attend as his illness has deteriorated and I knew as soon as he stopped coming for his healing sessions that he would be too sick to come again. If he didn't want to help himself then there was little I could do. His wife was with him when I asked her if she understood, she said she did. I had two people who both had Parkinson's disease I told them the same thing; that they should come more often for healing, but they were both too proud. All because of money. I told them not to worry about money until after they become better in health, but they would not hear any of it. I told them both that to just contribute a very small donation; if they didn't have that, there is nothing to worry about, just to forget it, as health comes first. That is what matters most of all. I cannot understand why people do not say their prayers more often. I always get a comfort from saying my prayers. I seem to know that Jesus did a lot of healing and praying.

I am very concerned about anybody getting cancer because it is so painful, especially for children. I remember when a young lad was being treated by me in 1988 and his adopted mother took him home. She told me a Macmillan nurse was waiting for him who was very cross. She said to his mother, "I have been waiting for you for quite a long time. Where have you been?" His mother said they had just come from the healer. The Macmillan nurse said she should not be going to a healer, so the mother asked why. Would she rather he died? By this time she didn't dream there was a healer out there who could heal cancer. If she did she wasn't very keen because the Macmillan nurses I have met along the way, in patients' houses, do not like me at all, just like the doctors and nurses and ministers in the church don't like me. They feel as if I am in competition with them, because I heal with my natural hands rather than with chemicals and butchering and amputating people's bits to cure a disease as they do. All because I can heal serious diseases. I would have thought these medical people would be very glad to meet me, instead of giving me the cold shoulder. They should realise that my source of power all comes from the Holy One, Jesus Christ. It is not very often you get someone like me whom Jesus Christ has chosen to work on his behalf. I think people should rejoice instead of complaining. What is wrong with these people? I am sure if they had cancer, they would be very glad to go to someone who could heal them. I know I would visit a healer if I had cancer. I would be over the moon with excitement. I would pray and thank the Lord. Maybe now I am writing this book, people will have a better awareness of me and the gift of my healing hands.

I went to Paris on a one-day ticket but going to further places was very tricky. I certainly did not want to be questioned on my birth certificate because I really did not know how it would turn out. I did not want to risk being embarrassed. If the woman who gave birth to me had not made such a mess of the early years of my life, then things would have been very different. I wondered if things had been different whether Jesus Christ would have still given me this marvellous gift to heal people. Somehow, I think Jesus would have given me the same gift because of my wonderful Mother Connie who brought me up in a special way. She was a dedicated mother who cared for me so much and raised me specially and dedicated herself that I should be brought up in a similar way to her. I loved it all and I still miss her very much. I would not have known Mother Connie if things had been different. So, you see, things would not have been the same. God helps everyone who help themselves, so my marvellous mother did just that.

I cannot understand how these people who live in the same block of flats as myself hate the birds so much. They even teach their children to hate the birds and they often stone the birds. Now I ask you what in the world can birds do to harm anyone? According to what my Mother Connie used to tell me, the birds I fed used to carry messages for our country to another country to keep us all safe, especially during war times. What is wrong with these people? Don't they know by now that English people like birds and don't ill-treat them? These sorts of people seem to treat birds cruelly; when I am feeding them, they throw things at them but I tell them to stop. Thank goodness someone has read the lease and told them that they must not use the grass outside my flat to play games. So at least for a time I got a bit of peace, and so also did the birds and they can enjoy the feeding.

The football had stopped as well as the throwing of branches at my window, but all of that did not last long! Some of these youths are so rude, but how did this start? The woman that lives at No. 10 directly beside my flat, is using her flat for a business that is definitely illegal. I say this because she uses her flat to run a sort of centre that looks after Jewish youths. They play football in my front garden and when I ask them to stop, they swear at me and abuse me, shouting at me to get out and move out. As this goes on, my neighbour does nothing to stop them, even when they broke the glass on my window she did nothing about it. I have never in all my life met such rude small boys and girls who don't seem to worry about anything – and some of the older children as well. When I open my window they are kicking the ball right near my face. Then we have to put up with the communal passage; they pile the passage up with prams, scooters, cases and bicycles and they know what they are doing but it does not seem to bother them at all. The fire service has already told them that it is a fire hazard, but they do not even take any notice of the advice from the fire services. The only thing that stopped them was when the fireman told the man who managed the flats that the passage should be left clear from now on. Of course, the chap that manages the building, Mr Marcus King wouldn't like to lose his job or to get into trouble; so he kept it clear.

Marcus King painted every flat in the building twice but painted mine once. He asked us all to stop paying insurance towards the property, and all the money we had paid towards insurance for the building was never refunded. Marcus King pocketed the money. Thank goodness he did not stay long running our flats. Marcus King owes me thousands of pounds to this day. That is just to show you what type of people they are; careless where money is concerned and instead of sending the money he owed me to my solicitor, he sent it to Brickman Yale and they didn't return it to me either. They stole the money. The flat got a new owner, a millionaire Jewish businessman. Brickman Yale claimed that the money owed me by them was given to this businessman, but I never saw this money at all. These people are quite appalling, how I kept my cool I will never know. Especially when one of the chaps who lives in the flats here told me the landlord of the flats had changed everybody's windows but mine. He was the main one trying to get me out of my flat. My solicitor had already told him that my window ledges needed repairing, but he completely ignored my solicitor and still kept a lot of my money, pretending I owed him. This millionaire in charge of my block of flats prey on other vulnerable people as well as myself. I got the worst of it because, this millionaire Jewish man wanted me out of my flat, so that he could give my flat to his daughter. She lives in No. 3 above my flat. This millionaire was only interested in how to squeeze as much money as he could get from me and anyone else that falls for his hocus pocus. As I mentioned before, he bought himself a Jaguar car. He was a very greedy man and he could not care less where he got his money from. I always wonder whether these types of people sleep in their beds at night. It was a good job I had a solicitor, otherwise he would have found some way to get me out. I do not really know how, but devious men like him are always ready to make up some story to suit themselves. He seemed to have lumbered himself with five very long boards. It seems he had bought them to board my flat up, so I could not get inside. These types of people never seem to stop doing what they do for their own greed. Of course my solicitor put a stop to that, and for now things are solved in spite of Marcus King doing everything he could that wasn't right (including as I mentioned hiring a hit man) and giving everybody but me new windows and having the cheek to steal a lot of money from me. I got sick and tired of his behaviour. Though I have mentioned him before, I suppose I will still be mentioning him again.

That is to show you how determined Marcus King was to get rid of me, but he didn't know God is much stronger than he is, and I walk with God all the time and trust in him always. I always feel that when you trust in God you never go wrong. I know that things will go wrong sometimes, but remember God helps those who help themselves. As a matter of fact, there is something called continue, and to continue means to cherish; when you cherish something you continue in it but if you don't cherish something then you don't continue in it. Again, listen – to accept is easy but to continue is difficult, and I am a person that cherishes the power of God and I am grateful for my healing hands, and as I have accepted my gift from The Creator it is now up to me to continue the mission on my journey of life without fear and to never run from difficulties and life's challenges, but to tackle them and defeat them using quality wisdom.

What a business getting a cleaner is today. The first one was a lovely girl called Andrea. When she and her partner went on holiday, I hired a cleaner for the day. I told the cleaner not to move anything on a particular side of the table in the kitchen. She moved everything that I told her not to move, she made such a mess on the side because she was stealing tins of fish. It took me hours to put everything right and she did not clean anywhere. She was too busy trying to get as many tins of fish as she could into her bag. When her time was up I asked her what was in the other bag. She was only given one bag for all the rubbish to dump in the bin. She told me she had split the black bag into two, but of course the split bag is where she had all the tins of fish she had stolen from my safe! Thank goodness she was only there for one day. She asked me if I wanted a cleaner. I told I did not. My usual cleaner was on holiday, so she was only needed for that one day.

I told the cleaning company not to send that woman again. These cleaning companies seem to hire anybody; even professional thieves. Why don't they send them to places where they have nothing to steal? I have another cleaner story. We shall call her Sue. Now the first day she came to do her job at my premises she wanted more money from me. I did not give it to her. Then she wanted to come an hour earlier than what we had arranged. I asked her why she did not arrange that before she came. When she realised I was not going to put up with her rules she changed her mind. I reminded her I was paying her for her labour, and not her paying me for my time. Anybody would think that these cleaners do the hiring. I do not know what we have to put up with these days. It is unbelievable. You just have to have your wits about you all the time.

If it was not that I had God in my life I do not know where I would be! I put my whole trust in Jesus Christ, and it is from Jesus Christ that I get my whole strength from. I ask the Lord to stay by my side and never leave me, and I know for sure I have a guardian angel with me all the time. I am never alone; even people who have come for healing have told me they have seen someone with me. I must say I have never seen these guardian angels but I have felt their presence and heard their voices. Though some people will not believe that I even saw Jesus Christ's face in 1983, and when I tell people that I have healing hands they always seem to be in doubt, but not all of them. You are going to read about my healing hands as I put some of my experiences in a book. Why would I lie about such a wonderful gift? Why is it I can heal cancer, arthritis and other diseases? Surely you can only get that from the Son of God, the saviour of the world. But you have people who do not like me. I think that is why God made me so strong and very outspoken, so that I can carry the burden all by myself. I have been carrying these burdens and dealing with all obstacles in my way.

The woman who has taken over the flat, as well as the woman putting the dangerous chemicals around my flat are still continuing with these criminal activities. They both think it is funny, but I do not. This is what I have to put up with – years and years of being harassed. It is terrible and rather sad that you do not know who to turn to for help. Even with being blessed with a special gift you find the people near to you are not the people you would like to approach. This is what is the most frightening. I am very sorry if I repeat myself a lot, but remember this is my life and I feel I should be able to repeat myself as many times as I want. Believe me, some things you never forget.

You feel if you do not repeat them people will forget them, so towards the end of my book on my life I will be repeating things all the time. Sorry.

At the moment, I am happy to tell you on 4 October 2015 these people who live above me have gone on holiday. What a lovely peaceful and quiet time I am having!

When Mother Connie was not with me I always missed her. Everybody thought she was my real mother and she treated me better than the woman who gave birth to me. She always took me for walks, bought me very strong ankle boots. She looked after my legs and tried to improve them after what the woman who gave birth to me did to my legs. Without Mother Connie I do not know what I would have done, but God always looks after children who have been neglected by their parents. I just wish I could have visited Mother Connie and looked after her when she became ill. I was 16 years old at the time, but as I said before, the nuns wouldn't allow me to visit her because they wanted everything my mother had to go to them and nothing to me.

I was not worried about what I may have inherited, all I wanted was to see her once more before God took her to rest, but those nuns prevented me from seeing her and they pretend to be holy. I am very sorry I did not call the police, but to tell you the truth at the age of 16 I did not think of it. I suppose if I had thought of calling the police, the nuns would have hated me even more. When we are very young, things do not occur to us. I had nobody to turn to. I would not like to tell you how I felt very alone and sad and did not know where or who to turn to. I know it would have killed my mother. She would have worried about me, just as I worried about her throughout it all. What those nuns did is something I will never forget, and I hope it will never happen to another child because it ruined both our lives. I feel that when one passes away perhaps there is transition to another life. I will admit I do not know much about the other world or where you go, but I do believe there is another world after you die. I cannot really talk about it as I only talk about what I know and have experienced. I only feel that my mother knows all about these nuns and what they did to me and that surely she would be very sad about it all, and hopefully that she can see me all the time now, as I can't see her. I do know she is in Heaven, wherever Heaven is. I wish it to be a place of total peace.

I had a phone call from a gentleman who asked if I could help him with a very bad pain that he had in his knee. I said to him I could help him. I asked him if he had seen his doctor and he told me he had. He had been sent for an x-ray and then they had told him it was arthritis. They offered him an operation on his knee but he said he would not want one. He had heard what I had done for a woman who was about to have an operation. He told me someone told her about me and that I had healed her two knees, but it had taken some time – that is why he came to me.

I told him I would give him two hours a week of healing sessions and he said that was fine. He would prefer that to an operation. So, I started on his knee. He was very tall and very interesting. He asked me if any of the doctors had met me. I told him a lot of them had heard about me but I had not met any one of them except one that had told me it didn't seem fair that God had given me such a powerful gift when doctors have to study for years to treat people. I told him we all have gifts and his gift is to be a doctor, but he still insisted that it was not fair. I told the gentleman that this patient I was treating had something wrong with her stomach. The doctor had given her three operations at different times, but the problem kept coming back. She then heard about me and came to me for treatment. She got better and went and told the doctor who had been treating her. Her doctor asked her if she could bring me with her so he can look at my head and chest. I told her he wouldn't find anything because that is how the Lord works. What is more, it is my hands that heal and not my head or my chest. The gentleman thought it was strange for a doctor to ask a patient such a strange question. Of course, I would not dream of going to see the doctor. I know the doctors have heard of healers before, but there are some healers who are stronger than others. As I told the gentleman, it is a pity that natural healers like myself and educated doctors could not join together to help each other. He said he did not think that would ever happen. He said that doctors do not like anybody being able to do anything better than they can. That is a shame, but it is the truth.

I told the gentleman that Prince Charles once said on the television he would like to meet anyone who could heal cancer. I told him that I had written three times to Prince Charles to tell him about my gift, that I had the proof I could heal cancer. He would just have to write to the church at Stoke Newington; there he would find some people who will always remember 1984. I also said to him that if I ever get ill and had to go into hospital, I would not breathe a word that I was a healer due to all the experience I have had with patients who have visited hospitals. Fortunately, a lot of people I healed who had cancer have visited me at my home. They told me themselves they prefer my method of healing, and how comfortable and relaxed they feel after being healed with my hands. I have healed arthritis as well, and yet the doctors tell their patients that nobody can heal arthritis, so can you imagine what they would do if they found out I could heal it. That is why, I told the gentleman, I have a lot of enemies. The gentleman was quite appalled and he said it is better if I keep away from them all. I quite understood what he meant. He said I need a bodyguard, and he could not be more accurate because that is what I need to do in the very near future. He himself was a very interesting person and he said he could listen to me talk about all the people I have healed. He said, "You tell me I am interesting, but I feel that there is no one as interesting as you", and he said, "You don't mention people's names, only first names". I told him people who come to me for healing are very private. I told him some people do not want anyone to know they have been ill. So he said to me, "But what if they have to go to hospital, wouldn't people know then? That is why they like somewhere very private to go to, very comfortable", and he said, "To tell you the truth I feel very private coming here, so I understand how they all feel. We only have to thank you, Dorothy; it is because you are so kind and patient". I told him it was very nice of him to say so.

I feel as if I am appreciated much more. I told him how I healed a woman who had multiple sclerosis (such a terrible disease). She told me that 12 people came to see her, all with the same disease, to enquire how she got better. When I said to her that I hoped she told them about me, she said, "Oh, I didn't tell any one of them at all of whom I was healed by, as none of them were my friends". I told her that was a terrible thing, not telling any one of them about me, because it would have been helpful for them to receive help just as she had, rather than for her to only think of herself and not consider other people. I said to her, "You chain smoke; who do think is going to help you when you get ill?" She looked at me as if she could not care less. I said to her, "Do you remember when I asked you how your mother-in-law was? You told me she was getting on very well. I heard sometime after that she was getting worse. Don't you ever call on me again". My friend said that woman didn't sound very nice. I said to him she was full of herself. I told him even before I saw the holy vision, I would always tell people of anything I found out that was good. As a matter of fact, I was always like that.

Since I became a healer I was surprised to find out people deliberately didn't tell other people of who or where or how they got healed. Once this sort of patient gets healed they never bother to spread the news. Or could it be that perhaps these patients are concerned about my safety? I guess it's about who to trust. I said I know some of them were worried about my safety. I certainly appreciate that, because these days you don't know who you are dealing with, neither do you know who to trust, even in nature – considering that everything is in nature, yet nature plays tricks on what itself created and we all as human beings are children of nature, fed and nourished by nature.

I was very glad when the gentleman told me his knee was getting very much better. He said he knew of a lot of people who have arthritis, some of them he trusts, but they do not believe anyone can heal arthritis because the doctor told them so. He really could not be bothered to argue with them. I said to him I know what he meant. I said, "Many people I know tell me that no one can heal arthritis. As a matter of fact doctors tell them that no one can heal arthritis. So, can you imagine when I do write a book, what in the world are they going to say when they hear that someone can heal arthritis?" My friend said to me to be very careful. I told him I would and not to worry. I told him I pray about it all the time. I have a guardian angel and often things come to me. My friend said to me, "I often worry about you, even when you are healing me; now that is why I have not got you a patient yet. As I told you those people I know only believe that the doctors are the only ones who can perform any sort of healing on people with arthritis, and truly, I feel very sorry for them that they are going to remain crippled, but there is nothing you or me can do to change their views. I know for sure if I ever suffer from anything else, even if I go abroad, I know where to come to when I want help".

He was a very nice man he said he did not know how to thank me. He said, "When you have pain and you think you are going to suffer for the rest of your life, and you hear about someone who can get rid of that pain you can hardly believe it when it happens. You just do not know how to say thank you because he said it is a miracle. You want to tell other people, but you are afraid of the people who you tell because some of them are full of sarcastic remarks or they won't believe what's been told. Then again you have to trust the person anyway, before you tell them anything because you are on your own and I would be worried for you just in case the individual has psychotic tendencies". I told him not to worry because I will not be healing anyone, unless I have an assistant with me. I told him I think that would be the best thing. He agreed and asked me never to go back on my word. I promised him that I would not. He said that made him feel much better because these days you can hardly trust anyone. He added, "Like you said, Dorothy, even the doctors, the nurses or the church ministers don't like you, so you have to be very careful".

The gentleman asked me what the minister said when I healed my friend that had cancer. I told him he was not very pleased, and would you believe, that he came to see me, and I had a patient with me. When I went out to make a cup of tea for the both of them, the patient told me while I was gone he told her that I would not be able to heal her. When he left, the patient said to me, "What a horrid man, he knows you have very powerful hands. He had the cheek to tell me you wouldn't be able to heal me". I said to her, "Some of the ministers are very jealous; they would love to have my power in their hands and because they haven't got such power as I do have, they say things that are not nice about me which is all made up and full of lies". She said to me she would not stay at that church while he is there. She then told the church minister that he had no right to say such a horrid things about me as and he knew I had healed my friend who was dying of cancer. How could he say such dreadful things like that? She told me she gave him a good telling off. I said to her she should not take any notice of people like him. I told her some people you just have to ignore; they do not know any better. My friend said to me, "That is just to show you, it was a good job you had a patient with you, and this guy is supposed to be a church minister and still he is full of envy, very abrupt, always wanting to be on top of everyone else as if to say he knows it all. How obnoxious he is". I can do things he cannot. I told the church minister never to visit me again because he upset people all the time. I do not want my patients becoming upset when they visit me. When it is time for them to leave, I want them to feel very contented and happy, looking forward to coming again. I told my friend I remember this same minister when they were talking about me healing Brenda who had cancer all over her body. He kept saying that he uses oil to heal and when one of the curates asked him if he had ever healed anyone, he didn't answer. He was quite annoyed because he did not know what to say. He gave me such a look, but I did not say anything. My friend said to me, "You did the right thing. Silence is much better when you have to deal with these types of people. You are going to have to deal with people like him all the time, but you are a very strong

Chapter Eleven

woman. I can see that in your healing hands and how you deal with most of your patients. Keep it up, your faith is very strong. You tell me you always feel you are not alone; you feel someone is always with you all the time and that should make you stronger. That is why I don't tell anyone about you unless I am certain of who they are". I told him not to worry. I am not taking in anyone else to heal unless there is an assistant with me.

I was telling a friend how I always make sure to lock my lounge window before I go to bed. I check it and double check it again so as to be sure. I remember when we had snow a few years ago. I opened my window and could see big footsteps coming towards my bedroom and going towards the lounge and towards my kitchen. Thieves never seem to stop; they are always on the go. You always have to be ready for anything. My friend was telling me he felt that I was safer since I am becoming more organised and he was getting better. He did not know if he would ever see me again because he was migrating to America, but he told me if he had not been healed, he would not know whether he would be going overseas. He said it is thanks to me that a change of life would be all he needed, as he had a lot of his family in America. They were thrilled that he is now completely better. He also said he wished I would come to America. They would certainly appreciate me there, much more than in Britain.

I had to explain to him about my birth certificate stating that I was English white, but my hue is brown. I was told the American authorities would be very suspicious of my status. He was very upset that I had this terrible problem over my head, but he quite understood. He thought that if that happened to him, he would feel the same because English people are white. He said he had never heard of an English person being brown. I said to him the woman who gave birth to me really messed things up for me. I can only thank her for giving birth to me, but as a mother she doesn't exist in my life. It was fortunate for me that I was adopted when I was quite young. By this time my birth certificate had already been registered, but I had a wonderful life with my adopted mother. She never married and her father was a priest in the Anglican church. Although the woman who gave birth to me was Jewish, my adopted mother was just the opposite, a dedicated Christian. She had three sisters who also never married and sadly they all passed away. She was the only one left. We had a beautiful chapel where we lived, and we had prayers every morning. It was a place where we all felt safe and very close to the Lord. I was a very small child when I first went to live with my mother, so all that she taught me stayed with me all times, even up until now. I do not suppose I was ever as good as she was. I could honestly say I never found anything bad about her. Everything she did was always good, even when we travelled by bus and the bus pulled off before we could catch it, yet she never got angry. My adopted mother fell once as a result of trying to catch the bus. I was a very young teenager at the time, and I was furious, but my mother remained very cool and calm. I called the man stupid and that he should have got the sack, but my mother told me to pray and thank God that she was all right. Of course, I would have done that anyway, but sometimes her being so good quite surprised me, given that there are so much wicked things going on in the world.

I was always very careful over anything, even when a man had put five new pennies on the window ledge and expected me to go out and collect it. I went straight to tell my mother. I could see the man peeping around the corner and my mother told me he wanted to cut all my lovely hair off. As I was just a small child then, I thought to myself what a strange thing for anyone to want to do. Of course, later on I realised if I had gone out I would not be alive today. I am not daft. I knew right away that there was something very fishy and what my mother told me made some sort of sense. I did not mention this to my mother, but I realised he was some nasty man that no child should go near.

When my friend had completely recovered after the healing sessions he went off to America and he telephoned me twice. I thought that was very nice of him and he said to me, "Believe me, I have met no one I could tell about your wonderful healing, because to tell you the truth I was frightened. They didn't seem the type of people I could trust". Now I realised why so many people never told anyone, they just could not trust them and as they were aware that I was on my own they had to think of my safety. That was the main reason as well. I think really and truly they are just worried for me and I can understand why of course; that is why when I start healing again, I will always have an assistant with me. That will make me feel a lot safer and I will only open my door to people who have already made appointments whom I know for sure are ill, although I know there are a lot of people all over the world who need help with cancer.

Believe me, I will treat as many people as I can because this is what the Lord has blessed me with; the gift to do good with such a powerful hands and I always wonder if there are many other healers who can heal cancer. If so, why don't they make it known to the public? Many more people could be healed, but people must remember that it is only me. I am writing a book about my life because I want it to be known that I am a natural healer. You see, there may be lots of other people who can do the same as I can and that have been blessed by God with a gift, just like I am blessed by the Almighty. I am aware that it is difficult for some healers to let people know what they can do because they have so many enemies, like myself. I am not very well known yet, but I have the church to verify my healing of cancer. Adrian King (Brenda's husband), who now lives in Birmingham can also verify this. I healed him of cancer. Though I have healed quite a lot of people with the same diseases, wouldn't it be wonderful if we found out that a lot of healers who could heal cancer? I am sure a lot of people would be happy also because being healed with healing hands is better than having pieces of your body chopped off. Besides, it is painless healing people the natural way.

I met a woman who told me she could heal, and she gave me a big pinch which quite hurt. I told her never to touch me like that again. She said to me that I was a stronger healer than she was and honestly, I could not make head or tail of what she was talking about. She told me that she knew five more healers beside herself. I asked if she had ever tried to heal herself or been to one of the five healers that she knew. She said they were not strong enough. I asked her if they had healing hands and she said none of them did. Well I couldn't understand how she could heal without having healing hands. There must be a lot of healers out there with healing hands but I haven't met any yet. Maybe with this book about my life they will discover what powers they have.

I had a call from a woman who had cancer in her breast, and she asked me if she could visit. She told me that someone in Hertfordshire had told her about me. I asked her if she had been to see her doctor she said she had. He had sent her to have an x-ray and that it was confirmed that she had cancer. She said that she certainly would very much appreciate having treatment from me rather than having the treatment they have on the NHS. I told her I would give her three hours a week of healing sessions; that is what I normally give to cancer patients. She said that would just suit her very well. We started immediately. She told me at first she didn't believe it because she had never heard of anyone giving cancer treatment, but the gentleman who told her said she had better believe it because I had healed quite a few people. He told her I had healed a lady at the Stoke Newington St Mary's Parish Church in 1984 who had cancer all over her body. She was dying and I healed her completely. She told me she was very grateful that I had started giving her treatments. She said to me that these days there are few people like me who have such powerful hands. She asked, "If you don't mind Dorothy, could we both think of something to make people aware?" I said to her, "I will, because I am going to write a book about my experiences and journey in life. My goal and purpose right now is to get my book published so that my story will spread around the world and those who read it and are in need of healing will know where to find me; because that is what Jesus Christ gave me the gift to do". The lady agreed. I have been thinking about this for a long time, but I told her I have never written a book before and I know it will take me some time to learn how to use a laptop. I know how to use the typewriter very well, but it will take me some time to be quick on the laptop. If I had been able to go to America that would have been very much different. I said to her, "Where there is a will, there is a way". I suppose it needs more patience and sometimes we all run out of patience. I told her not to worry. I know for sure I will find a way, and I know what that will is – I will write a book about my life and then I can write about the people I have healed, all the people who have come to me for healing. Of course, I do not mention full names only first names because I will always respect their right to privacy.

The lady said to me, "I hope I am around when you write the book. I know it will be very interesting, but I may not live in London so I will have to keep an eye on any new books published because I certainly would not want to miss it. I do not really go out to buy books, but I will certainly keep a look out for your book. I know it will take a long time to write a book, especially as you have never written one before". I told her when I worked in the Civil Service the keepers sometimes would ask me if I would type a book for them, and I know it is a lot of typing; it seemed to go on forever. I will be glad when the book is finished. My friend who I was healing at that time was getting so much better. She said to me, "What in the world would I have done if I hadn't met you, because cancer is such a dreadful illness? People are always talking about the disease and to think you can heal it, few people know that, what a shame. It was a pity that Diane Abbott when she first got into power and you told her you could save lives and heal pain; she ran you out of her office. She should be ashamed of herself. Being an MP, she should have no excuse taking the details of those healed by you, and verify it herself so as to match your claims". I said that she is quite right.

My friend by this time was quite better and she said to me, "Well Dorothy, I don't know how to thank you. What surprises me is that you do not make any money out of this wonderful gift you have. That is to show you, I do not know if I will ever see the chap who told me about you. I must try my best to see if I can find his address or his phone number to thank him. I know he was very grateful, and he told me, I was the only person he has told because he knows me very well. He said to me I would not be telling anyone else, but he warned me to be very careful who I told, and I have not. I would not tell anybody else, but all I want is that your safety is assured".

I did tell her when I start to heal on a large scale again, I will make sure I have someone with me, and she told me never ever to forget to do so. I told her I would not and that she must not worry anymore. She said to me it is such a shame the amount of people I could have saved, but because people who are all for themselves, few people know about me. I said to her that will all be solved when the book is written, though it may be a very long time. I will try to ensure that it will not take too long. I realise that will be the only way that people will get to understand me, then I can heal a lot more people. Believe me, every day on the television you hear about people who have cancer, and want help and as a matter of fact people all over the world want and need help. Of course, I can't heal everybody, but certainly will heal as many as I can. I suppose most people know of someone who is ill and suffering from pain, and maybe some who are not in this world today. That is why I have to write this book – to let people know just what Jesus Christ has blessed me with. Otherwise people would not believe me. Let's face it there are not many people who can heal cancer. If and when people know that they have an opportunity to get better and know where to go, I do know without a doubt, that I will have a lot of people healed. I do hope my book gets to the United States of America and beyond because a lot of people around the world, especially there, would be very happy to get some help and be willing to travel to England to get healed. You don't hear of many healers who can heal cancer and I think it is about time that people realised the Lord Jesus Christ is the power giver and the true saviour of the whole world, and we should all know this and praise his name. I sometimes wish I could preach the word of God all over the world, but my calling and mission in this physical realm is healing; that is what God has blessed me with and that is what I will be doing for the rest of my life. I look forward to healing as many people as I can.

I have just been trying to help a young lady who was in terrible pain and has been that way for quite some time. Neither she nor the doctors know what is causing the pain. I do not know what it is, but I put my hands on her; the hands bring out what the problem is. Even when I have not got a clue of what the problem is, I still heal people. Some patients put most of their trust in doctors and when the doctors disappoint them then they run looking for me to get healed. I tell them of course they can come to me, but I do warn them that it will not get better right away – it always gets worse before it gets better. I tell them depending on what it is I will give them either one or two hours a week of healing sessions but If I feel the illness is so bad that it needs treatment every day, I will then tell them that it wouldn't be possible for me to treat the illness because other people are on the waiting list, and if I delay their treatments then their symptoms will worsen. I only wish I could meet someone who has healing powers like me. We would be able to heal so many people as partners, but even on my own, I hope to heal a lot of people. I will always have an assistant with me while I am healing, for my own safety.

My neighbours do not like me feeding the birds, but I have always loved the birds and horses. I grew up with loving animals. Mother Connie always made sure I visited the zoo very often when I was small. I remember when Mother Connie used to give me a banana and put it in my hand and tell me to give it to the elephant; I thought that was lovely. I am so glad to see so many different people in England looking after animals.

In my healing I have only healed one dog. One of my friends, Myrtle, brought the dog to me and asked me if I could heal it. I used to give it healing sessions in their car. The dog had cancer. It was a very big dog, and it seemed to know what I was doing to it was good. I always wished I could heal dogs with arthritis because it is such a painful thing to have; but of course, some of them would have to have their faces covered for protection to the person who is healing them. I gave the dog three sessions of healing with two hours each. The dog healed and I asked the owner if she had told the vet. She said that she had not as she knew that the vet would not like what she had done. The vet, however, had confirmed that the dog was cancer free and although he could not explain how the dog had been healed, he seemed to think it was "one of those things" and that he was responsible for the dog's recovery.

I wonder if I have heard this information correctly – that you can take a person to court if they make too much noise which stops you from sleeping. I heard that it is called The Noise Act. I hope that someone will tell me of it when they read my autobiography. I do not know if any of you have heard a chair being pulled along, scraping across a floor without a carpet. It is simply awful, and this goes on every day upstairs in my block of flats. It never stops. I couldn't understand how this young boy's mother just listened and did nothing; and if he wasn't dragging the chairs, he was running and stamping his feet all over the place. The noise never stops. He is certainly well out of control. This goes on from morning until night. His mother is very irresponsible; nothing seems to bother her. I suppose running a laundry and a factory, which are both illegal, keep her too busy to be bothered. I had a number of items in storage in the communal storage area on the ground floor, they have all been damaged and ruined due to the detergent chemicals used in the laundry. They were all in four large plastic bags: a duvet, clothes, an expensive carpet and the last one full of lovely handbags. All had to be disposed of. I am hoping to get some compensation for the cost of damage and replacing these items.

I think it is a shame that ministers in the church like to talk about politics. They should stick to the church and get more people in. Instead, some of them like to take people for granted and leave them destitute. It is disgraceful; no wonder the churches are empty nowadays. I have heard quite a lot of people telling me how the churches like to take liberties. I heard on the television that some of the bishops stated that the Prime Minister is not giving enough food to children. What is wrong with these politicians? Don't they know that nobody should starve in England? Why do you think so many people like to come to Britain? They know it is so easy to get jobs and free food. Some people of course, you can never satisfy. I think Britain does very well when helping people.

The library never seems to be open when you need it to be. I went there once not long ago, and it was closed. Even when you telephone there is no one there to answer. So, I would like to know in which days the libraries are open. It seems as if the council are trying very hard to close them. I wonder what they will be closing down next. It is just like our passage in the flats. The Fire Department says that the passage should be left perfectly clear because of the amount of people living here but they could not care less. The passage is certainly in a real mess. Sometimes when I come home from shopping, even my door is blocked.

I always wonder if we all pay a lot in council tax. I often wonder when I am healing if any of my patients pay a high amount of council tax. I remember asking just one of them, she said to me, "I just pay rent, so I don't pay council tax". She lived in a council property, and it left me thinking...

The lady had cancer so I didn't like to question her too much as she already had enough to cope with, but as she said to me, "Dorothy I have never heard of anyone else being able to heal cancer". I said to her, "You just haven't heard of anyone yet, but I'm sure there must be someone else who can heal cancer". She asked me if I knew anyone else who could heal cancer, and I replied I have not heard of anyone, but I don't go out very often and meet many people. She knows I can heal lots of diseases. I tell her that I know it is a God-given gift. I had to tell her exactly how I came to know I could heal.

It was because I saw the face of Jesus Christ in a vision in 1983, and Jesus told me I had healing hands. I told her the other day I was cooking. I burned my arm very badly and all I did was just to sit down and put my hand where

I had burnt it and left my hand there until I could not feel the stinging anymore. Then I knew it had completely gone. I also remember being stung by a big black bee that was on my windowsill, and again I just sat down and put my hand on the sting until I couldn't feel the sting anymore. I once got a splinter right down my nail as I was getting ready for bed; it was very painful. I just held my thumb and when I woke up in the morning the splinter had completely disappeared. I thought how fortunate I was that Jesus Christ had blessed me with such a powerful gift. There was another time when I was at the office when somebody closed the door right on my arm which gave me one big bruise. The bruise got very big by the time I got home. I just put my other hand on it and held it tight until the bruise disappeared. I did not tell anyone because they would not have believed me. I once sprained my ankle, so I sat down and held it for about an hour. No one would ever know that I had sprained my ankle. I completely healed it. I have always thought the whole world should know of this power given to me by Jesus Christ, and he has certainly blessed me after my terrible early childhood. What a way to have been handled by the woman who gave birth to me.

I was very blessed to have been adopted by a Christian lady who loved and cared for me. I can honestly say I have never met a lady like her before, with all her kindness and very high qualities, including patience and a most adorable nature. I never tired of being with her and always wanted more of her company. I thought I was very blessed to have been given the honour to have had her for my mother. Never a day goes by that I do not think about her and how she raised me to be polite; never to swear and always to be caring to people. If I saw people limping or that they had something wrong with them, I was taught never to laugh at them and always try to be kind. Though where I live it is very hard to even think about being kind to someone who is trying to kill you or cause you harm.

It reminds me of a gentleman called Edward who came here for healing and he saw people bringing in factory equipment. He said to me, "What in the world is that rubbish they are bringing into your passage?" When I told him, he could not believe it. He said, "Doesn't anyone try to stop it?" I told him I was writing a book about my life and that I am putting it all down. He said to me, "I hope it doesn't take you long to write this book because I have never heard of anything like this before". I said neither had I. I told him these types of people seem to get away with everything. He asked me if they know who I am and what I can do. I told him they don't know anything and I don't tell them anything. He said maybe that is why I have come to live here; for a purpose to bring these types of people to justice. I thought to myself he may have a point there. I myself never thought of this but somehow it makes sense. They may have been getting away with this kind of thing for a very long time. It is about time someone brought them to justice. I said to him, "I think you may be right. I do not even think that the law knows what they have been getting away with. Let us start talking about you now. What is wrong?"

Edward said to me, "I was pretty overjoyed when someone told me about you. I certainly had never heard of a lady who could heal cancer. I was over the moon because the person who told me had cancer himself and had come to you and you got rid of it". I asked him if the man who told him about me had been to his doctor. He told me he hadn't, but he went to a private doctor to get an x-ray. They told him that all his cancer had gone.

I told Edward I could treat him also, and that it gets just a little more painful at first, then it starts to slowly get better, little by little. He said he did not mind, as long as he gets better and better. He did, and said he did not know how to thank me. He said, the money was another issue – why is it I am not a very rich woman? "With all those qualities that you have you should be very rich. You honestly need a manager or some sort of bodyguard. I do not think it would be wise for you to continue by yourself in this day and age. With the world the way it is you can't trust anyone today". I told him I intend to have an assistant when the book is written. I will always have someone with me. He had cancer in his stomach, and I told him the story of Brenda I had healed who had cancer in her stomach just like him. I told him how I hoped one day I can bring the doctors to justice for damaging her lung, causing her death. It did not matter how long it took.

Edward said to me, "I know, Dorothy, when people know what you can do, I am sure they will be brought to justice. I certainly will pray to God now, Dorothy, as you told me if it was not for Jesus Christ you would not have this wonderful gift. I know you are blessed. I will always pray to God and thank him". I said to him I felt very happy that he would not do such a foolish thing like Brenda did, though I still feel very sorry for her.

I felt that Brenda's eldest son was trying to please the doctors when he told me that he allowed the doctors to experiment on her. I told him he should be ashamed of himself, causing the death of his own mother, and he said to me he would not do that. I asked how was it that her other three sons and her daughter did not want her to have any experiment done, only him. Now he was trying to make an excuse. Well he is the only one who has to live with this dreadful decision he made for his mother. Edward said to me there must have been some reason why he allowed the doctors to do such a dreadful thing to his mother, and I told him I will never forget when I looked at her she was pleading with me to help her and I could see the pain in her eyes. When something like this happens, as I told my friend, you can only pray to God because he is the only person who can give you peace of mind. I could see the dreadful pain she was suffering. I told Edward I would never like to experience that ever again. He told me if ever anybody comes to you with the same complaint she and myself had, tell them what happened; that should put them off. I quite agreed with him. I will certainly warn them before I start anything at all. He said to me, "I am feeling very much better now but I know I have a little way to go yet". I said to him, "It is very remarkable how you know exactly when you are completely better, especially with cancer. Your whole body feels different; it feels much stronger and fitter all over".

Chapter Eleven

Edward was a very nice man and he said that he would never forget me. He used to tell me all sorts of things such as what happened to him when he was younger. He told me he did not know quite what to do. He thought he would love to be a journalist, travelling all around the world and seeing how other people live. He thought that would be very interesting. He told me he had been to quite a few places. He was quite shocked to see how some people lived, and never seemed to care about their health. He said to me he always thought it might have been something he ate while he was abroad that made him ill. He asked me what I thought it was. I did not think it was to do with anything he ate while he was abroad because a lot of people in England get stomach cancer. I told him I thought it was just one of those things, that nobody really knows how these things happen. I told him a lot of women have their breasts removed to avoid having cancer. I told him I thought cancer is one of the worst illnesses. There are other very bad diseases as well, and he said to me I am just very fortunate to have met you. He said to me, "When you do write your book, even if I am abroad and come across it, I will know right away that it is your life story and I will treasure it. I will be able to tell my grandchildren all about you. I know they will say that they would love to meet you". He said he would never stop telling them everything about me. He told me that I would always stick in his memory. I said I would love to meet his grandchildren too, but I told him at the moment he would have to get himself completely better and healed.

Then I told him he could dream as much as he wanted to, and he said I could not be more right.

Edward said to me, "You must have some disappointments when you advise people to do certain things and they don't take any notice". I said this is absolutely true. He said to me, "Why do you think the doctors wanted to experiment on her in the first place?" I said it was because she told them she could eat now, had no pain, and they wanted to know and understand why the cancer had gone. It was me who had taken out the cancer through my healing hands, they could not believe it and because of that, she had to lose her life. I think it is one of the most terrible things I have ever had to see. It was so upsetting. I cannot imagine how her family felt except for the eldest son who gave the doctors permission to experiment on her. When I spoke to him about it, he did not seem very concerned. My friend said to me, "I hope you don't have to experience anything like that again. You give people so much time". I said I will just have to warn all patients who come to me and tell them to be very careful.

Some people do not realise things until it is far too late. It is natural for some people to believe in the doctors, but at first, they mostly have to hear about me from other people that I have healed. That gives them more confidence to come to me. I did hope he had faith in me already and would not do anything foolish. Edward was getting better already and the doctor wouldn't have done that for him; I mean the healing of his cancer. Doctors just give you treatment, which is not very nice, but at the moment they have not got anything else. As I told my friend, I have treated a lot of people with cancer and they have been very grateful, though some people try to hide their illness. My friend said to me he thought that was silly because as he said, if anyone tried to hide their illness, how in the world would the rest of the world have found me?

Edward was glad to hear I am always going to have someone with me when I start healing again. I told him he would have nothing to worry about as he was getting completely better. I would certainly miss him; he was such good company, such a caring man. When you get patients like him you are bound to miss them. I wished him all my blessings and I told him I would pray for him all the time.

I hoped he would pray for me, and he said he certainly would and that he would never forget me.

Once upon a time, this was before I saw the vision of the Lord, I had a terrible paralysis right down my left side. I thought I was going to have a stroke. I did not tell the doctor for some reason. I did not think it would last long; at least I hoped it would not, but the thought of the outcome frightened me. It did pass away, but all the while I was praying to the Lord Jesus Christ and asking him to help me. It seemed very odd because when I went off to work one day and was standing at the bus stop, I walked towards the edge of the pavement looking for the bus, when I found myself walking almost into the road. I stopped myself right away and still kept praying and asking the Lord to help me.

The very next week I saw the vision of Jesus Christ telling me I had healing hands. If only you know how relieved I was. A little while after that I had a very bad pain in my chest. Of course, I knew that was a heart attack. I just kept both of my hands on my heart. I did not tell anyone because I knew then I could heal myself. I kept my hands on my chest for two hours. Quite a few years after that, my doctor sent me to have a heart test. I never told anyone about my heart attack, but after I had the test at Homerton Hospital the medical man told me my heart was very strong and that I was very lucky. I still never told anyone about my healing hands and how the Lord had blessed me. By this time, the only people who knew about me being able to heal cancer were the people at St Mary's Church, Stoke Newington. Of course, I had been healing quite a few people with all sorts of different diseases.

This is why I am determined to write a book about my life and the gift God gave me so that I can heal lots of people. I know there are so many people looking for help and thank goodness I have nearly come to the end of writing my book. I am very anxious now. I have someone who is proofreading all my thoughts and opinions of life, and my own personal life experience. Given the fact that I've written a book, perhaps I will be in need of a solicitor. When Marcus King took over the running of my estate, he and the people above my flat were trying to run me out of my flat. It was my solicitor who I turned to and he made sure that nobody could run me out of my own flat, though they were trying to do me harm. I never mentioned that part to my solicitor because I just didn't want to keep bothering my him, so I reported this to the police. I

Chapter Eleven

thought it would make sense to put all these experiences in my book.

I am so very anxious to get a makeover with the Scottish makeover man I saw on the television called John. I would employ him to make my flat into a comfortable flat to call my home and he has a way to fix chairs for healers, hairdressers, restaurants, and so on. I would like him to design a suitable healing chair. My intention in the near future is to make sure I will always have someone with me.

I heard through the grapevine that when you are a genuine healer you cannot heal yourself, though I do not believe it for one minute because up to now I get dreadful pain in different places and I'm able to heal myself. Illnesses that other people get and have to go to the doctor for, I do not, because I can heal myself. When I try to heal myself at night, I deliberately lay fully on the hand where my hip is. Because the body is so big, naturally the hand starts to hurt so I have to take my hand away and allow the other hand to heal it and it does. You see, I can still heal myself; it is just that a person's hip is in a very awkward position and the hand can't stand the pressure, so it is very good that both hands can heal. They are both very strong. I will say that my hip does not hurt all the time. As long as I can save lives and stop the pain of arthritis and other dreadful diseases then I think I am very privileged to be able to do all these things through the Lord Jesus Christ.

Remember I mentioned already that I had a heart attack and never told a single person, and I explained to you that my doctor sent me to get a heart test and that I passed the test (which did not take long time) with flying colours, all thanks to my hands. So you see, I can heal myself. It is such a pity that the hip is in such an awkward place, but I feel with a lot more help I will get it better.

I remember a very long time ago there was a man who claimed he could heal cancer. I saw him on the television. This man who could heal cancer looked very ill and the presenter of the show asked him what he thought now he could heal cancer, but not on himself. I always wondered what happened to him. This was of course a very long time ago. I did not know then I was capable of healing people, but then again, I had not seen the vision of Christ until 1983. It was then I was told I had healing hands.

I remember, also quite a long time ago, when we had a severe winter and a lot of snow. I was not very happy going down the steps because there were very dangerous and slippery. I took a few steps, and someone held me right back. I could see I would have gone headfirst and that would have been a terrible accident, but I realised that my guardian angel was right there to save me. I remember when I was going to the office, I slipped in the snow and a very kind gentleman came to rescue me. I thanked him very much. He asked me where I was going. I told him to the office which was right across the road, and he took my arm and walked me straight to my office. I thanked him and told him it was very kind of him to take the trouble to guide me safely across the road. He told me it was a pleasure. I thought to myself there are still a lot of nice people around, and that very same day when I was going home in the afternoon, I was carrying

Chapter Eleven

a couple of shopping bags, and as I was crossing the road a big red bus came very close towards me. I dropped one of the bags and my shopping went all over the ground. It seemed the bus driver deliberately came too close to me. Two gentlemen at the side of the road ran to help me pick up my groceries and shouted at the driver. As he left, a policeman saw what was happening and stopped him. I suppose he gave him a good telling off and the two gentlemen said they didn't think he would do that in a hurry again, and they thought he was showing off. They asked me if I was all right. I told them I was, and thanked both of them for helping me off the ground and retrieving all my groceries. Now these were gentlemen just like the one who picked me up when I slipped on the snow. So you see, there are a lot of nice people still in this world. I was very fortunate to meet them, especially under those circumstances. I remember also when I got lost once and a gentleman gave me a lift in his car. He took me straight to my door. I certainly was very thankful, and believe me, I had nothing to worry about. I always think that my guardian angel is with me, even at home.

With regards to the woman who ran a laundry business and put the dangerous chemicals underneath my windows for 18 years, I always knew my guardian angel saved my life, because I know I have a lot of lives to save myself, so it is good that I have a guardian angel. I always know that there is someone with me and on my side at all times, fighting my battles at any given time.

I remember a man called Michael rang me and asked me if he could make an appointment with me. I asked him what was wrong with him and he told me he had very bad eyesight and if I could treat him for three hours a week. He said to me he thinks that within three weeks of treatment his eyes will get better. I started to treat him for the three hours he asked me for and after about two months he said that he could see much better and he thanked me very much. He told me that someone told him about me. He said he couldn't believe it because it's so difficult to hear of someone like me. When the person told him, he could hardly believe it and now he said he was thrilled to bits. He asked me how I would let other people know that I am a genuine healer. I told him about writing the book and he thought that was the best thing to do. I told him I always wanted to write a book about my life, even before I knew I was a healer. He wondered how I ever found out about being able to heal people. I told him about seeing a vision of Jesus Christ's face. I told him I know some people will not believe me, but I know what I saw. He said he believed it because with such powerful hands, I must have been told by someone powerful. He said it would be only by a special force like the Almighty Creator, otherwise I would not be so strong. He said he would look forward to reading my book when I told him I had healed a friend of mine who was dying of cancer. He said he had never heard of anyone who has ever healed someone who had cancer all over their body. He told me he was so pleased to meet me because his eyes felt wonderful after receiving his treatments. He told me he had plans to go to America and he will go now that his sight is better. He was in awe that in such a short time he had got healed simply with my bare hands. He said, "You certainly have patience. I am so grateful to you". I said I hoped he would pray and thank God for the healing. He said he certainly would from now on. He will always thank God for the healing. I was very pleased to hear that. I told him I never stop thanking God. I say my prayers very regularly. I cannot count how many times of the day. He said he would never ever forget me. I told him I was glad that his eyes were so much better and that he could see much further than what he could before. He told me when he walked into his lounge, he would have to go right over to the clock before he could see what time it was, and now as he entered the room, he could see the clock without any hindrance. He thought sometimes that it was a dream.

After Michael's eyes got better, he started to have doubts because he asked me if his eyes will become doggy again or for how long his eyesight will remain good. I said it will last for evermore. He felt he had not done enough for me. I said to him the very fact he is going to pray, thank God and also pray for me is quite enough for me. He said he must have done something good for God to have blessed him to ever meet me. I told him, as he travels to America, to make sure he remembers Jesus Christ, because he is the saviour of the world. With him you will never go wrong because he is the true healer. I am the channel working on his behalf. I told him I would miss him because his company had been very rewarding. I had learnt a lot from him and by this time he was completely better. It was time for him to go. We said our goodbyes. I knew his driving would be much better, but I told him never to drive too fast, to always try and stick to the normal speed limits. I would pray for him all the time; and I hoped he would be happy in America, get all he wished for and that God would go with him all the way.

When you have patients, some are very nice but not all of them. You have to take the not so nice with the good, but it is a wonderful thing that God has blessed me with, to see people come to me very poorly and get completely better – it is just a wonderful feeling. A few years ago, before I saw the vision of me as a healer, I was quite ill. It was something to do with my stomach. It was such a long time ago, but I remember it like yesterday, and I told so many people about it. What I do remember is that I went to University College Hospital. The doctor was not very nice to me. She said to me that there was nothing wrong with me. I really did not know what she was talking about. I left the hospital, but a little time later I went back into another hospital and that was near King's Cross, and there they found out that there was something wrong with me because I had an operation. That was a nice hospital, and the nurses and doctors were very nice. I was one of the youngest in the ward and the food was not bad. They kept telling me I was the youngest in the ward. How time goes so fast. I certainly will not forget that episode at all because it left a very bad scar on my stomach, and that was long before I saw the vision of the Lord. I certainly would never like to have another operation. Of course, I will never ever have another one because I can look after myself now, by healing myself; even though it is difficult

Chapter Eleven

for me to get to my hip. I still would never ever have another operation. Even when I was very much younger, one leg was shorter than the other due to my leg being tied to a chair when I was a tiny baby. The doctors asked Mother Connie if I wanted an operation to get it right and she said certainly not. I did not know then that I was going to be blessed with such a wonderful gift. I have never been very keen on operations. I still do not like them today. I always feel you are never the same after having had one.

I am just finding out how many things that dreadful girl stole from me who came from Amy Cleaners. How in the world do they employ those kinds of people? I do not know. She was complaining to me that they put her to clean in a big kitchen and that there were few things in there. I suppose that was to prevent her from stealing. Half the things she stole from me she was helping me to look for. Talk about brazen! She actually stole a nightie, bed jacket, six spoons, so many tins of food I cannot count, and so many bottles of cleaning fluid. In all my life I have never seen anyone quite so greedy. They should send her back where she came from. I think if they knew this woman was a criminal, they would send her back because I am not the only person she has stolen things from. Why in the world would the cleaning company employ her? They should have reported her a long time ago for her behaviour. I found myself having to spend so much more money because of having to replace all the things she stole. I think she thought she would get away with all the things she stole from me, because I was on my own and not able to get about quickly. Even when I hear on the television about people stealing things from shops and people's houses, I feel cross and I hope that the police will catch them, but this girl is the limit. Amy Cleaners, the agency where she was hired should be held responsible, and they should have never sent her to me. I have to now stock up in every room. She practically stole most of my utensils in the bathroom and in the kitchen. When the new cleaner kept telling me what she was short of, at first I couldn't believe it, then I realised I hadn't been watching the previous woman at all because I didn't realise she was a professional thief. It is a shame that people can come right into your home and steal; you have not got a clue until all the things that you have worked very hard for are missing. I am spending extra money each week, buying things I need for the bathroom, kitchen and bedroom which I never had to do before because I always bought little things every week to make sure I had enough. Now it is different; every single week something that woman stole has to be replaced. How in the world she got them out of my flat I will never know? What a good job I told the agency to get rid of her, but I can't understand how they can keep hiring criminals and letting her get away with this behaviour.

I certainly have to thank Mr Tom Whitemore, who runs The Hackney Volunteer Befriending Service renting at Unit 2, 15 Ramsgate Street. He has been so helpful in getting someone to help educate me on how to use my laptop. They are the type of unit that when you join, they try to help you as much as they can, and they do not expect anything in return. It makes things so much easier for you, especially when you have no relatives. As I heal people I made a few friends, but some of them, as soon as you have healed them, after a while forget all about you. As life has to go on, you cannot blame people because they all have their own lives to get on with. I would very much like to thank Rebecca who helped me a lot to get used to the laptop. I have had this book on my mind for a long time. I have never written a book myself before and I am never likely to write another one after this, so this book is mostly about what happened to me when I was a child and the wonderful gift I got from God; to heal people's pain and saving their lives. Without a book written about my experiences, lots of people would never know I have already healed quite a lot of people, but not enough.

It is hard for people to believe because few people can heal cancer, but when the force behind my healing hands chooses a person to carry to the work, then such work must be conducted. Nothing is impossible with the Almighty. It is a pity that both doctors and natural healers could not work together to help one another. That would help remake our wonderful world. I do hope one day this will happen and that it will not be just a dream. Trust me, I am aware that so many people need help right now in this world. I like watching police programmes on television, and how they try to keep order. I also like to watch 'Nothing to Declare' in the UK. This is a programme that shows what customs and border controls do. As with other countries they have a very difficult job keeping drugs and firepower out of their countries. At customs control they have to watch the food that comes into the countries.

That must be quite a big job. I think if you believe in God, things eventually seem to come right though. I know we all should have a lot of patience and knowledge, but most crucial is having wisdom and applying wisdom in all things that we do. For example, we all have been given brains by nature and nature tests out our brains on how to survive in nature and live in harmony with nature; so let's imagine nature gives each one of us a tomato and gave us all free choices on whatever we choose to do with it, now some of us might decide to share the tomato, some will eat the tomato, some will take out some seeds and plant it, and some will just throw the tomato in the bin – now which amongst these people applied wisdom? The one that took out the seed and replanted it knows that a seed makes a plant and plants make a forest and in that forest is money because money grows on trees and in the seas; so apply wisdom in whatever you do because you are what you think, your thoughts are who you are; just as you are what you eat, all medicines should be natural because your food should be your medicine, your plant and trees are your medicines, anything else is poison. Without it there is not much anyone can do. Everything today is about being patient and applying wisdom.

I once remember meeting a woman who needed my help and when she told me that she had a dreadful pain. Her name was Ayana. I asked her if I could help her. She looked at me and said to me how in the world can you help me? She told me her hand was hurting her and if her doctor could not help her, how could I help her? She thanked me for asking me but was afraid it would be impossible. I said, "Perhaps you don't believe me, but I am a healer. Let us both sit on this seat and give me your hand and I will hold it for you".

I held Anyana's hand for a little while she said to me. "I am sorry I didn't believe you, but I can feel your hand right now on my hurting one; it seems like I am in a little less pain. How long might it take for you to heal my hurting hand?" I told her not too long, just a few weeks. She came to my home the next week in need of treatments and when her hand started to get better she said to me, "Isn't it strange that I spoke to you because if I hadn't, I would have never known that you were a healer?" She told me I have very big and strong hands but why didn't I charge a penny? I told her that money is not everything, but perhaps one of these days I shall receive my rewards from whoever that might be that truly appreciates a genuine healer as myself. Once her hand got better, she told me that she did not know where to begin to thank me. I told her to pray and thank God for the healing, and she told me she did not believe in God. I told her as from now, she should think of what has just happened to her and start praying and thanking God. She told me she would start praying all the time now. I explained to her if it was not for Jesus Christ, I would never had been given such a gift; a very sound one. I told her about people I have healed through the Lord Jesus Christ quite a few years ago, like the one in 1993, who along with his wife, still keeps in touch with me. I said, "Once I heal you, that illness never comes back to you again; that surely is something to pray and thank the Lord Almighty for, because you said already you had been to see the doctor and he couldn't do anything for you". I told her to be very careful on what she says to the doctors because the doctors are very jealous and bitter when they find out that a natural healer healed someone.

Doctors are funny characters who thinks that their titles are entitlements for life, but it's about time that doctors recognise that overtaking is allowed. I think it would be better not to tell her doctor at all of who healed her. Anyana said to me in all her life she had never met anyone who could heal arthritis, she said she knows if she told her doctor he would hardly believe it and would not like it. I have heard him say time and time again that nobody can heal arthritis, but that I have proved him wrong. She went on to tell me there is nothing impossible with God, and I said to her I do wish that everyone believed that. This world would be a much better place for us all to live in. I told her that in America you have only to show them what you can do and then they will always believe, but in England it is very much different. Even if they see the proof, they wish not to believe in what is in front of their eyes, because in England the people are like sheep and only do what the politicians asked of them or what has been certified by a person in authority. I told her I had so many ministers in the church not liking me at all because of the gift the Lord Jesus Christ has blessed me with. The doctors do not like me and neither do quite a lot of the nurses also. I told her it was quite a miracle meeting her because if I had not, she would be in pain and suffering with her hands.

Ayana said, "I feel much happier now you told me. I just met two of my friends. I told them my hands were almost better now and they did not believe me. What do you think about that?" I said to her that is why I need to write a book, where it can be verified just what power is in my hands and how blessed I am; I give thanks and praises to the Almighty Creator. I suppose it is hard for some people to believe in what I am capable of doing as I told her I hope I can get this book written, proofread and published, so a lot more people can be helped. I know there must be a lot more people who do healing besides myself. I know for sure because I have heard about them, though I have never met anyone who heals the same way I do with my hands. It would be nice if all the healers got together as I told my Ayana.

I remember a woman coming to me and telling me she knew five healers. Her name was Joan. I asked her why she brought her children to me for healing when she knew so many healers and she said to me that none of them were as strong as me, but I could not quite understand what she meant by that. She was insisting she could write my life story. I told her the only person who could do that was myself. She was not happy about that at all and from then on, she did not want to talk to me. I could not understand why she was so upset, but Ayana told me that some people are like that. It is because she could see you had so much power, therefore she wanted some of the credit. I thought that was rather strange. I would not want to write a book about anyone else's life story. I suggest that all people should write their own life story by themselves. This is my first book and it's a story about my journey in life, and it will be the last. It took me a long time to put this book together but I realised if I didn't write my life story, people would never know what I could do, that would mean I wouldn't be able to save a lot more lives and help people with their pain. I know I would never forgive myself for that, and also be able to fulfil the wonderful gift that the Lord Jesus Christ had blessed me with.

Ayana's hands were completely better now. I wished her all the best, and that she would meet someone, get married, be happy, have children, and that her trip to America would be a permanent one. She had the whole of her life before her because she was very young. She was very anxious to secure a job where she could help other people. She had all the right ideas but was never happy living in England. She had not met the right person. I hope that she will find her happiness in America.

I have also just this last week seen a friend of mine who has been suffering with pain for a very long time. She came to see me, but she could not stay very long. She told me her doctor was going to send her to see a specialist. I told her if she doesn't get any good results then she could visit me as she had only come to see me once for a very short visit. We all suffer from pains in different parts of our bodies, but most times we don't know where the pain is coming from, but we do feel it.

I remember attending to a very small boy, His parents were showing me where the doctors told them the cancer was. I was quite surprised. I told his parents I could not feel anything where the doctors told them the cancer

Chapter Eleven

was. They inquired at the hospital where he had been, and the cancer was in a different place altogether. I was quite shocked when they inquired from the doctors at the hospital. They said that it did not matter because there was nothing they could do anyway. That is why I do not keep telling people about the church where I healed a young lady who was dying of cancer. I thought to myself the doctors would not believe me anyway. That's why it is quite urgent that this book I am writing is written as soon as possible. At least some people can get help, and as my friend said to me as soon as she visits the specialist, she certainly will tell me the results and then she will visit me. I told her it will take quite a few visits. She said she did not mind because she said she was fed up with the pain and that she had suffered with the pain for years. She wondered if it had anything to do with what we eat or drink, but when she goes to the specialists let us hope they will be able to solve what is wrong, otherwise my hands will have to solve it for her. I am quite amazed of what my hands have solved. So many different diseases, and it always seems to solve whatever the problem is.

I am just about to start healing someone right now who has varicose veins. I don't remember ever healing anyone with this complaint before; but I do remember long ago having varicose veins myself, but after I saw the vision of Jesus Christ and being told that I had healing hands, my varicose veins disappeared because I healed it myself. My cleaner told me she too had varicose veins. I was glad to help her with them. The woman I am healing right now told me that her varicose veins were bruised so I will just have to see the way to deal with this woman and maybe I will be able to do a lot more.

I remember meeting a woman whom I know, and she asked me if I could help her. She was a diabetic. I asked her if she knew where the diabetes was in her stomach, but she did not know. I knew that even myself I could not help her because the pancreas in the stomach was so thinly fine. I would not have a clue as to where it was and as she did not know either, I told her it would be impossible. She insisted I should put my hands on her stomach where she had a feeling it might be; she knew where it was. I certainly was not too certain about it at all. She was demanding if it was possible that I fix her a dinner. I was quite surprised because I thought diabetics were on a special diet, but not her. She demanded meat and everything else that goes with it – roasted potatoes, cauliflower and so many other things. I was quite surprised. I wondered if she was having me on. She even wanted a pudding, then I became very suspicious. Was this woman taking me for a ride? I had a word with a nurse that I knew, and she told me to be very careful of her. She went on to say, "It looks as if she is taking you for a ride; it is very difficult to find the pancreas in the stomach and where she is telling you doesn't seem to be the right place. I think she just wants a good dinner every time she comes to visit you. If I were you, I would just tell her it is very difficult to find out exactly where the problem is and to stop treating her right away. It is a good job you are going to have someone with you all the time in your healing theatre sessions because there are so many tricksters. You just don't know who to trust". On taking the advice of the nurse, I told her I was very sorry, but I could not continue. I do like to know what I am doing, and it was awkward for me to continue.

I then heard from a woman I did not even know. She telephoned me and asked me if I could look after her husband. I was quite shocked. I asked her what in the world was she talking about. I do not know her or her husband. She then told me that her husband was a diabetic and the doctors had operated on him. She sent him down to me all on his own in a very weak state. I was quite appalled, and I told her so, and when I asked him where they had operated on him, he showed me. I was very cross, and I telephoned his wife and asked her if she went with her husband when he had the operation. She said she had not, and I asked her why. She told me she had other things to do and that made me very cross. I wondered to myself how long this gentleman was going to live because I realised that the operation was not done in the right place. I was not surprised when the wife phoned and told me her husband had died. I had only seen him once. I asked her what the operation was all about, because she had told me he was a diabetic, and the operation was nowhere near where the diabetes was. I told the wife that the medical people must have given him the wrong operation. She did not seem a bit concerned, and I told her I have never heard of any doctor giving any operation to a diabetic. She told me she had never heard of it either; so much for her looking after her husband. Sometimes I get so cross when I see these kinds of things happening with no consideration at all to the person in question. It makes my blood boil and it reminds me of Brenda with the doctors very busy experimenting on her to see if the cancer had gone, and they had no right to touch her at all.

What you have to go through when you are a healer is quite strange and stressful on hearing how some of the patients have been living in pain before they come to me. Most often they tell me all their life story in one session and expect me to heal all their worries in one go.

I remember this woman talking to me on a cold winter afternoon about my healing hands, and she said to me she wished she had my gift because all I do is just to sit down and place my hands on people. I said to her, number one, you have to be very dedicated and have a lot of patience because if you haven't got patience it wouldn't be any good at all. You have to have integrity and you need to have relationship skills. I asked her if she is capable of placing her hand on a person steadily for three hours non-stop. "Ooh no I couldn't do that!", she said. She said she did not realise I had to stay all that time on a patient when people are very ill. I said to her, believe me it is not easy. I told her when the Almighty gives you a gift like mine, The Almighty knows who deserves to receive such gift and the purpose of the gift and how to make use of it. Patience is most essential; without that you could never be a healer I told her.

I love what I do and I very much like to see when people come to me very ill and I able to make them better – it is the most wonderful feeling. I can never stop thanking Jesus Christ because without Jesus Christ I would have nothing.

Trust me, when you are able save people's lives and take away people's pain, well that is something very special. I would very much like to continue for as long as my creator allows me to do so. I hope for long life because so many people need my help.

As I am coming to the end of this book which is all about the experiences of my life, the people I have met and dealt with, and the people that have stuck in my memories; I would very much like to thank Peter who helped me quite a lot and I am so sorry that I missed him when he came to see me. I was just across the road looking through the window and I do not know how I missed him, but if he ever reads this book I would very much like to thank him for all he did for me. He was a perfect gentleman and very kind to me. I would also like to thank Henry who I met in Jamaica. He was very kind to me when I needed help and he was also a perfect gentleman. I always think when I meet these kinds of people that the almighty Creator is always there. I would also like to thank the gentleman who was in charge of the place where I worked in Jamaica. He was also very kind to me and even helped me to get a place to live. He was an Englishman and very helpful. I always feel very safe with these types of people.

When I came to live in London, especially when I came to live in this flat where I currently reside, at first things were beautiful but when Marcus King took over managing my flat, that is when I felt that my safety was threatened. It is a good job I have quite a strong constitution. If I didn't I suppose I would be dead by now because for more than 18 years is a long time to be breathing in dangerous fumes coming from the laundry operating business above my flat; and up until now it is still going on. I hope when I get this book published, it will expose the council and there lack of concerns for my health. I just can't wait to start breathing in fresh quality air again. I just want to be able to open my windows to get air every day and to feed the birds in the garden. It is amazing what some people will do to get what they want, but I somehow feel I was definitely chosen to come and live here to teach some of these people a lesson. They seem to think that they can get away with anything and they do get away with quite a lot and I wonder why. I have been told quite a few times that these guys living above me think they are better than anyone else. I certainly do not think that they are better than me, though some of their actions are quite underhanded; they are not straightforward people, they like to question you but never tell you anything about themselves, and my bell is forever ringing even when it isn't someone coming to see me. I cannot understand why they cannot ring each separate bell, and in all my life I have never heard so much door slamming. This goes on all the time in the block of flats where I live.

    I remember getting a phone call from a man who said to me he did not know if I could help him and I asked him what the matter was. He told me that his ear was hurting him, and I asked him had he mentioned this to his doctor. He said he had and that his doctor had sent him to the ear hospital. They had tested his ear and they said they could not see anything wrong with it. A friend of his gave him my name and number and told him to phone me and

Chapter Eleven

ask me if he could make an appointment. I then told him I would be able to heal him. I told him that I only use my hands to heal people and he said his friend told him the same thing. So, I booked him an appointment and started to give him one hour of healing session each week, but as my hand was on his ear I felt something, and I told him I didn't think that his ear would take very long to heal. I made it clear to him that his ear will get a bit worse at the beginning due to clearing what was wrong, and after that then it will slowly get better. He asked me what I thought caused it. I said to him I really didn't know. I told him I have healed so many illnesses and some I do not even know what they were. I said to him that is how things go sometimes. He said to me, "When my friend told me about you I realised you would solve the problem. Though as you say you didn't know what caused it, fair enough, surely the Almighty Creator has certainly given you very powerful healing hands". I told him I hope he will give thanks to the Creator for the healing I told him I pray every day and thank the Creator for such a wonderful gift. He said to me I bet you make a lot of enemies and I said to him, "How do you know that? You are quite right. The doctors don't like me, the nurses also don't like me".

I told him about a boy who came to me he had only six weeks to live. His adopted mother brought him to me and when she got back home the Macmillan nurse was there waiting for him on the doorstep and the mother told her they had been to a healer. She said you should not go to a healer. I was not at all surprised. I have met Macmillan nurses when I was asked to visit a cancer patient and they give me such dirty looks. Of course, now I refuse to visit people in hospital who have cancer. I prefer it if they come to me and I instruct them to be careful not to tell their doctor because most of these doctors don't like healers like me.

A book will be written by me so as to raise awareness and allow people to get to know more about me and the testimonies of the people healed by me. I told him about a dear friend who had cancer all over her body at the St Mary's Church and he said his friend had told him about it too. He said to me. "Look how many people would be glad for your help". He told me he was glad his friend had told him about me. He said he thought that writing a book is a good idea. He said to me there are so many people looking for help. His ear got completely better even though neither one of us knew what it was; but it did not take me very long to heal his ear. He was a very nice man and very grateful. He said I will always pray for you and that the Lord will keep you safe and sound. I thanked him.

I remember someone else who telephoned me and asked for help. She had cancer in her breast. I had healed quite a few women with breast cancer. I asked her if she had seen her doctor, she told me that she had, and he sent her for an x-ray. He then mentioned something about therapy, but she was not happy about that at all. When she got home a friend of hers came to see her and told her about me. She said I might tell you it was like a big burden taken away from me, so we made an appointment. I started to give her three hours of healing sessions a week. She enquired how

Chapter Eleven

long I had known I had such a wonderful gift, especially to heal cancer. I then told her I had seen a vision of Jesus Christ's face and Jesus told me that I had healing hands. I had a bad knee at the time and the Lord told me to put both my hands on my knee and heal myself. I then realised that only Jesus Christ can heal any illness right away. As for me, my healing depends on how serious such an illness or disease is; it is can take a few months.

"What do you think of a book being written by me?" I asked this patient. She thought about it and asked what the book will be about and I told her it will be about my life journey. She said to me that it is a very good idea, and I told her about my accident when I fell and couldn't move or get up, I laid on the floor for two days with a damaged back and hip and a big hole on my foot.

The other day, when I opened my window to feed the birds I saw a small hand on my window ledge, it was a boy, the boy was no more than about six or seven years old, he was trying to open my window and when I asked him what he was doing, I have never seen anyone move so fast. He was on a bicycle and he seemed to think that there was nobody in the flat. I was shocked to find that they start at such an early age, and it seems to be getting worse instead of better.

I started to concentrate on the woman's breast cancer. She said to me, "The Lord certainly gave you very strong healing hands and she continued. When the book comes out and it gets to circulate you will hear from a lot of people all over the world. If that be the case, then I would need an assistant during the healing sessions. She advised me to be careful. She never missed a healing appointment and she was a very nice lady and she told me all about her family. She asked me if I knew that some people like to hide their illness. I replied that I am aware of a lot of my patients hiding their illnesses, and it comes to me, quite naturally. I am used to it. I told her as I write this book I don't give away any names; only my dear friend Brenda who I healed suggested that I gave away all her names as a proof of a real person with real names.

Unfortunately, a gentleman I was healing of chest and lung pain, who was knocked to the ground by horses, and was suffering with breathing difficulties at Stanmore Hospital, started to make progress, yet still the medical people didn't like this at all They practically barred me from helping him. I was disgusted at their behaviour. I did not get his name, but if his wife ever reads this book about my life she will be able to explain. I do hope those doctors were able to save his life. I know if they allowed me to stay and continue healing him, he would've been all right, but after a performance of ignorance from the doctors, I don't know how anyone can subject themselves to medical people. It is such a worry when you wonder what happens to people in the hands of these medical people. To them a person is just a number. I have warned a lot of my clients to be very careful in what they discuss in front of these chemical people. It has become evident to most of my clients that the doctors and nurses, in fact the whole of the medical people do not like me.

One day while I was visiting the same guy at the same hospital, his friends also came to pay him a visit, then one of his visiting friends said loudly to the other friends, "Oh my God! I have never seen you looking so well". Of course, his friend who was ill didn't understand the position and he said, "This is Dorothy, my healer. I can't understand why my wife never introduced her to me earlier, I would've been better by now. I just don't get it". I was so frightened for him because I knew then that the nurses had heard everything and they would tell the doctors, and the next time I went to pay him a visit, I soon realised they wanted me out of the way. I was so sorry for him I just did not know what to do. I try my best never to go to the hospital. It is much better if the patients come to me because if I go to their homes sometimes I might meet the Macmillan nurses, and knowing how these nurses feel about me, it would be preferable that my clients come to me. If a patient is as sick as the one at Stanmore Hospital then that is different, because it is a matter of life and death and I choose life over death; therefore I will force my way into any hospital to heal such a patient. Now of course, as I cannot get around very much, the patients would have to come to me for healing sessions, but I do not expect it to be like this all the time. I know what I would like to do, but I will keep it quiet for the time being until the book on my life is published and I am able to get around much more.

I have been healing people over the years, but have been doing research since 2013, and also doing a bit of writing. I know that cancer is very painful, and I know a lot of people need my help.

People will think that it is very strange for me to be in a wheelchair; but when these people see me walk again, then they will know it is the blessing of Jesus Christ that made it possible. Having said that, I am able to walk, but not long distance or with speed as my balance is affected. If you have been reading this book from the beginning, I told you about the vision and conversation between myself and The Mighty One. This vision is so very real, though I have heard that some people keep saying that healers can't heal themselves. Of course, I do not believe that at all. If you are a genuine healer I think you can heal yourself. Of course, it may take some time because some illnesses take longer than others and I am afraid that my hip is taking me quite a long time to heal, but I know I am getting there. It is a good thing that I have a lot of patience. I will let you know later on about my progress.

Sometimes you have to be very careful, because people who know you can heal people try very hard to take liberties. They want everything for nothing and expect you to be at their call all the time. I am afraid I have to put my foot down and put a stop to all that because there are other people who are serious and want my help much more. You always have to keep your eyes wide open and look out for people who need you the most. I like to attend to the people who have cancer the most because their treatment in hospitals is so painful and I honestly would never like to have that sort of treatment myself. I was treating a woman once who had cancer, her mother had died from the disease. She told me that the doctor had told her that radiotherapy treatment might give you the feeling of living longer, but all it does is to enable you to live perhaps a few years, then you kick the bucket. She told me her mother went very stiff; she could hardly move during her treatment, and the doctors claimed that that is what happens to a person who is receive of radiotherapy. That is why she herself refused to have radiotherapy and she told me she felt so much better when someone told her about me. I warned her not to let the doctors touch her, and she said to me I would not even go near to any of them after you have removed the cancer. She told me she would not even discuss it with any one of them, not even the nurses. I told her about the book I was going to write and she said she thought that was the only thing to let people know what I can do. She said she knows I am going to help a lot of people, then she noticed I had a cough. She asked me if I had a cold, and I told her I do not get a cold. I get rid of colds in a couple of days. I explained to her about the cough. I told her the woman who moved into the flat above mine came with a complete laundry business with dangerous chemicals, and these chemicals give me a cough or cold and I heal myself.

I told her about the sergeant in the Stoke Newington police who came to visit me, and said he wanted to see me as it was something very important. I agreed for him to visit me but when he came up to my flat and I asked him what he wanted, I couldn't believe it when he asked me for sex. The cheek of the man! My friend said to me, "When you write your book, please do not forget to put that in". I told her some people told me I should have taken him to court, but I told them if he is so brazen to ask me for sex, do you think he will admit to the truth? He would certainly lie through his teeth; you can trust me on that. It would be my word against his word. I certainly think some of these police officers should be taught a lesson, especially those at Stoke Newington Police Station; their behaviour is terrible. I personally think that the police officers at Stoke Newington police station are the worst in London. I have spoken to quite a lot of people and not one person has said a good word about them. We all pay enough money in council tax so as to have decent policing.

A man across the road says he likes to help people, but he very much likes to help himself. He is a professional thief, but it is a waste of time telling the police.

My friend was completely better now, and she said to me she will be looking out for my book. I said to her, "When the book is finished you will know because the title will certainly ring a bell".

As this book is near completion, I would like to inform the readers that I have no hospital equipment at my house. I just use my hands to heal people, but I am getting on in age these days, so I have ordered a special chair for the patients; one that requires that I do not hurt my back during the healing sessions. When you are getting older it is rather silly to be careless, especially with your own body. Of course, I love to help a lot of people and especially those with arthritis and cancer. People have to remember I am only one person. I honestly think that the Almighty knows I have only a certain time to heal people, and as such the Almighty allows me to treat people much quicker. All the hours I used to take in healing people will not be

Chapter Eleven

necessary at all; if only these people came to me on time rather than delay , so the illness gets worse. This of course prolongs the healing.

I just feel with Jesus Christ's help, as I am only the channel working for the Lord, things will be very different when my book comes out and people get a better understanding that their illnesses can be cured without them going under a knife and having their bits cut off from their bodies.

I am very much looking forward to seeing Barbie Webster an old dear friend of mine from St Anne's on the Sea. Her parents used to run a lovely summer holiday for children when I lived with my adopted mother. I used to go there every year. Barbie used to take me out on the beach. She was absolutely marvellous on a horse. I am afraid I was not. I was afraid every time the horse moved its head, I kept thinking it wanted to bite me. She used to laugh at me because I was such a coward, but I do love horses; I just do not like to ride them.

I wonder what happened to my friend Ella Poole. When the nun told me to leave the home and I grabbed hold of her habit and brought her down to the floor, she had hit me on my right eye with what looked like a piece of iron, and I got really furious because it hurt so much. Ella gave me a home. I do not know what I would have done if it was not for her. When she left the home we became very good friends. She was such a lovely girl. I wonder if she is still alive. Also, I would like to know if my friend Dorothy Micklewright is still alive, and my friend Mary Langford. When you have friends like these you never forget them.

I always wonder what they would think if they know that Jesus Christ had given me such a wonderful gift. I know they would be happy and if any one of them is still alive and would love to see me, I would be happy to see them as well, but if they read my book they will know how much I look forward to seeing their faces again. Perhaps they may have even gone abroad; all I hope is that God will bless them all.

I am finding it difficult to heal one side of my hip as I healed the other side but to reach the other side is difficult for me. I want to seek help with someone that will help me on positioning myself properly so that I will be able to heal the other side of my hip, but I just do not know who to trust. I am asking my two best friends to say a prayer for me. I do believe in prayer and they know I saw a vision of Jesus Christ.

I remember a church minister once took me to see another church minister who claimed to be able to heal. When I told him what I had healed, he did not seem very pleased. He said to me, "That is a nice story". I was simply flabbergasted. I heard he did operations in the churchyard and I wondered how they all turned out. Two doctors, quite a few years ago, did an operation on a lady who had cancer. I felt very sorry for the woman; their hands were inside her body, and after all that she died. I thought to myself if they knew what I could do they would not like me at all. I still think it is a shame that doctors don't listen to genuine healers. When I was in the hospital myself after having an accident, I did not tell anyone that I was a healer. They asked me if I would like to have an operation on my hip and I said thank you very much, but I would rather not. I have always been very much against having an operation, more or less frightened of them. I don't know what it is. I suppose it is because I can heal myself and Jesus Christ gave me a gift of healing, so I always work very hard on healing myself and I know if I put my hands on the right place of my body I will be all right. Sometimes I will admit that certain places on my own body are very awkward to reach, but with determination I will get there and of course, with the blessing of the Almighty Creator, because without the precious Almighty I could do nothing.

When I first saw the vision, I was absolutely delighted that I had been chosen for such a responsible and wonderful task to be a channel for Jesus Christ the Son of God. When I first saw the vision of Jesus and was told I had healing hands I did wonder if when I put both hands on myself, or on anyone else, where exactly, what exactly, and how exactly do I begin? Do I just lay my hands on the patient, do I rub my hands on them? I decided to phone a few healers even though I didn't know any of them, but I wondered if they would explain to me what I had to do. The first thing they asked me was how I knew that I was a healer. I told them that I saw a vision of Jesus Christ and that Jesus had told me that I had healing hands. All of them said they wished they had seen a vision of Jesus Christ, but neither of them could explain to me how they came to know that they were healers. I thought that was very strange; but a couple of people who came to me for healing told me they each knew about five healers. So I asked them automatically what sort of healing they did and each one of them said their healing is not as strong as mine, that left me wondering how anybody could make themselves into a healer without getting it from the Almighty force, creator of all that is in nature, and they couldn't explain to me. Also they couldn't prove or provide evidence of what condition or illnesses they had healed. That left me wonder if that is why so many people don't believe in healers. People are always asking me if I know other healers who can heal like me and I tell them I have never met another healer. I am very anxious to meet another healer, but unfortunately, I have not, and what worries me is why so many people do not believe in God. I mean, personally I think that all bad things are caused by the devil's mind set and all the good things are caused by the Godly mind set. My Mother Connie used to tell me if ever you are doing anything, do not ever get annoyed because the devil creeps in, and that way you never get anything done. So that is to show you without the Almighty you cannot do anything in regard to healing; you need power and the source of that power comes from whom is in nature, and nature is whom we all belong to.

I have just had something happen to me which I have never ever heard of happening to me or anyone else. A couple of years ago I went across the road looking for the caretaker to ask him if he knew anybody who could help me to do things like cleaning my windows and moving heavy furniture that I couldn't manage to move. Right away a man approached me and asked me if he could help me, and I told him I was looking for the caretaker.

Chapter Eleven

He told me he was the caretaker, but at the moment he wasn't feeling well. I thanked him and told him that I would come back in a month or two, by which time I thought he would be well again. I went back home and returned much later. I still could not find the caretaker, but a man came up to me and asked me if he could help me in any way. I told him I was trying to get somebody to clean my windows and he told me he lived across the road from me and I could phone him and let him know when I wanted the windows cleaned. He came from time to time and did other things as well, like cleaning and emptying the rubbish because as I mentioned before, I could not get around very much since I had my accident. I did tell the man I was going to get a cleaner and he agreed that it was a good idea so I was quite appalled when one day after I got a cleaner from a company, I was looking for my electric hair straightener and my electric tongs. I could not understand when I found some of my things placed inside a black rubbish bag. I then realised the chap across the road had stolen them. He even stole from elderly lady he had been helping out, and hid them in my kitchen cupboard. I had never heard of such a thing like that happening before. I wrote to him and told him to bring my property back. I then heard that the elderly lady had died and that was why he had his bright idea of making some money for himself, by stealing my property and selling them. This man must be stopped; he is just a thief taking liberties with people and making as much money as he can. He must have stolen a lot of things from the dead woman and stolen a lot of things from me too. It would be useless telling the Stoke Newington police because they would not do anything about it; they are too busy making money for themselves unlawfully, so that would be just a waste of time. I do hope that someone will help me to stop this man right away. His behaviour is disgraceful and I am very worried who next, he will be stealing from, and how many people he is still stealing from. He has the nerve to give me a sad story and even borrowed money from me. He paid me back the money he had borrowed, but I then realised he was just about to ask me if he could borrow some more money. I started to get very suspicious of him and he started to back out. It was then I realised my special things were missing. I was furious because I make use of most of my things all the time; besides, I have one philosophy which means a lot to me and that philosophy is that, it is not what you want but what you need. Of course, these sorts of individuals are always looking for something to sell, especially what does not belong to them; in other words, stolen properties. I have never in all my life heard of anyone doing such a dreadful thing and I wonder why nobody has reported him at all – maybe they are too frightened, but not me. I am trying very hard to get a proof-reader and I am praying to the Almighty to guide me because I know that so many people need help.

I can't wait for this book to be published because it will open up the eyes and minds of people, and they will know the truth of a natural healer that can heal cancer and other illnesses naturally. Even though I found out that I am able to heal cancer in 1983, I have already written where you can get all of this verified.

Chapter Eleven

In Italy, one day was a very sad day for me. There was a young girl who had all her life before her. She was an assistant head-mistress and a very educated person, but she realised too late that she should have listened to me. I might tell you I was very upset and it took me a long time to get over the whole disaster. All the people I healed after that, I never mentioned a word to them about it, but I still haven't forgotten it. I suppose I never will. She was such a lovely girl. She sent me a beautiful card from Italy telling me how she had no pain and was eating very well. She said, "All through your help, Dorothy", but she really meant all through Jesus Christ who blessed me with this wonderful gift.

I am hoping to heal as many people as I can of cancer because it is such a dreadful disease. and so many people all over the world seem to be suffering it. According to the amount of people I have healed, I am knowledgeable enough to explain to anyone how painful cancer is to a person. I hope to heal a lot of people who have knee problems as well as people with hip problems, but it would be difficult to heal hips problems because I would have to stand up for a long time and I couldn't do that for long due to the accident I had, and believe me I am trying so hard to get around to my own hip as I myself have hip problems.

I am delighted to say that I have just found a proofreader for my book. She is such a lovely girl and quite clever. She started right from the beginning and she comes to me twice a week to proofread. I feel so much more contented and I feel as if I am getting somewhere with my book. It is like a load off my mind and she even helps me to get my watches fixed when they need batteries, and other things as well. I put all these things down to the Almighty. I know the Almighty is helping me all the time and always trying to lift the burden and make things easier for me. Without my trust in the Almighty I just do not know where I would be. I was so worried about getting a proof-reader, then all of a sudden God brings me one that is so cool, calm, and collected; and someone like that takes most of the worries off my shoulders. She herself does not even notice it and each time she is ready to go, she asks me if there is anything she can do for me and that is to show what a caring person she is. I just thank her for her kindness and extreme consideration. You don't meet people like her very often.

As all our memory works at times, things just spring up into your memory, and you have to write things down as you remember them.

When I lived with my adopted mother I used to roll my head from side to side when I was in bed. I remember in my nursery we had a cradle. When I came home from school I used to jump in it and rock myself to sleep. As I got older and went to bed I sometimes rock myself to sleep, but when I was young my adopted mother complained about this to my doctor and the doctor advised that it was not good for me to rock myself to sleep because I wasn't getting enough rest. Mother started to worry, but I know she did ask the doctor what she could do and I am sure he gave me some sort of medicine which seemed to stop it right away and I was so glad because

Chapter Eleven

rocking in the bed was giving me a bald patch at the back of my head. Off course, the hair soon grew back and even today I still have very thick hair, but I cut it very often. Before my accident in 2011 my hair was very long and thick and it was too difficult to handle, but now I am thinking of growing it long again.

I will be so busy healing as many people as I can, and after that, I will have a makeover in my flat and will stay with a friend who is in a hospice for a few days and heal whatever is wrong with my her leg. After the makeover of my flat, I am jumping straight into what I know best to do, and that is to heal people from their illnesses, but my friend comes first. I will not rest until I have got her better, but I am glad to say whatever she has got, it will not take me long to heal her. We all know we have to stick to our friends because at times friends too are like families.

The other day I opened my window to feed the birds and there is the millionaire from across the road. He had invited a lot of his colleagues to the ends, there were about nine of them looking at me from across the road. What he had been telling them I don't know, but after a while they moved off. I guess England is a free country and I don't let these types of things bother me at all. The millionaire very much wants me out of my flat, even though he has two very big flats. He wants to please his daughter by acquiring more properties and he is managing the flats where I live; and I am tired of him trying to please his daughter at the suffering of other people. Thank goodness his daughter is now living in America, but she is still determined she can run me out of my flat with the help of her father, and this has been going on for 18 years. As I have already mentioned, the dreadful laundry she has been running all this time with the dangerous chemicals; nobody should have to put up with such things. I do want to go to court and clear up all this mess and I am sure the courts would stop this nonsense immediately. This sort of nonsense should never go on for so long, and what's more, it is very dangerous to be surrounded by chemicals. They themselves would not allow anyone else to do this sort of thing to them. I certainly have not been able to fathom this out at all; is it because her father is a millionaire? Well I myself think it is disgraceful. I am hoping and praying for this nonsense to be stopped and of course what makes it worse is that the Stoke Newington police get paid for the privilege of allowing this illegal laundry business to operate above the flat where I reside. Lots of us are very surprised that nothing has been done about their behaviour as far back as before the 1970s, when I first came to live at Clissold Crescent. According to all the people I met it had been going on long before I moved into the area. How in the world did it go on so long and still be going on now?

As I mentioned earlier, I have a lawn beside me and I was pleased when those using the lawn to play football were told to stop it because in the lease it specifies that the lawn must not be used as a playground. Once this stopped it was so nice to get a bit of peace and sleep, but just the other day, they started to use it again as a playground. When will they ever stop? Personally, I think they should be given an antisocial behaviour order labelled against their names by the court or justice department. People like these sorts make my life a misery.

I am not moving, until maybe after I have finished my book. I have healed quite a lot of people in my flat and I am going to heal a lot more once they realise what I can do. and I am going to heal the dreaded cancer what so many people have and want is help, and it is only through my book that will let people know what I can do. Christ blessed me with healing hands and I think it is a most By this time I will not be healing in my flat. I will have to find somewhere else more appropriate to heal people. I remember some time ago when I found it very difficult to heal this woman; even going through the door she was very unsteady on her feet and I was trying to show her how to walk steady and she nearly knocked me over and I thought to myself this would certainly have to change when I get a lot more people to heal. I know a lot of my friends will rally around when needed; that will make things a lot easier for me. This particular lady had come to me far too late, and as I told her family, when you wait until it is too late, then it can also be too late to heal whatever illness you have. Besides, to treat a person that only attends healing sessions once a week is not enough, especially when the illness has been ignored for too long. It is simply impossible to get you better, I told them, and they understood what I was saying; but I didn't feel good about this myself because I like to know that when people visit me to be healed they are absolutely fit and well before leaving. If they are coming from a far distance it is rather difficult for the person to come to me more than once a week; I am aware of that, but your health is your wealth.

I remember having a man coming to me once a week for healing. He did not live very far but for his own interest he should have come for healing every day, but he was far too sick to come even once a week. It is very awkward when someone tells you they can only come for healing once a week and expect miracles to happen overnight. In cases such as that, I am afraid I just feel very sorry for them and there is nothing more I can do. My friend Brenda was a good model for a patient because she understood the importance of having good health, and also for recognising that she was in poor health; so when I told her of the importance to attend the healing sessions each day she took my advice and attended. I healed her every day until she told me she was feeling on top of the world. She had a very rapid cancer and was on death's door. I was very happy for her as she made progress on regaining back her health. She was such a lovely young girl, but as I've said earlier, it was such a shame she didn't listen to me. In the end and against my advice she gave herself to the medical people to examine her so as to establish she was cancer free, and that was the end of her life. I try to explain to people if they are very ill they need more than one healing session a week. Some people of course only need once a week if their illness does not call for any more time, depending on if their illness is not so rapid. It is much less stressful if they come along as advised, and as the healing progresses, so too will they start noticing the changes with the illness and of their bodies.

Chapter Eleven

Often whenever I am healing my patients and they become relaxed, it wouldn't be long enough. Do you believe any one of the doctors would ask you for help? People often ask me, and I would say to them if it became well known through this book that I've written then perhaps they might seek my help. I am sure they would come to me for healing if they were desperate enough and seeking to get better, but I would say I think most of them would be far too proud, unless of course they knew someone else who was very ill and I had got them better; then things would be different.

I just remembered a few years ago when my husband was alive, we lived at Stamford Hill in a ground floor flat. This was quite high with many floors. The bathroom was right on the top floor where lived a woman who took a dislike to me for no reason. In fact I became terrified of using the bathroom because each time I went upstairs to the bathroom I got abused by her. As for me, I did not say a word to her because she was very a large woman and my husband was always at work. I mentioned it to my husband and he was very annoyed and said that I should be able to use the bathroom if there was nobody in there and that she didn't own the property, so I said to him don't worry about it, I will only go there when you are here so one day my husband met her coming into the building as he was going out and he spoke to her about it and would you believe it? She started to fight with him throwing punches and kicking. She was such a bully she would always boast that she could fight any man and my husband was not the only man living in this building that she had had a fight with. She wanted everyone to be frightened of her. I begged my husband to ignore her next time and not to even notice her, but he told me he would never do that. Later on, I noticed that she was pregnant so I told my husband that he should completely pretend he had not even known her, because as she liked to fight with everyone, she might accuse him of doing some harm to her baby. He certainly took my advice this time. This was the time when women were being given the wrong pills and I guess she too might have taken one of those pills because when she had her baby, one of the tenants from our building told us that her baby was born with one arm and one leg. Neither of us ever saw her again, but this dreadful disaster happened to a lot of babies during that era. People in the building kept asking what had happened to her but we told them we did not know. I thought that was rather strange. It was as if she had disappeared altogether.

I must say, some very strange things went on in that building, such as the woman who lived next to us on the ground floor. She told us that her brother was coming over from Jamaica to live in London. I asked if was he coming to do a particular job and she told me he was disabled, so he would not be able to work at all. That struck me as very strange. I asked her if he had permission to come and live in England as he would not be able to work, but she never answered me at all and when I told my husband he could not understand it either. Then one day I heard he had got a council flat. I just could not understand it at all.

I certainly have very bad memories of that very high building that my husband and myself found ourselves in.

Chapter Eleven

My own husband got very ill in that building and that added to more bad memories; we just had to move out of there and we did. We moved to another flat. Life is so strange; sometimes nobody knows what is going to happen to them.

I met so many different people and they all seemed to suffer from one illness or the other, and most of them will tell you they feel fine even when it is obvious that they're in pain.

I used to help this woman who drank a lot. She was on welfare, and she asked me if I could help her. She lived only a few doors away from me and I would check up on her to see how she was getting on. She would tell me that she had stopped drinking, but every time I went to see her or when she came to see me, her whole body smelt of drink. I told her that she must try a lot harder and give up on the bottle and she told me she would, but it is was always the same. I often prayed for her and I asked her if she would come to the church with me sometimes, but she always made an excuse. I still tried very hard to help her though. She lived on her own because her husband had died from alcohol abuse, so I suppose life was very difficult for her.

There was another woman I knew; she certainly was very ill and was always shaking. When I asked her if she ever went to church she said she had never stepped inside a church, and the gentleman she was with, said he too had never been into a church, but he had his hand pointing upwards and then said to me, "Whatever I want from the big man upstairs, he provides it". I was quite astonished.

I wondered why she did not ask Jesus Christ to get her better. When I asked her if she wanted me to help her, she told me that there was nothing wrong with her. It is quite strange that some people are ill, but they pretend that there is nothing wrong with them. I always wonder how they can get help if they don't reach out and admit that they are in need of help. I suppose it is just one of those things; it seems as if some people don't want help at all.

I am surprised about some mobile phone companies, especially T Mobile, EE and Orange. If you top up £50 credit on your phone it seems to disappear in minutes. I think something should be done about these phone companies, as often most people wonder where their money has disappeared to, and you can't ask these phone companies; if you do you don't get a nice answer. Vodafone is just the same, if not worse. I am trying my best to switch to a more reliable network provider that won't rob me of my credit. It is sad to see £50 top-up credit disappear so fast even when I don't use it. I once put in three £50 top-up credits on my phone which I had hardly used, then the second £50 top-up credit which was never used, so when I asked them where my money had gone to they said to ring 191. When I rang 191 they kindly asked me if I wanted to put another £50 on my mobile. I just could not believe it. Why do these companies get away with these wrongs? They earn so much money and they have a cheek to tell me such a load of nonsense. Imagine I cannot get about very much by myself at the moment and they are telling me that all my credit must have gone when I went on holiday, which is a lie because I have not

Chapter Eleven

been on holiday for ages. Why in the world do people have to put up with so much dishonesty and lose their money to these companies just like that? So, I am going back to my old network provider and will finish with Vodafone. I prefer to top up at Sainsbury's; I feel much better and safer with them. It is a pity that Sainsbury's doesn't provide mobile networks anymore.

The Amy Cleaning company I ever signed up to was quite a disaster. They do not seem to check the securities of any of the staffs or for criminal records. Though the first girl was very honest and hardworking, she was having trouble with her accommodation. I was so sorry to lose her when she had to move very much further out of town. While she was on holiday they sent a woman in her place she hardly did any work she was far too busy stealing from me. The last one told me such a very sad story and stole £260 from me and I never saw her again. She told me that when she telephoned Amy Cleaning they sent her straight to me with no investigation of any sort, and the cleaning companies she has worked for knows her for stealing money. She goes by the name Suzan and she has been stealing wherever she works. why hasn't anybody found her out? It is because of her behaviour I was left with no cleaner. This was the first cleaning agency I had ever been to for a cleaner and they do not seem to mind who they send over to you to do the cleaning. Even a thief can come and clean your house due to the negligence of Amy Cleaning. I have lost monies and properties. I am now paying a proof-reader. I cannot afford to pay money to a company for just sending me over a cleaner, and also to pay money to the cleaner. How right is this? All of this is very expensive, so I am just very anxious to get the book published and put a stop to paying any more money to my proof-reader and the next stage is to get my hip done in America so that I will be able to walk properly and not go about in a wheelchair.

After having my hip done, then I can start healing people and getting down to the gift Jesus Christ blessed me with and saving more lives. So many people want help with cancer and arthritis but do not know where to seek help. It is amazing how many people I have met who have had operations on their knees and are sorry they had had an operation because the operations hurt them more than before. Someone told me it depends on how experienced the doctor is, but when I do the knees healing on my patients it does not hurt them after I have finished with the healing sessions.

Of course, all I do is use my hands to heal people and as such, most doctors and ministers of the church houses do not check for me; neither do they show me any love. I have been insulted so many times by medical people and church preachers that I cannot count anymore. God chose me because I have strong nerves and that is why I am so anxious to start doing my healing again because so many people want help, and some people think as soon as they are told they have cancer they think it is the end of their lives. This has got me worried. I have healed so many people of cancer by simply using my bare hands, but those that I have healed of cancer told me that when they told other people of being cancer free and being healed naturally, they refuse to belief it, and often question how it can be possible to heal cancer with just bare hands.

I am in search of a first-class publisher; one that will witness my healing sessions first-hand and interview those healed of cancer by me. Of course, I have to get the operation on my own hip first and then I have to get to one certain gentleman who works for Pick because my flat certainly wants a makeover. I know his name is John and I think his other name is Taylor. I do hope I have the right man because my flat certainly wants a makeover and I like the way he does his work. My flat is overdue to get something done to it. As for now, all healing sessions are put on hold until I sort out my flat and the spaces for the patients.

I do know my special friends Christian Luke Barker, who I healed of cancer and his wife Wendy will always make sure there is someone with me at all times during the healing sessions, and that will make me feel much safer. They have been my friends for a very long time and I trust them both. Christian Baker has put me in the limelight by advertising me and telling people how he only had six months to live and he thought his life was over, but I healed him.

A woman I used to know is in a very distressed state. She came to see me and asked me if I would help her. She has skin cancer in her forehead. I have never heard of this before, but what can I do? She's in a lot of pain all over her body, so I gave her a couple of hours healing sessions and she has asked me if she can come over every week, and she also asked me if she could bring her youngest son who has some sort of asthma. Although I am in pain myself with this dreadful hip of mine, I just have to help her get better.

Once this book is out, I hope those who read it and get the message should pass it on.

Sometimes things seem to take so long you just don't know which way to turn to, but I always know that the Almighty Creator is with me, so I try very hard to have patience because without the Almighty I would have nothing, and Jesus Christ knew when he gave me this remarkable gift, that I had broad and strong shoulders and that I would be able to put up with a lot of insults and abuse and with people who dislike me at a glance. People ask me why the Lord chose me and give me such a powerful gift and I tell them I simply do not know why, but I am very proud that I was chosen. Now as often, one of the people coming for healing asked why I am not rich. She thought people should be paying me thousands of pounds and she said that I couldn't be very good, because when people are dying they would be glad to give me a lot of money. I said to her I just tell people to give a donation. Some people are very mean and don't appreciate the healing, but when I resume healing again I will always have someone with me, and people will have to give a much larger donation because you can't expect people to work for nothing and live on water; so this time around it will be much different. I myself have never been greedy. I am too kind. It is always good to be kind and when people take liberties with me, I enjoy correcting them.

I will have to keep going to the library where I met this man who told me he didn't work there, but he went there sometimes, but I can't find his number. I will just have to hope and pray that I will see him soon today. It is hard to get people you can trust in this day and age, but I seem to know this man looks very trustworthy, so I am hoping to see him soon. I will just have to keep going to the library.

I do wish I had kept up my driving lessons. Things are so much easier when you have a car. You can get around so much quicker and you can get to buy things you need instead of depending on people all the time, but it is no use for me to worry over having an accident which I couldn't help and end up being confined to a wheelchair and not be able to get from A to B; but I always trust in the Almighty and I know something will come along. As it says in the Bible, God helps those who help themselves, and without Jesus Christ I do not know what I would do. I always seem to know that Jesus Christ is with me all the time and I know that prayers help, and going back to the church where I used to go to a few years ago, St Mary's Church at Stoke Newington. I just mentioned the trouble I was having getting a proof-reader to the church members and the Almighty immediately introduced me to a lady who told me she would be happy to help me and she came to see me the very next day. Her name is Pat. Pat is not used to my computer because I only bought it just over two years ago and she had bought her own computer many years ago. They changed them so much that it requires studying it all over again. When I went to a computer school nobody understood my computer because it was so very new; only one man understood it and he turned out to be a real con man. I really appreciated Pat's help and she said she would try and get somebody in the church who had a computer similar to mine to help me with some of the difficult things that she does not understand, nor I do myself. Pat certainly knows her English language. She was able to put quite a few things right, so I am hoping we can slowly put things together.

What really upsets me is when people want so many things for themselves and yet they do not believe in Jesus Christ. I always wonder why when the Bible tells you so much about Jesus Christ and how he suffered for everybody in the whole wide world, that quite a lot of people don't believe. This makes me very sad. I always ask them to explain to me why they don't believe in Jesus Christ and some of them tell me that there are too many bad things going on in this world, and I say to them, do they think that Jesus Christ is responsible for the ills of this world? I tell them right away that it is the devil, and some of them say they do not understand. I tell them not until Jesus takes control over the entire world, the devil will always be there and in charge, running things in this world, and we have to be strong and make sure the devil does not take over. I feel so much better now that Pat from St Mary's Church is going to help me when she can. I am sorry that I ever left St Mary's Church. It was just because one of the ministers in the church didn't like me at all and I felt rather embarrassed to stay there, but he has left the church, as I have been informed, so it is all right for me to go back there.

Chapter Eleven

The church I grew up going to in Manchester is so beautiful and I have never seen such a church like it in London. I look forward to going to church every Sunday, but the church I want to be part of must be sincere because there are so many fake pastors who are into churches only for the money and showmanship. I feel that at the end of the week I must thank God for all the blessings given to me, as there are so many people in the world going hungry, and I am at last getting genuine help with my book and since it is the only book. I will write about my life and many of the things that have happened to me.

I feel much more contented and I feel that so many people would like to know more about me so that I can help many more people than I already do; but getting my hip repaired is on my mind, so as soon as I get my hip fixed it will be nice to walk again instead of going everywhere in a wheelchair and then hobbling around at home. My wheelchair is not electronic, but I wish it was. My doctor advised me to make use of my wheelchair more often and even ordered a wheelchair for me, but nothing came of it as she soon retired, and I received a wheelchair from the hospital. At least with the help of someone pushing me, I can go to places. Besides, I make use of the Dial a Ride services which I am grateful for. I miss my doctor; ever since she retired, things at the clinic have never been the same.

I have just remembered a patient that visited me; a lovely woman with twin children. She was very poorly and her husband brought her over to see me so that she could get healed. Her husband was of Chinese origin. I advised them both to visit me regularly so that she can get better quicker, but as usual, her husband fed her up with drugs which were making her even more ill, but she was too frightened to ask him to stop. I advised her to inform family members, but she told me that her relatives all sing the praises of her husband. She said, "Little do they know that he goes out nearly all day. I suppose that is what all the pills are for and I can see he is getting fed up with me, and all these pills he is stuffing me up with are making me worse, and to think there is nothing I can do".

I feel helpless, but as for me, you see, I do not like to interfere with things like that. I do what I can to get her better and I cannot do anything more, and after she told me about the pills, it quite distressed me. He never brought her again to see me for more healing sessions, and it took me a long time to forget about it all, and it is just at this moment I remembered. What I have to put up with sometimes and I can't do anything about it, especially if it is cases to do with other people's domestic affairs. I can't report it to the Stoke Newington Police Station because I don't trust them.

THE END

I would like to extend a special thank you to Hackney Volunteer Befriending Services, Unit 2 and to Rebecca for typing this book. A special thank you also goes to Brother Muta Kilimanjaro for proofreading this book; a special thank you goes to Emily for her friendship; Brother Ali I thank you for being there for me and helping me to get rid of all those flies that invaded my flat due to the inappropriate behaviours of Marcus King; Christian Luke Baker, I thank you for being truthful always and for your kindness towards me, especially telling people how I healed you and extended your life; thank you Brian for introducing people to me.

I emphasise that being independent does not mean doing everything by yourself, but rather it is doing what you can do for yourself and other people, and knowing when and where to seek assistance with those things you cannot manage.

This book is a biographical depiction of my life experiences to heal people, about getting to know and understand people better and why they behave the way they do and what causes them to do so, and why some seek help and others don't. It is also my fight to live a fulfilling and meaningful life, and be as independent as I can be in the face of enormous obstacles.

I also like the readers to get a glimpse of my mind, hopes, ambitions, feelings, and ability to heal all of any race and to love all regardless of race. Most importantly I want people to come to the understanding that the mind, and not the external features, is a truer measure of a person. A person must always be of the right mindset.

Mrs Dorothy N.L. Rodgers
(Author)